Luke Alfr

Testing times

The story of the men who made SA cricket

Published by Spearhead
An imprint of New Africa Books (Pty) Ltd.
99 Garfield Road
Claremont
7700
South Africa

(021) 674 4136
info@newafricabooks.co.za
www.newafricabooks.co.za

First edition, first impression 2003

ISBN 0 86486 538 4

Cover design by Cinnamon Graphix CC
Design and typesetting by Cinnamon Graphix CC
Editor: Mike Marais
Project Manager: Marita Nortjé
Body text typeset in Berkeley Book in 10.8pt
Printed and bound by ABC Press, Cape Town

ACKNOWLEDGEMENTS

I would like to thank three librarians in particular who were of immense help in writing this book — cheers David Khukhele and Anthony Kuthar of the Central Lending Library in Johannesburg, and Johann Greyling of the SABC Radio Archives in Auckland Park.

A special thanks also to several former South African cricketers who went beyond the call of duty in dealing with extra questions and those fine points of memory: Osie Dawson, Kennie Funston, Roy McLean, Clive van Ryneveld, Johnny Waite and John Watkins.

Big thanks too to: Denis and Dorothy Begbie, Colin and Hilton Bland, Bert Blewett, Linda Boswell, Syd Burke, Norman Canale, Michael Chubb, Steve de Villiers, Denis Done, Brian Edwards, Dougie and Lennie Ettlinger, Norman 'Mobil' Gordon, Daphne Greenwood-Mann, Clive Grinaker, Derrick High, Dave Ironside, Richard Knowles, Tiger Lance, John Landau, Denis Lindsay, Chris Mann, Alan McCarthy, Mike Melle, Cyril Mitchley, Peter Muzzell, Jack Nel, Sid O'Linn, Joe Pamensky, Hamish Paterson, Aubrey Paton, Tony Pithey, Joan Plimsoll, Roger Prideaux, Gerald Ritchie, Peter Rowan, Andrew Samson, Mike Shafto, Harry Shapiro, Di Thompson, Mike Thompson Sr, Arthur Tayfield, Ian Tayfield, Lindsay Tuckett, Carol Viljoen, Colin Wesley, Paul and Moira Winslow.

I would also like to thank Mike Marais, Jeremy Boraine, Marita Nortjé and Chris Dawson for their expertise and support.

Finally, a big thank you to my wife, Lisa Lyhne, for her patience, love and understanding.

CONTENTS

INTRODUCTION

For many contemporary South Africans, South African cricket history begins in late 1991 and early 1992, with the hastily-arranged one-day series in India and subsequent World Cup in Australia and New Zealand. In a narrow sense, this interpretation of our cricketing past is true. In the broader sense it is quite wrong — as I hope to show in *Testing Times*.

Why should South Africans be so committed to the willed amnesia that neglects the cricket played before 1991/2? We are committed to amnesia because dismissing the cricket — both official and unofficial — played before 1992, brings with it a parallel series of dismissals. In forgetting the cricket played we forget about history; in forgetting about history we forget about politics — most notably apartheid — and in forgetting about politics we can, in a sense, forget about the pain of the past.

Such a deep and abiding forgetfulness is illustrated only too well in an item which appears every so often on SuperSport. Entitled 'Great South African Sporting Moments', the images show post-1992 sporting achievements, such as Jacques Kallis going to 4 000 Test runs and 100 Test wickets. This is all well and good until one realises that the footage illustrating Kallis' achievement has been doctored so as to appear old. The footage suddenly turns black and white, a certain jumpiness intrudes, the film is scratched to appear authentically old and valuable. Given that the distant past is fraught, even untouchable, best we confer the trappings of history on the recent past. It's far safer that way.

This book implicitly takes issue with the fact that South African cricket history started in late 1991 and early 1992. In contrast, it puts forward the novel idea that the seeds of modern South African cricket started flowering approximately 55 years ago, with Alan Melville's 1947 tour to England. Melville's tour was a watershed because it initiated a long process — a process strengthened during the war, in which many of South Africa's cricketers participated - to slip free from the imperial chain. Of course, such a process was primarily achieved politically, as the National Party self-consciously sought to limit and then amputate completely any lingering vestiges of imperial ties. But it was also achieved on the cricket field, as South Africans went about defining a cricketing identity for themselves which had little to do with batting in the Union Jack's shadow.

In the post-war period South African cricket was dominated to an incredible degree by what was correct and worthwhile, and what was correct and worthwhile was nearly always English. English coaches, such as Lindsay Tuckett's coach, Len Bates, used to coach South African schoolboys. Some, such as 'Bok' Hannah, Melville's master at Michaelhouse, went further and laid some of the first turf pitches at South African schools. Clive van Ryneveld, like Melville a captain of South Africa, remembers not only the English coaches. 'When I was young one stood for "God Save the King" at the end of a cinema show,' he says. 'The main news service that we heard was the BBC news bulletin, starting after the chimes of Big Ben. When I grew up there was a fairly common sense that the imported article was better than the home-grown one, and it applied to cricket *inter alia*.'

One man during the immediate post-War period only bought part of this. Although a royalist — and in the South African context an ardent Nationalist — Eric Rowan chafed at the narrow, class-conscious strictures of South African cricket. He was loud, irreverent and at times vulgar, and in him South African cricket was brought face-to-face with some of its own prejudices. Rather than confront them, however, the cricket establishment chose to wash Rowan from the system. It never explained to either Rowan or the South African cricket-loving public why. Predictably self-righteous until the end of his career, Rowan railed at the injustice of it all, but it was to no avail.

Rowan's last tour abroad, to England in 1951, coincided with Steve de Villiers' first trip outside of South Africa. On the flight to London, De Villiers was befriended by fellow-commentator, Charles Fortune. De Villiers ended up falling in love with England — and cricket — and went on to popularise the sport for a generation of Afrikaans-speakers through the decade and well into the sixties. Lacking facilities, schoolteachers and cultural reference points, Afrikaans-speaking South Africans were not pushing for places in the Test teams of the fifties and early sixties. But people such as De Villiers (and before him, Dana Niehaus) played a small part in patiently preparing the ground.

Caught between the competing claims of Afrikaner nationalism and British cultural imperialism, South African cricket before Jack Cheetham's tour to Australia in 1952/3 was a timid affair. But Cheetham, who had toured Britain with Rowan in 1951, and Ken Viljoen, Cheetham's batman in Australia, changed that. Their encounter with a society more homogeneous and egalitarian than their own inspired them to leave their cultural diffidence behind. It was a happy tour, full of strong performances, particularly from Hugh Tayfield and Russell Endean, but also from Kennie Funston, Michael Melle and John Watkins and, because it ushered in a uniquely South African cricket based on sharp catching and the creation and perpetuation of relentless pressure, it became the most important tour of the period. Cheetham was at it again in England three years later. The 1955 tour was similarly important for South African cricket and, although the series was narrowly lost, the tour demonstrated South Africa's continuing place at the international cricket's high table.

Cheetham's departure from the team coincided with a period of self-conscious doggedness from both South Africa and England. Scoring rates plunged, public interest ebbed and flowed. South Africa seemed not to know whether to burn or fizzle; in the end they did neither.

One man arrived as a saviour. Making his debut against John Reid's incoming New Zealanders in 1961/2, Eddie Barlow galvanised South African cricket. He didn't do so immediately but against Australia in 1963/4 (the final tour covered by this book, the subsequent three-Test tour to New Zealand is omitted) Barlow fashioned South African cricket in his image: he was bold, super-confident and prepared to occasionally chance his luck. The series against Richie Benaud and Bobby Simpson's team (the Australian captaincy was changed mid-series) was shared, but halfway through the South Africans discovered how to really play cricket. They also discovered themselves as cricketers and human beings. Perhaps this had something to do with Viljoen's antiquated style of management; perhaps it had something to do with Trevor Goddard's formulaic style of captaincy; perhaps it just had to do with the sixties and the heady chemistry of the times. No doubt it had to do with a combination of factors, but in Australia in the summer of 1963/4, South African cricket — free at last from the imperial yoke, South Africa, after having recently become a republic, was no longer a member of the Imperial Cricket Conference — finally came of age.

Of course it also came of age because of players other than Barlow. Players like the hardworking and uncomplaining Joe Partridge and players of his kind before him. If anything, this book is dedicated to players such as the late Partridge, to 'Goofy Lawrence', to Syd Burke and Dave Ironside. It is they — and those more famous — who made South African cricket what it is today. These men are the real heroes of this book. This book is dedicated to them.

Luke Alfred, Kensington, December 2002.

CHAPTER 1

The war — 'we'll doddle it.'

'A ship without an engine and 63 Hawker Hartbees'

Hitler is reputed to have burst out laughing when he heard of South Africa's entry into the Second World War. Back at home, the decision was taken at significant political cost. On Monday, September 4, 1939, *The Star* reported '[A] Grave Crisis in South Africa' ahead of the day's special session of the Union Parliament to debate whether South Africa should enter the conflict. The following day the newspaper reported Prime Minister Barry Hertzog's resignation after his decision to oppose the move was defeated by 12 votes and, a day later, Jan Smuts was busy moulding a coalition government. It was the same day that the Union declared war on Germany, an act which made a mockery of talk about 'benevolent neutrality' which animated South African political circles in the years before the war.

Commitment to the Allies' war effort was one thing, the ability to contribute to and sustain such an effort quite another. When General Smuts opened the Museum of Military History in Saxonwold, Johannesburg, in late August 1947, he made public for the first time the impoverished nature of South Africa's military arsenal upon entering the fray eight years previously. Hardly the envy of the free world, South Africa's reserves of military hardware, at that stage, consisted of six Hawker Hurricanes, 63 Hawker Hartbees, many of them non-operational, several South Africa airways Junkers and two First World War tanks. To this motley collection of tanks and planes could be added a six-inch howitzer, which had first to be commandeered from Cape Town's war memorial, as well as one navy ship – although she had no engine.

If South Africa's military establishment was not quite shining with the spit and polish of over-preparation, her men and women were prepared to volunteer in numbers for the war effort. (Union forces remained volunteer-based through-out the war, ostensibly because Smuts doubted his ability to pass conscription legislation through a divided Union parliament. Parliament was so divided that Herzog mounted another challenge to its decision to enter the war on the side of the Allies in January 1940. After an all-night sitting on January 27, Hertzog was once again defeated on the war issue, this time by 81 votes to 59.)

According to Hamish Paterson, a historian at the Museum of Military History, 342 692 South African men and women volunteered for service between September 1939 and September 1945. The voluntary spirit was most sharply developed, says Paterson, in the settled communities of Natal – a community which, incidentally, also provided a high proportion of South Africa's pre-and post-war Test cricketers – and least developed in the mainly Afrikaans-speaking heartlands of the Northern Transvaal and the Orange Free State. Of those who volunteered 6 215 died or were presumed dead outside South Africa's borders, whereas 3 317 lost their lives within the country, either on active duty or engaging in basic training.

South Africa's military contribution tended to be most substantial in the early years of the war – during the East Africa campaign between June 10, 1940 and November 11, 1941, when she committed between 57 000 and 65 000 troops to Abyssinia – and the campaign in North Africa and the western desert. As the war crossed the Mediterranean and crawled up the spine of Italy through the European summer of 1944 (the South African Sixth Armoured Division landed at Taranto on April 20, 1944), so South Africa's involvement tended to fade as a proportion of the collective Allied effort. Whereas she contributed approximately 20 percent of Allied troops to the East Africa campaign, she only contributed, or so estimates Paterson, about six percent of the one million Allied soldiers involved in the Italian campaign.

Denis Begbie, who played cricket for South Africa after the war, saw action in all three theatres featuring South Africans: east Africa, the western desert and Italy. He played cricket in two of them and well remembers posing for a photograph with the rest of his team-mates in the first battalion of the Transvaal Scottish at the Metaga Cricket Club outside of Nairobi, all of them wearing their regimental berets – with pom-poms. 'Yes,' he says, 'we played two matches there in 1940. I remember it well. We had a very good side. Ronnie Grieveson, "Dooley" Briscoe, Bruce Mitchell, Owen Wynne, "Guido" Keightley-Smith. And "Shunter" Coen, who was flying for the RAF, he played for them. I can't remember much about the match although there was another photograph taken at the same time. It shows "Dooley" presenting Bruce [Mitchell] with a big empty basket. It must've been because Bruce dropped a catch.'

Begbie admits to both skirmish and battle with the retreating Italians but says that his slog through east Africa was characterised mainly by sore feet. Occasionally there was heartache. Following three months training at Gil-Gil, west of Nairobi, Corporal Begbie and colleagues tramped to the foothills of Mt Kilimanjaro and from there on through the National Frontier Defence (NFD) to Juba, El-Waq, Kismayu, Mogadishu, Addis-Ababa, Asmara and Masawa on the Red Sea.

In April 1941 near Komboltcha in Ethiopia, he was not 10 metres away from Briscoe when he was shot. 'He was a great captain, Dooley, and a very confident kind of fellow,' says Begbie. 'By the time I arrived at King Edward [School] he had left but we played for Old Edwardians and Transvaal together. His favourite expression on the cricket field was: "We'll doddle it" And this was in Abyssinia at a place called Komboltcha, after Addis Ababa, and we were held up in the mountains. My company, the support company, was supporting Dooley's company, the A company, the rifle company of the Scottish, and we were pinned down. Dooley wanted a better o-pip, or observation post, and there was some open ground that he wanted to go through and I said to Dooley "no don't, this is impossible, you'll never make it. We've got these snipers, they know our position, you just put your head up and they have a shot at you." And Dooley's remark, his last words to me were, "We'll doddle this". So he took his runner, who was a chap called Lightfoot, Fleet Lightfoot, and they went over the top. I'd say that they got about ten yards from us and they got cut right down. That was in the morning. And we couldn't move, we couldn't get up, Lightfoot was wounded, Dooley was killed outright. We didn't get them out until dark.'

Begbie, Mitchell and Athol Rowan, a fellow member of the first battalion of Transvaal Scottish, survived the travails of east Africa and Somaliland. All three arrived at Suez on June 27, 1941, approximately eleven months after sailing from Durban to Mombasa on the SS Dilwara. Begbie and Rowan went through the north Africa campaign unscathed – this included both the setback at Tobruk, where an entire South African division was captured, and the victory of El Alamein – but on October 21 of the following year, Mitchell received a gunshot wound on the right-hand side of the neck. His military file makes light of the injury, noting that he was discharged and returned to his regiment on October 23.

Despite dropping catches in Kenya and receiving wounds in the desert, Mitchell's sardonic sense of humour was a constant companion. The late Stan

Eldridge, former sports editor of the *Natal Witness* in Pietermaritzburg, told the story of Mitchell's artillery regiment suddenly being attacked by Rommel's panzers while on duty in the desert. A jittery officer chided Mitchell for the unavoidable delay in getting a heavy weapon into action, this as the Panzers thundered closer. Mitchell, unperturbed, is reputed to have muttered to those around him: 'Does he expect me to fire it from the hip?'

Like Mitchell, the pages of Rowan's military file are not thick with tales of adventure: apart from a minor indiscretion involving a day's absence without leave on March 4, 1943, an offence for which he was forced to forfeit 12 and a half days pay, only one item stands out. Under 'Battle Casualties' we are told that Rowan went missing and was presumed to have become a prisoner of war on June 20, 1942. A week later, Rowan had miraculously reunited with the Transvaal Scottish. Paterson notes that June 20 was the day before the official fall of the garrison at Tobruk, when some 20 000 Commonwealth soldiers were captured by the Germans. He notes that in the chaos before the garrison's fall it would have been quite possible for Rowan to have escaped back into Egypt on whatever transport was available.

In fact, this is exactly what happened. Paterson estimates that it was 450 miles 'as the crow flies' back to comparative safety and a journey east would account for the apparent discrepancy between the dates when Rowan went missing and when he was rediscovered (that is, 20.6.'42 and 28.6.'42). 'During the retreat my dad's company, in order to avoid being captured by the Germans, stole two ambulances,' remembers Rowan's son, Peter. 'While racing through the desert, and on one or two occasions through German camps, they crossed German mine fields. The one ambulance was blown up altogether, possibly killing all occupants, but my dad's ambulance wasn't too badly damaged and the occupants managed to escape.'

In a pigsty somewhere between Padua and Venice

Unlike Begbie, Mitchell and Rowan never saw service in Italy. But even Begbie's experiences in three theatres paled in comparison with the time spent in Italy by Norman Bertram Fleetwood Mann, born in Benoni three days after the Christmas of 1920. Norman had a nest of curly hair perched on his forehead and, as a result, was nicknamed 'Tufty' by his older brother, Noel. The nickname stuck and to thousands of South African cricket fans in the immediate post-war period he became known as Tufty.

The Mann family lived in Benoni and Tufty's father was a medical practitioner on one of the east Rand mines. Tufty's high school education took place at Michaelhouse, from February 1933 until December 1937, where he played cricket and, extra-curricularly, golf, winning the Natal Amateur Championship at Umkomaas before the war. According to the school records, the major influence on Mann's fledgling cricket career was Bobby Woods, a schoolmaster and former Natal cricketer who had played against the visiting Marylebone Cricket Club (MCC) side of 1929. The second major presence in young Norman's life was a maternal one. 'She [Tufty's mother] took them to golf tournaments across Johannesburg,' says Daphne Greenwood, Tufty's widow. 'She knew Bobby Locke very well and the boys were with her whenever the school holidays allowed.' It was Locke who introduced Greenwood and Mann while Tufty was at Cambridge in pursuit of a blue for golf.

'We were introduced on the Addington Palace golf course just before the war broke out,' Greenwood recalls. 'His family then recalled him to South Africa. He joined up and we were married in Johannesburg in September 1940. When we returned my parents and I were three of the last six first-class passengers on the Winchester Castle. It was literally the last trip the Winchester Castle took before she was converted into a troopship. We zig-zagged the U-boats across the Bay of Biscay all the way to South Africa. We went to bed fully clothed. We needed to be ready to run for it if necessary. We were completely blacked out. You lit a cigarette on virtual pain of death.'

Having studied at the Royal Academy of Dramatic Art, Daphne made a small name for herself as an understudy to Kitty Prince, playing in *Aladdin* and *Robin Hood* on the Bournemouth pantomime circuit before the war. After marrying Tufty she found herself in Potchefstroom, where he had been billeted for basic training. In mid-1941 Mann went north, was captured and was interred in an Italian prisoner-of-war camp. News from him was non-existent until Daphne miraculously received word. 'I somehow got some sort of card from him and in it he said that he was about to take up farming. The Italians had surrendered and they turned a blind eye to the prisoners if they wanted to make a dash for it. He thought he could make a better life for himself and after an awful walk north an Italian family took care of him. He was in the open air for 23 months. He lived in a pigsty. He came out looking like nothing on God's earth. He looked absolutely ghastly. And you do all of this for your country. I just don't know how they managed to survive. I really don't.'

For 23 months neither Tufty's wife nor his family heard anything from him. They knew he had escaped in the chaotic hiatus between the Italians' surrender and the Germans' assumption of control of the Italian prisoner-of-war camps, but nothing more. Some presumed the worst. 'I had a strange feeling that he was alive. I didn't doubt that he was,' Daphne says. 'Somehow I hung onto hope, I suppose. I hung onto some kind of certainty that he was alive. Other people weren't so sure.'

Daphne Greenwood can't remember the exact date but some time in the late South African winter of 1945, she was reunited with the handsome young man she had fallen in love with. When asked if she remembered what she said to him when she saw him for the first time she replied: 'I don't remember, I just suppose we fell into each other's arms.' After being debriefed, Mann joined his wife, who was acting in an African Theatre production touring the country. In one capacity or another, whether touring with his wife, the Eastern Province side or the South African team, the next five years were years of almost ceaseless travel.

Due to the length of the demobilisation process, no Currie Cup cricket was played in the 1945/6 season but a full programme was scheduled for 1946/7. The competition was squashed into a few brief months around Christmas, with the national selectors announcing the team to tour England the following South African winter in early January, 1947. 'This is essentially a season of grading,' wrote seasoned cricket journalist, Louis Duffus, in late October, 1946, 'of placing new post-war values on a variety of talent. It is one of those exciting summers of high hopes and ambitions with incentive and inspiration for cricketers of every class from the international to the schoolboy. With the tentative reconstruction stage now passed, clubs in all centres are now returning to competitive league cricket. The Currie Cup provincial tournament is to be revived for the first time since 1937/8. The Nuffield schoolboy gathering is to take place in Cape Town in the New Year. For the first time, if the efforts of its founders are supported, a new 'Varsity Cricket Week will be launched in Natal. And, above all, for those in the higher strata of play, there looms that glamorous prospect, the most cherished dream of all who would sense the richest emotions of a sentimental game – the four months' tour of Britain.'

By December of 1946, Mann was back in whites, turning out for Eastern Province against Transvaal in the first game of cricket ever played at Ellis Park. To celebrate the occasion, the respective captains, Bruce Mitchell of Transvaal and Sid Heard of Eastern Province, raised the Transvaal Cricket Union's flag.

Symbolically it signalled a new chapter in the book of South African cricket. Post-war cricket was back in the groove. 'Instead of having a formal opening of the ground,' wrote 'mid-on' in the *Rand Daily Mail* of Friday, December 13, 1946, 'with some well-known figure bowling the first ball, the Transvaal Cricket Board have decided to do things very quietly. They have agreed that the honour of breaking the Transvaal Cricket union's colours at the flagpole should go to the captain of the Eastern Province side. It is almost certain that Sid Heard, the visiting captain, will not decline this honour.'

As a result of overnight rain, play was slow to begin and, eventually, just after lunch, Transvaal's openers walked out to start the innings. Mann was brought into the attack almost immediately. Before close of play on the first afternoon he wheeled through 39 eight-ball overs of orthodox left-arm spin, taking three for 41. 'It was a wet wicket and Eastern Province looked as though they were going to beat us but we played out time,' says Begbie, part of an imperious Transvaal team which included Mitchell, the Rowan brothers, Athol and Eric, Owen Wynne, Tony Harris, George Fullerton and a young Russell Endean. 'But Tufty bowled and, my word, he was on the spot all the while, he was a wonderful bowler.'

Mann resumed his spell on the second morning, denting the home side's innings still further in taking two wickets for 28 runs in 26 overs. After lunch the 'Durban law student turned Port Elizabeth wool dealer,' as he had been dubbed in the *Rand Daily Mail*, damaged the Transvaal innings irreparably, taking the last wicket to fall and reducing the home team to 232 all out. Mann's figures finally read: 67.6-38-69-6. At the time his 542 balls bowled were a record for the most balls bowled in an innings of first-class cricket. (The record was overtaken not long afterwards by Alf Valentine, the West Indian. In the 1950 Trent Bridge Test, Valentine bowled 552 balls, passing Mann's record by ten deliveries, until his record was itself passed by compatriot, Sonny Ramadhin, who bowled 588 balls against England at Edgbaston in 1957.)

Reports of Mann's feats suggest that he didn't bowl more than half-a-dozen loose deliveries throughout the Transvaal innings, but his achievement wasn't simply a case of conspiring with a negative Transvaal team intent on creeping to a massive total. In fact, only when Ola Grinaker, batting at nine, came to the crease was Mann forced to change his seven-two field – his two leg-side fielders consisted of a silly mid-on and an orthodox mid-on – and post fielders on the long-on and long-off boundary.

Begbie's 50, Endean's 48 not out and Grinaker's sprightly first-innings 34 turned out to be invaluable as the match unfolded. Replying to Transvaal's 232, Eastern Province were bowled out for exactly half of that. Adding to their 116-run first innings lead, the home side cobbled together 141 for nine declared in their second, giving Eastern Province a target of 258 to win. Batting last, the visitors folded meekly, only managing 100. Athol Rowan finished with match figures of 11 for 69 and Transvaal won by 157 runs. Although the victory was definitive, Transvaal and Eastern Province shared third place in that season's Currie Cup. First place went to Natal, led by Dudley Nourse, who pipped Western Province to the trophy by a point.

A tight cluster of schools and assumptions

Some years senior to Tufty Mann at Michaelhouse was Alan Melville, Mann's captain on South Africa's first post-war tour – to England in 1947. The son of a Carnarvon bank manager, Melville was born on May 19, 1910, five days after another esteemed pre-and post-war South African cricketer and cricket administrator, Ken Viljoen. When Alan was aged two, the Melvilles left the Karoo and moved to Greytown in Natal. When of school-going age, Alan was enrolled in St David's preparatory school and, in October 1924, aged 14, moved to Michaelhouse as a border.

While at Michaelhouse, two figures were to play an influential role in Melville's cricket career, the first being CW 'Bok' Hannah, Melville's housemaster, and the second, Herby Taylor, the South African captain. In interview with the South African Broadcasting Corporation's (SABC's) Charles Fortune, four days before his sixtieth birthday, Melville says the following about Taylor, a colossus of the inter-war period and a man who played the bulk of his 42 Tests between 1921/2 and 1931/2: 'It improved my technique by watching great players like Herby Taylor in the nets. Now Herby was a Michaelhouse old boy and used to come up and play against the school on old boys' day and always made a point of having a net on the Friday afternoon before the match in which he paid very great attention to the detail of his batting. He didn't make a farce of it and a lot of us were privileged to stand behind that net. He certainly taught me an enormous amount about the game.'

School records tell us that the Michaelhouse first X1 were pitted against the old boys in October, 1928. Melville made a round 100 for the school but even his five wickets' worth of leg-spin for 57 were not enough to keep the

Old Boys from passing the school total. Taylor made 124 not out but Melville had done more – he had made an impression.

Hannah, the son of the Dean of Chichester, was less obviously and immediately influential but helped Melville – in many ways the definitive *soutpiel* – bridge the world of Natal with that of southern England in the decade before the war. Hannah was no great cricketer (in early 1930 he laid the school's first turf wicket and in the subsequent festival match scored a pair), but he was a man of standing and social reach.

Due partly to ill health and partly to the fact that he had a brother who was stationed at the garrison in Eshowe, Hannah visited South Africa for the first time in 1897. According to the official Michaelhouse historian, Mike Thompson, it was early in the following year, while staying with the Bishop of Natal, that Hannah met Canon Todd, the founder of Michaelhouse, at a dinner party. 'Todd persuaded him to join the staff and at the age of 20 he began his long association with the school which lasted intermittently until 1930,' says Thompson. 'He chose the present site of the school for Todd and when Todd left in 1903 he became the first principal of Cedara Agricultural College and later farmed in Mooi River. He helped the school on occasions until 1917 when he became a full-time member of staff and stayed until June 1930, after a six-month period as rector. He coached the first X1 throughout his permanent tenure.'

Six months prior to Hannah's departure, Melville left for Oxford. He had obtained an ordinary – class three – matric in the December of 1928 but the path to Oxford was nonetheless assured. He arrived in 1930 with an established reputation, having played in the senior Natal team before leaving school. During his Oxford holidays Melville used to stay at Hannah's Sussex home and in 1932 he made his Sussex debut, having completed the two-year residence qualification prior to being allowed to play county cricket.

An amateur, a batsman of grace and renown and a WASP of almost faultless pedigree, Melville was bound to attract attention and this he did. He was approached by Douglas Jardine to tour Australia on what was to become the 'Bodyline' tour in 1933 and was also hounded by the SA Cricket Association (SACA) to make himself available for South Africa. On the advice of his father he refused both overtures, biding his time at Sussex (1932-'36) before returning to South Africa to play for Transvaal in the 1937 South African season. Melville made a string of important centuries for Sussex but none more so than his ton against the 1933 West Indians. Batting first, the visitors' scored

431, ELG Hoad scoring 149 and George Headley 79. In reply, Sussex totalled 549, John Langridge, one of their two openers scoring 172 and Melville, batting at three, scoring 114. The following August and Melville could only manage two and 40 against the visiting Australians (560, Alan Kippax scoring 250 and Don Bradman, batting at seven, scoring 19) as Sussex were beaten by an innings and 19 runs. Despite the reverse against the tourists, Sussex, with Melville as captain, finished second in the County Championship for the third successive summer. 'Melville, when set, was the most graceful batsman in the side,' reported *Wisden Cricketers' Almanack*'s Sussex correspondent. 'He made his runs with delightful ease and against any type of bowling he drove superbly.'

The following season was again successful, despite Melville suffering the minor irritant of having his appendix removed. The South African scored 1 555 runs at 44.42, which included a memorable 90-minute century against Nottinghamshire's Harold Larwood and Bill Voce at Hove, this despite being handicapped with an injured thumb. But in 1936 the Sussex dream began to sour. Wisden wondered if it didn't perhaps have something to do with the fact that Melville only played in 10 matches. 'Far from improving their doings in 1935, Sussex fell away in such marked degree that that they dropped from seventh to fourteenth in the championship. Not since 1911 had they occupied so lowly a place in the competition. The fact that Alan Melville, one of the finest amateur batsmen in the country, who has now returned to South Africa, seldom played, may have influenced in some degree the fortunes of the eleven.'

Melville's time at Sussex was not without its social tensions. 'It was a little embarrassing in those days because I was the only amateur playing at the time, and there I was, sitting in this enormous dressing-room, with six armchairs and two couches and every possible comfort, while my professionals were a few yards down the road – so to speak – sitting in a tin hut with hard wooden benches.' The awkwardness inspired by antiquated divisions in the game could have had something to do with Melville's lack of ease. But what is less commonly recognised is that Melville was never a well man, the source of his incapacity dating back to an injury received after Transvaal's match at the old Wanderers against Ronnie Stanyforth's England tourists of 1927/8. 'After the game I was involved in an accident, travelling as a passenger, which fractured my spine,' he said in 1970. 'It is an injury which has worried me ever since.'

Despite its severity, Melville did not dwell on his spinal injury or allow it to become an excuse. Norman 'Mobil' Gordon, who played with Melville for both Transvaal and South Africa prior to the war, remembers Melville as spindly and elegant but never frail. 'I'm definitely not aware of any such injury,' he said. 'He was tall and thin, not frail. He was prone to strain, I will say that. I remember once he suffered from a muscle strain. He had a big plaster strapping on his thigh, this was in that final series before the war in which we played the "Timeless Test".'

Even Melville's war exploits were dominated by the injury. Hurting his back again, he was in a strait-jacket for 14 to 16 months during the war, this while working as a lieutenant in the quartermaster's stores. Afterwards, the injury re-surfaced. 'I got myself really fit for that tour [to England in 1947] but half-way through the injury began to worry me again. The second half of that tour was a bit of a trial actually.'

CHAPTER 2

'Stationed at the Park Lane Hotel'

One happy imperial family...

When the ageing South African gang of seventeen arrived in England on the 18th of April, 1947, they found a country not cowed in defeat but one chipped and cracked in victory. Duffus complained that the men were shabbily dressed, the trains late and the shops stocked with luxuries no-one could afford. In a phrase, England was 'irritatingly thwarted.' Thwarted though it may have been, England welcomed South Africa's cricketers with open arms, enjoying the opportunity to repay the hospitality that had been shown to British servicemen as they stopped off at Durban and Cape Town during their voyages across the Indian Ocean or their crawl up the east coast of Africa during the war. 'We practised at the Nursery nets at Lord's prior to the start of the tour,' says Begbie. 'We were stationed at the Park Lane Hotel. We were there for a fortnight before the cricket started – our first game was at Worcester. Monty came in to meet us, in our dressing room. And we were all in the Eighth Army excepting Ian Smith, he was too young. Monty just greeted us and he said: "hello, my boys".'

Melville's men were Monty's boys all right. With the exception of South Africa's captain and Smith, the young Natal leg-spinner, all of the South Africans had fought in the war. Some, such as Tony Harris, had flown Spitfires before being shot down over the Adriatic. Others, such as Osie Dawson, had risen to the rank of second in command of the Durban Light Infantry during the Italian campaign, winning the Military Cross. 'I don't know how that happened actually,' says Dawson, to this day bemused by the achievement. 'It was supposedly for bravery but I was never that brave a sort of fellow.'

Dawson's provincial colleague, Dudley Nourse, was less fortunate. He was admitted to hospital in Alexandria on April 3, 1945 with a stricture of his urethra. Nearly two weeks later we read that Nourse's condition was improving – his medical file notes 'renal insufficiency' and continuing problems with his kidneys and bladder. On July 21 of that same year Nourse, well enough to be moved, was released from the military to return to the Durban Municipality so that he could resume duties as a health inspector. 'On my return to South Africa my friends were immediately alarmed at the growth of my girth,' says Nourse. 'The increase in my waistline made it uncomfortable to get about with the old-time agility. In fact, it became impossible. Stooping quickly became a hazardous business.'

Nourse needn't have bothered worrying about his girth. When the '47 team arrived, England was gripped by rationing; plaice and kippers substituted for red meat, eggs and butter were rare and bread was seen more frequently at dinner tables than the team would have liked. Big-boned Athol Rowan – christened as the team's 'master trencherman' – tugged unhappily on the leash of rationing, sometimes slipping out for a second meal when he found the one offered at the team hotel insufficient. 'The conditions were good overall,' remembers Dawson, the team's only genuine allrounder. 'The food was a bit of a devil. We always somehow found ourselves short and had to scrounge for more.' With an attention to detail characteristic of a seasoned journalist, Duffus records that he ate no more and no less than 131 kippers while on tour. 'Towns were recalled not because of their cricketers or fame in history,' he writes, 'but because of the quality of their menus. "That was where we had bacon" identified a place more clearly than to say it was Shakespeare's birthplace.'

The first game of the tour took place against Worcestershire at Worcester on April 30 and May 1 and 2, 1947. 'The Severn water had receded from its invasion of the ground,' writes John Arlott, 'and from its ten-foot mark high on the pavilion bar, to its normal charter channel, leaving only a white ghost's robe on trees and walls and buildings to tell of its record-breaking rise of only a few weeks before, but traces of it were expected to be found still lurking in the wicket.' Worcestershire won the toss and elected to bat in the gloom. Rowan must've eaten well the night before because he took four of the first five Worcestershire wickets to fall (with Mann taking the other), as the home side crumbled to 37 for five before rallying to reach 202 (Rowan: 30-11-59-5, Mann: 21-6-40-3). At close on the first night, South Africa had reached 50 for one. The 'master trencherman' must have eaten well again because he top-scored in the

South African first innings with 28, as the visitors' were bowled out for 167 in reply, Dennis Dyer scoring 26, Ken Viljoen 26 and extras 26.

Worcestershire struggled again and, despite a solid opening stand by the brothers Cooper – Eddie (22), Fred (20) – were all out for nelson, leaving South Africa 147 runs to win the match. The task was beyond them as they surrendered by 39 runs. Only Dyer (12), Melville (14), Rowan (14) and Nourse (16) reached double figures. Extras numbered ten and South Africa revealed their innate and timeless vulnerability against spin. Between them, Rowan (five for 34) and Mann (five for 36) took all of Worcestershire's second innings wickets. With Tuckett's two for 38 in the first innings, the three took all of Worcestershire's twenty wickets.

After the loss against Worcestershire, the South Africans only lost once more before the first Test – this to the MCC, despite Bruce Mitchell carrying his bat for a century. They beat Leicestershire, Cambridge University, Oxford University, Surrey, Glamorgan, Combined Services and Northamptonshire, and drew with Hampshire and Middlesex. Melville scored the South Africans' first century of the tour against Leicestershire. Mitchell and Viljoen with centuries, and Nourse with 92, prospered with the bat in the match against Middlesex and Tuckett strengthened his claim for inclusion in the first Test through sheer consistency of performance, bowling well against Leicestershire, Surrey, Glamorgan and the MCC.

A medium-fast right-arm over the wicket bowler, Tuckett was something of an anomaly in the touring team in that he came from the Orange Free State, whereas 12 of the seventeen came from either Transvaal or Natal. Tuckett was educated at St Andrews in Bloemfontein, preferred bowling to batting and, like most of his team-mates, sacrificed the best years of his cricketing life to the Second World War. 'Five very nasty years best forgotten,' is how he describes them.

Turning 28 in the February prior to the team's April 5 departure on the Cape Town Castle, Lindsay was the son of Len Tuckett, who played for Natal and Orange Free State and once represented his country – against JWHT Douglas's England side in the third Test of the 1913/14 series. His father was a major influence on his sporting career, as was Len Bates, a county professional employed by St Andrews on a regular basis. But, while they refined his technique, it was only Tuckett, extraordinarily willing at the best of times, who could inspire himself. In all, he bowled 724 eight-ball overs on tour, a total only exceeded by Jack Plimsoll of the fast bowlers. Tuckett took one more wicket than his good friend – 69 to Plimsoll's 68 – but, unlike the left-arm Western Province seamer who played only at Old Trafford, he featured in all the Tests – and what a debut his was.

Fried eggs at Blackboys...

As if to remind her readers that England hadn't cornered the market on hardship, the City Late edition of *The Star* on Friday, June 6, 1947, ran a South African Press Association (SAPA) story about the issuing of an extraordinary item in the Government Gazette. The story noted that while rationing wasn't expected to be a feature of South African life, meat, jams, jelly, marmalade, breakfast oats and oatmeal were all about to increase in price. Elsewhere, the same newspaper reported that Durban's 11 000 registered dogs were suffering from malnutrition. 'A little realised result of the meat shortage and one which veterinary surgeons and kennel owners agree could be easily overcome by the immediate supply of whale meat.'

Meanwhile, in the same edition of the newspaper, the cricket correspondent was weighing the respective claims of blind hope and sober analysis. 'Judged by the erratic record they have achieved in six weeks of climatic extremes, the South African cricketers have no logical right to expect to win the 65th Test match against England which opens the four-day series at Trent Bridge tomorrow,' he writes in his Test match preview. 'But their volatile talents give them an exciting outside chance of victory. Reason is against their winning, but this is a team that flouts rational assessment.' So splendidly did Melville's men flout rational assessment that on the evening after the first day's play they were 376 for three, after having won the toss. They lost Mitchell for 14 with the total on 23 and Viljoen fell leg before to Edrich for 10 with the total on 44, but after that it was plain sailing for Melville and Nourse as English resolve leaked away in the sun-filled afternoon.

According to Nourse, Melville greeted him with a pointed look when he arrived at the crease. No words were exchanged between the two of them. 'He was worried, naturally, as any captain would be,' says Nourse. 'A stand had to be made. The first over gave him my answer. I was going to attack the bowling from the start.' Both, in time, mastered the England attack and both went to centuries as well as the record for a South African third-wicket partnership against England.

As Melville (189) and Nourse (149) marched in harmony through the fading afternoon, Dawson, the next man in, was shuttling between emotional extremes. 'I was in bloody agony waiting for those two,' he says. 'I was very pleased for them, I really was, but it was a trial getting my chance to bat. And it was my debut. Eventually, just before the close, I got my chance. I took a swish at something and it went flying over the covers. I should have been out but it fell safely. I got back in on the Monday [Sunday was a rest day] and the nerves of Saturday night had gone. I got 48 but I was crooked out. Bloody [Godfrey] Evans. [Eric] Hollies was the bowler. I went to hook him and Evans did one of his stumping tricks. He was well known for that, you know.' The South African innings snagged on 533, with Tony Harris chipping in with 60 and Athol Rowan making 34 not out.

In conversation with the SABC's Charles Fortune eighteen years later, Harris remembers that his free-spirited knock was not met with universal acclaim. 'I went in and managed to get about 60 and had a very good chance to be one of the chosen few to get a hundred in my first Test match,' he says. 'But Norman Yardley, who was skipper of the English side and a very great friend of mine, suggested that I try and hit Hollies for a six. And with the score on 530 for six or something at that stage, I said, well, tell Hollies to pitch one up and I'll give it a go. And I promptly proceeded to do this and I was caught by Hutton at deep mid-on, right on the boundary. I was very unpopular when I got into the dressing room. This was my first taste of how stern a Test match is. I certainly felt with the score on 530 I had every right to try and lift the ball over the boundary.' 'But you soon learned that you hadn't,' says Fortune. 'Well I've never learned, that's why my career wasn't so wonderful unfortunately,' replies Harris.

Play on the third morning began with Bill Edrich (44 not out) and Denis Compton (65 not out) at the crease, England having lost Cyril Washbrook (25) leg before to Tuckett and Hutton (17) leg before to Rowan the previous afternoon. Compton swatted at Tuckett's second ball of the morning – '…apparently failing to realise that play had officially begun,' comments Arlott acidly – steering a chance to Mitchell at slip. After a quick boundary, Horace Dollery (nine) played on to Dawson, as Edrich and Norman Yardley inherited a withering innings on a true pitch.

With Dawson, Rowan and Mann having come and gone, Melville introduced Smith and Tuckett was tossed the second new ball. When Edrich was on 65 and the total on 198, he received an apparent full-toss from Smith; but the ball dipped disconcertingly, the batsman missed and was yorked. The last five

England wickets fell in 16 minutes for the addition of 10 runs. Before one o'clock England were following on to South Africa's 533 all out. 'In one of the worst exhibitions of batting in English cricket history,' trumpets Duffus, 'eight wickets fell today in 75 minutes for 54 runs.' Tuckett, having snuffled Washbrook the previous evening, recorded the figures of 14-7-16-4 for the day. Smith added magic to Tuckett's line and length in taking three for 14 on the day and Mann recorded the intriguingly back-to-front figures of 20-13-10-0.

Hutton became Tuckett's fifth wicket of the session when he was bowled for nine before lunch but, through the third afternoon, South Africa, with their bowlers tiring, had to prise every Englishman from his wicket. Still, with Washbrook (59) and Edrich (50) out for fifties and Dollery out cheaply for the second time in the Test, South Africa were well-placed when Yardley joined Compton with the total on 170 for four. Unfortunately for Melville and his wearying men, they were still there at close of play on the third evening.

As the South Africans congregated for breakfast at the Blackboys Hotel in Nottingham on the final morning, the manager of the South African team, Algy Frames, realised that his bowlers needed protein. He went in search of eggs. 'At breakfast the South Africans were treated to an unusual luxury of fried eggs,' writes Duffus, although he fails to mention that the additional rations did not succeed in separating Yardley and Compton – who were still steadfastly barnacled to the bulkhead of the English innings at lunch on the fourth day. By this stage, Melville had limped off the field and Nourse was captaining the side.

Just after lunch, Mitchell made amends for dropping Yardley off Tuckett when he was on 51, by pouching Compton off Mann for 163. The fifth wicket was worth 237 and although Dawson had the consolation of capturing Yardley's wicket one short of his century, Compton's dismissal had not relieved the pain. 'It was Evans who did it,' comments Nourse on the arrival of England's number seven. 'If it hadn't been for Evans those two fellows at the end couldn't put up the show that they did.' Evans scored a swashbuckling 74 (with ten boundaries and a five) as South Africa continued to chase imperial leather on the fourth afternoon.

Eventually Smith pocketed a caught-and-bowled off the England wicket-keeper, Harris caught Bedser (two) and Dawson accounted for Cook (four). At 3.37 on the final afternoon the last England pair came together. The England second-innings total was 500 for nine, a lead of 175. Martin and Hollies then had the audacity to do the unthinkable – they hung around. They were still there at four o'clock and stuck firm at 4.15. At four minutes short of 4.30, the innings finally ground to a halt but not before Martin had savaged the South African attack with two sixes – he and Hollies had used big blows to hammer together a tenth-wicket stand of 51.

Depending on the sources, South Africa had either 138 or 140 minutes to score the 227 required for victory. They fell short by 61 runs, the injured Melville scoring his second century of the match. Viljoen supported him with a not-out fifty after Mitchell went early for four. 'A moral victory isn't much good,' comments an ornery Nourse. 'You want the victory noted in black and white as yours, outright and unmistakably.'

The crown prince of the lost cause

The next time South Africa were similarly well placed in the 1947 series was in the fifth Test at the Oval. Thanks largely to Edrich and Compton the series had come and gone by that stage – the South Africans were three-nil down with one to play – but enter nonetheless Bruce Mitchell, crown prince of the lost cause.

Born on Ferreira's Deep Gold Mine and a product of St John's College in Johannesburg, Mitchell was never one to set an innings alight when he could fan it gently with ones and twos. Possessed of a slightly ungainly technique with a functional rather than extravagant backlift, Mitchell was not one to keep the scorers sharpening their pencils. (As a 20 year-old he took well over 400 minutes to score 88 on Test debut against England at Edgbaston in 1929.) In later life he admitted to his slow-scoring ways when, reflecting on his exclusion from the South African team to face Lindsay Hassett's 1949/50 Australian visitors, he said: 'I was bitter at the time but they were probably right. I had become very slow and tended to get bogged down.'

In hot, cloudless conditions at the Oval – Arlott describes the outfield as 'half-way between jaundice and peroxide outside of the diligently greened middle' – England batted first in the fifth Test and totalled 427, no-one making a century but Hutton scoring 83, Compton 53, Yardley 59 and Evans 45. A photograph published in the *Rand Daily Mail* on the day after the Test shows men in newspaper hats, shirtsleeves and folded jackets, sizzling obediently in the London sun. Mitchell and Dennis Dyer opened for South Africa and put on 47 before Dyer failed to get over one and thumped a drive to Cliff Gladwin in the covers. Viljoen and Nourse parted for 10 runs apiece and Melville, batting at five, had come and gone for 39 by the time the second day's play came to an end with the South African total on 204 for four.

Mitchell and Dawson, the not-out batsmen overnight, duly went to their hundred and fifty respectively before lunch on the third morning. When their partnership was worth 79 Mitchell lost his fifth partner of the innings, Dawson falling leg before to Doug Wright with the total on 243. The sixth (George Fullerton for six) and seventh (Athol Rowan for nought) wickets fell on 253 and 254. Mitchell was eighth out, guiding a rising delivery into Evans's hands as the South African first innings spluttered and died with the total on 302. Mitchell, who had taken 130 minutes to reach his fifty, had batted 380 minutes for 120. The other South African contributions of note came from Dawson (55), Melville (39) and Mann (39).

The England second innings was light-hearted. Compton breezed to his fifth century of the summer against the tourists with a breathtakingly fluent 113, and Cyril Washbrook (43) and Hutton (36) chipped in. Howorth and Evans compounded Melville's misery, stitching together an unbeaten 68 for the seventh wicket, and England eventually declared on 325 for six, leaving South Africa to see out half an hour on the third afternoon.

Before the close Mitchell had lost Dyer, his opening partner, but on the fourth morning he was still there on one not out, with South Africa resuming on eight for one as they began their march on the winning total of 451. 'The whole match had seemed, at its outset, to lack point,' writes Arlott. 'There was a complete lack of high hostility about the English cricket, and yet the South African batting had not taken advantage of it. Only Compton had saved the major English batting from looking pedestrian on a wicket which gave the bowlers occasional encouragement but no real help. But on this last day Mitchell lifted the game on to the plane of the heroic, and Nourse and Tuckett stood with him by right.'

Viljoen had scored 33 of the morning's 40 runs when he became the first wicket to fall – stumped by Evans with the total on 48. This brought Nourse to the crease. He started to attack immediately, survived a sharp chance when he was dropped by Hutton in the slips when on 30, and South Africa lunched on 147 for two, with Nourse 63 not out. Mitchell, at the other end, was not about to be accused of recklessness – or, for that matter, shooting from the hip – having taken three hours for 38.

But the South African innings found greater momentum after the interval and thundered on after lunch, with the two putting together 184 runs all told in 145 minutes before Nourse was the victim of an umpiring decision which looked suspiciously hometown. TD Nelson, the *Cape Times'* special correspondent at the cricket, explained the dismissal as follows: 'The decision which sent Nourse to the pavilion was a little confusing. In trying to turn the ball to leg, he missed and was hit on the pads. Evans, taking the ball wide on the leg appealed, first for leg before and then for a catch behind the wicket. Hutton, noticing the bails on the ground, appealed for bowled. The decision was referred to the square-leg umpire who gave Nourse out.'

Mitchell, still at the crease, then saw a run on partners as three wickets fell for 34 runs, leaving South Africa perched precariously on 266 for six. Mann was next man in. Had he blinked or turned away he would not have seen Mitchell apologetically touch his cap as he went to his second century of the match. Tea was taken with the total on 294 for six and South Africa still needed 157 to win. They had 135 minutes in which to do it.

Mann's departure for 10 with the total on 314 effectively cancelled any chance of an unlikely South African victory. The more immediate problem facing the visitors was that they still needed to bat out the 90 minutes left in the day: Mitchell was exhausted and Tuckett, the next man in after Mann, had only scored 47 runs in eight innings so far in the series. But survive they did, scoring an unbeaten 109 for the eighth wicket of which Tuckett's contribution was a handsome 40 not out. Mitchell carried his bat for 189. He had been on the field of play for all but 15 minutes of the duration of the Test. 'When I saw him, sitting motionless in the dressing-room with his pads still on, he looked an old man,' wrote Duffus. South Africa had failed by 28 runs to win the match.

Mitchell's feat was all the more remarkable for the fact that he was 38 years old. Moreover, his captain, demoted down the order for the Test, was clearly struggling with the physical and emotional rigours of the tour and, by the time the tour was over, had lost 47 pounds in weight. Other than Melville the only South African batsman who could be relied upon consistently to score runs was Nourse (who totalled 621 in the Tests compared to Mitchell's 597).

Still, Mitchell wasn't over-inclined to praise his exploits as the crown prince of the lost cause. He was always of the opinion that his undefeated 164 not out against England at Lord's in 1935 was his greatest innings ever. On a pitch affected by rain and infested with leatherjacket grub, Mitchell's score allowed Herby Wade to declare the South African second innings on 278 for six. Xenophon Balaskas, the leg-spinner, added to his five for 49 in the England first innings with four for 54 in the second as England imploded for 151 and South Africa won the Test by 157 runs.

No doubt tired by news of Mitchell's heroic caution, the *Rand Daily Mail* of

Tuesday August 19, 1947, ran a photograph and deep caption by way of a corrective. 'John Cobb's Railton Mobil Special is unloaded at Wendover, Utah, ten miles from the Bonneville Salt Flats speed course, after its 7 000-mile trip from England. Cobb will attempt to break his own world land speed record of 369.7 miles an hour on the Bonneville course.' Not everyone, then, was as diligent in his doggedness as Mitchell. While some tottered along bravely in perpetual second gear, Cobb was pursuing the ecstasy of speed.

Melville's merry men?

As far as the Tests were concerned, the 1947 tour to England was a self-evident failure. Other than the three Test defeats, Melville's men only lost twice, to Worcestershire in the opening match and to the MCC shortly before the first Test at Trent Bridge. Their problems against all but the strongest teams in the land stemmed from the fact that the team relied too heavily on the exploits of too few, with the rest of the South African side consigned to bit parts and frustrating cameos. Significantly, in this regard, Melville, Nourse, Mitchell and Viljoen, the senior batting vanguard, scored all but four of the 28 centuries on tour.

Correspondingly, Melville persistently over-bowled the bowlers he could trust, a captaincy trait he revealed before the war. 'I found him a very unimaginative captain,' says 'Mobil' Gordon, the bowler Melville said he would have loved to have taken on the cancelled tour of England in 1940 because he believed Gordon had the ability to prosper in English conditions. 'When you bowled at my pace you had to be careful but he wouldn't think twice about bowling you for 15 or even twenty overs.' Nowhere was Melville's reluctance to bowl any but the chosen few better illustrated on the tour itself than in the fourth Test at Headingley, where he bowled Athol Rowan unchanged after lunch for three and three-quarter hours – with only tea for an interval – although the off-spinner didn't take a wicket. 'Melville,' writes Duffus, 'had the Micaber-like belief that something would turn up.'

Despite physical frailties, a constant battle with insomnia and dispiriting weight loss as the tour progressed, 'the Rake,' as he was known to his mates, saw to it that the tour didn't plunge into embarrassment after the final Test at the Oval. Melville played in every one of the games after the fifth Test, leading by example if not by inspiration, a state of affairs which suggested he didn't want his gentlemanliness to be confused with softness. 'One morning, at breakfast, we opened the papers in Ireland and big headlines read: "Sir Learie

ove: The Transvaal Scottish cricket team at the Metaga Cricket Club outside of Nairobi, 1940.
*te Denis Begbie, sitting on extreme left.

low: Alan Melville, hands folded in front of him and wearing a cravat, leads the 1947 South
*icans onto the field at Leicester. Melville, an insomniac, was known as 'The Rake' by his team.

Above: The '47 South Africans take on Oxford University in late May. Athol Rowan is the bowler.

Below: Ellis Park, the temporary venue for Tests in Johannesburg after the demise of the old Wanderers, and before the 1956 birth of the new Wanderers.

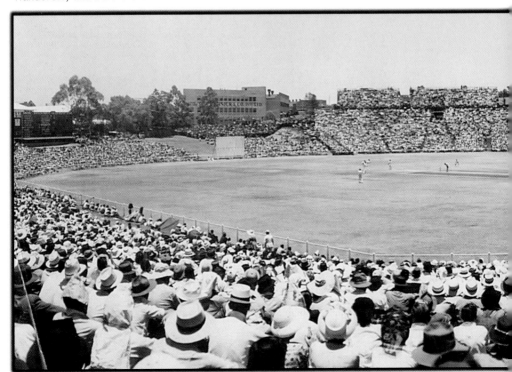

Above: A combined team photograph featuring England and South Africa in 1947. Dudley Nourse and Alan Melville flank England captain, Norman Yardley.

Above: The '47 South Africans prior to their departure. In front, from left to right, Ken Viljoen, Athol Rowan, Alan Melville, Algy Frames (manager), Johnny Lindsay, Denis Dyer and Ian Smith.

Below: Old Trafford, Manchester, venue of the third Test of the 1947 series.

ol Rowan, with club in hand, takes time off for a round of golf in 1947.

Above: Len Hutton slides Osie Dawson through the covers — Headingley Test, 1947. George Fullerton is the 'keeper and Bruce Mitchell is at first slip.

Below: Crowds as they used to be: a slice of the crowd that watched the fourth Test at Leeds, 19

bove: Eric Rowan scuffs one to leg during the first (unofficial) match of the 1951 tour of the
nited Kingdom. Keeping wicket is young Johnny Waite.

elow: Eric Rowan in characteristically loud voice: as Athol kisses his wife goodbye at the Johannesburg
ation, 1951, prior to the team's departure for Cape Town. Russell Endean looks suitably shocked.

Above: Prior to docking at Southampton in 1951, from left to right: Mick Melle, Russell Endean, Johnny Waite, Jackie McGlew, Geoff Chubb, Roy McLean, Dudley Nourse, Athol Rowan, George Fullerton, Percy Mansell, Eric Rowan, Cuan McCarthy (obscured), Clive van Ryneveld.

Below: The cold of a '51 England summer — note the clasped hands.

nother '51 team photo, from top of stairs: Johnny Waite, Clive van Ryneveld, Athol Rowan, Cuan cCarthy, Mick Melle, Percy Mansell, Jackie McGlew, Norman 'Tufty' Mann, Roy McLean, George llerton, Russell Endean, Eric Rowan, Geoff Chubb, Jack Cheetham, Dudley Nourse and Syd Pegler, e manager.

Above: Percy Mansell in the nets.

Below: Trying on new Stetsons, from left: Athol Rowan, Cuan McCarthy and Dudley Nourse.

Above: SA team for first Test at Trent Bridge in Nottingham: from back, left to right: McGlew, Waite, van Ryneveld, McCarthy, Cheetham, McLean, front: Mann, Chubb, Rowan (E), Rowan (A), Fullerton.

Below: The traditional tour opener: at Worcester in 1951.

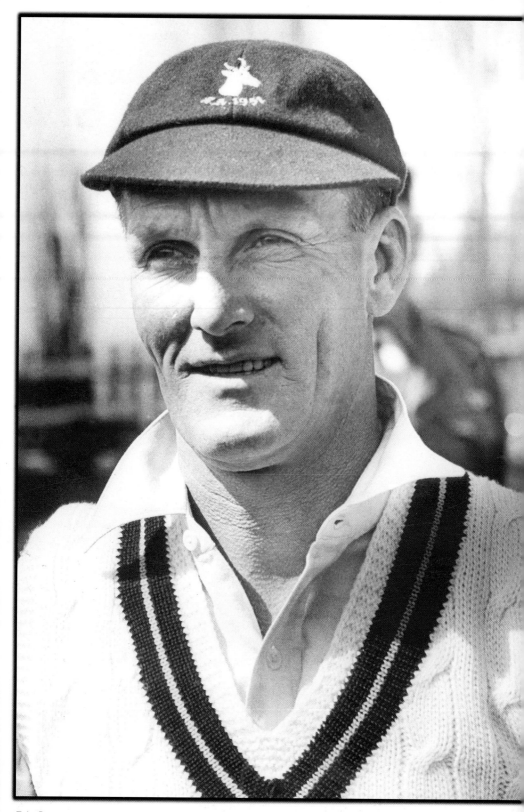

Eric Rowan

above: Johnny Waite faces up to Brian Statham during the second Test of the 1951 series; the non-triker is Eric Rowan. Note the leg-slip and short midwicket.

below: A reception at Lord's: from left, Waite, McGlew, Alec Bedser, Roy McLean, Athol Rowan nd Cuan McCarthy.

Above: 1951 — with Worcestershire cathedral in the background.

Below: SA v Derbyshire, Derby, 1951: Athol Rowan has the bails off in a flash.

Above: Dinner for both teams during 1951 tour of England. South Africans nearest the camera near the foreground are: George Fullerton, Russell Endean and Jack Cheetham, with Mick Melle on opposite side of the table.

Below: Athol Rowan snicks one through the slips during second test at Lord's. Standing up is Godfrey Evans; Len Hutton is the fielder.

Jackie McGlew and Johnny Waite opening the SA innings versus New Zealand, Basin Reserve, Wellington, 1952/3. McGlew went on to make 255 not out.

Constantine has no desire to meet the South African cricketers,"' says Begbie. 'And a reporter came up to Melville and said, "What do you think of this?" Melville looked at it and said "I don't think I ever indicated I wanted to meet him" and he left it at that.'

Despite Melville's resolve that the tour should not plunge into failure after the fifth Test, the South Africans were possibly over-concerned with their status as colonial guests. In one of the most revealing passages written about the tour, Arlott attempts to get to grips with Tuckett, a bowler of big heart and little venom. 'What, then, stopped him from reaching the highest class as a pace bowler,' asks Arlott. 'The answer lies in his complete lack of hostility, in the easy gentleness that went so well with his slouch and his shyness. When Yardley came in to bat in the second Test at Manchester, his first ball from Tuckett pitched on a good length and rose to strike the batsman in the jaw. For the remainder of the over Tuckett bowled half-volleys.'

There is evidence to suggest that the tourists and their wives felt compromised by association – the war was still too close, the countries, in sentiment and feeling at least, too near. The Tuckett example suggests that the South Africans, if only unconsciously, found England's cultural influence difficult to overcome. England's cricketers, therefore, were difficult to beat.

Ties between England and South Africa were, after all, still taut with feeling. In the February immediately prior to the start of the tour, a royal party of 29 – including Queen Elizabeth's detective, Inspector AE Perkins, her two dressers and her hairdresser – visited the Union for the first time. The Queen's wardrobe was appropriately African, with millinery colours such as 'Springbok,' 'pale mealies,' 'Rhodesian gold,' 'Limpopo' and 'Cape Mist' predominant. Four days after the Royal Party landed in Cape Town, King George V1 opened the Union Parliament and, shortly before their return, Princess Elizabeth (later to become Queen Elizabeth II) honoured Cape Town again by choosing it as the city from which to give her twenty-first birthday broadcast.

After their initial arrival in Cape Town the party, which included the King, Queen Elizabeth and the two princesses, toured the Cape Province before travelling through the Orange Free State and Basutoland. In Harrismith, Field-Marshall Smuts, the former member of the Imperial War Cabinet and Winston Churchill's long-time friend, entertained them. Smuts escorted the party to Ladysmith before they moved on to the Natal National Park in the Drakensberg and Bonza Bay, not far from East London. 'The Queen had great personal success with everyone, including the formidable South African

Dutch,' writes Dorothy Laird, a royal observer. 'The nationalists would have liked to have boycotted the tour entirely, but did not do so, partly out of respect for Field-Marshall Smuts, and the Queen charmed smiles onto many stern faces which had initially looked more than a little dour.'

As far as royalty on the 1947 tour itself was concerned, the players met King George and Queen Elizabeth shortly after the resumption of their follow-on innings at Lord's during the second Test. The King is reputed to have said to Melville during the introductions that his father was 'England's best change bowler' and that he hoped he didn't inherit his talents. It is not known how Melville saw fit to reply; what is more widely acknowledged is the fact that Melville and Viljoen lost their wickets soon afterwards.

As well as shaking the hand of royalty, the tourists and their wives rubbed shoulders with the aristocracy. George Fullerton was tossed sixpence when opening gates on the Duke of Portland's Sherwood Forest estate and Dorothy Begbie remembers an outing to Sutton Place in Surrey, home of the Duke and Duchess of Sutherland. 'I can only remember seeing bowl after bowl of golden azaleas,' she says. 'The Duchess told us how it brightened up the place and how they brought the flowers down from their shooting estate in Scotland. She had turned all her damask tablecloths into curtains. I can remember tickling Lady Lovett's feet...'

Characteristically, perhaps, Dawson remembers a different smell to that of azaleas. 'The tour was actually very ordinary,' he says. 'We used to go from the hotel to the ground and back again – there wasn't much time for sightseeing. We played 33 games all in all. We used to get 80 pounds pocket money a month, I think it was, and we spent it on shows like *Oklahoma* and *Annie Get Your Gun*. There wasn't much time for dancing and that kind of thing. There was a shortage of soap and the females used to smell a bit.'

Behind the cricket and the socialising, the tour was riven with significant tensions. The more well-to-do South Africans such as Melville, Mann, Mitchell, Nourse and Begbie brought their wives. Others, such as Viljoen, Tuckett and Dawson, were less fortunate. Algy Frames, the tour manager, attempted to keep the players and their wives apart wherever possible, even going so far as to not allow the wives onto the Cape Town Castle, the mailship which brought the team to England. Instead, the wives flew – and consorted with their menfolk when Frames dropped his guard. 'I loathed Algy Frames,' remembers Daphne Greenwood. 'He was very unkind to us. We had to go across on a different ship [others, such as Dorothy Begbie, flew]. We came diddling on behind. They wouldn't even allow us to take the same ship on the way back. That Algy Frames made life very difficult for us.'

The real victims in all of this were those outside of the inner sanctum. In Dawson's opinion it meant that the team was less cohesive than it should have been. 'The team could have been closer together but were not,' he says. 'There was also the jealousy between Dudley [Nourse] and Alan [Melville] and because of that the team didn't combine as well as it should. Dudley always had this chip on his shoulder about his breeding and the fact that he wasn't captain.'

CHAPTER 3

The Unthinkable

Man's inhumanity to man...

I n 1948 the unthinkable happened in South African politics: the Nationalists, under Dr Daniel Francois Malan, won the election, defeating Smuts' United Party as Smuts himself lost his seat in parliament by virtue of losing his by-election. The Nationalists' victory came about largely because of two things. Although they had been a spectacularly divided party through the war and had lost the 1943 election, they reconstituted themselves prior to the May 26 election around the emotive theme of 'native affairs'. Secondly, the 1910 constitution gave preferential weighting to voting in the country districts and so although the United Party and its allies polled almost 60 percent of the vote in pure numbers, when inflected through a system of country weighting, the Nationalists ended up with 79 votes as opposed to the United Party's 65, the Labour Party's six and three token votes by African representatives.

Once in power, the Nationalists did everything to tighten their grip. In time they flooded the police, the military and civil service with Afrikaners and passed a series of repressive bills through parliament. Such legislation introduced a series of infamous acts including, at one end of the spectrum of repression, the 1949 Citizenship Bill which limited British immigration and, at the other, such heinous bulwarks of apartheid as the Prohibition of Mixed Marriages Act (passed on June 29, 1949), the Population Registration Act (passed on May 16, 1950) and the Group Areas Act (passed on July 7, 1950). In 1951 the Illegal Squatters Act was passed and later that year the Abolition of Passes Act ruled that all black men were required to carry passes at all times. The latter act in particular was a high point in the theatre of the apartheid absurd – an act which appeared to signify an abolition was in fact designed to create the detested pass-book system, the very opposite of what its name suggested.

Along with this unified front of legislation, the post-1948 period brought forth a number of smaller symbolic moments that not only served to entrench Nationalist power, but also were designed to send unambiguous messages northwards. With Smuts and his imperial affections having fallen by the wayside – Churchill described their relationship as that between 'two lovebirds who can still peck' – Malan was free slowly to alienate South Africa's allies. Malan used the occasion of his swearing in as prime minister (on June 4, 1948) to make it clear that South Africa would not tolerate any 'external' interference in her domestic affairs. An oath of allegiance to King George V1 was taken, but the intent was obvious – don't meddle.

Nearly two years later and Malan announced a bill abolishing the right of appeal in the South African Appeal Court to the British Privy Council, whose members, not surprisingly, were appointed by the British Government. In keeping with the Nationalists' increasing fixation with sovereignty, it was felt that one of the last remaining bridges linking South Africa and Britain should be dynamited – and so it was.

While the Nationalists were on the one hand severing imperial ties and on the other refining double-speak to a virtual art, there was one realm in which imperial intimacies were still observed: on the cricket field. After Melville's men had returned empty-handed from England in 1947, a full Currie Cup season was played in '47/48 – this prior to the arrival of George Mann's MCC tourists the following year. The 1947/8 domestic season was dominated in general by Natal – who won six out of eight matches – and in particular by Dudley Nourse, who scored 863 Currie Cup runs at an average of 96. Natal's dominance was so complete that her nearest contenders, Transvaal and Griquas, only managed three victories apiece but, better than that from Natal's point of view, was the fact that their bush telegraph crackled with news of an unknown, eager and appropriately wet-behind-the-ears fast-bowler.

Fresh and flaxen-haired, Cuan McCarthy was barely out of school when he became the object of the Natal selectors' attention. Initially doubts were expressed about the legality of his action. 'It seemed at one stage of his delivery as though the arm did not quite belong to the rest of his body,' says his provincial captain, Nourse. 'We were mainly concerned with his elbow at the time because it was suggested that his delivery was not quite legitimate... After a thorough inspection we expressed ourselves as completely satisfied about the fairness of his delivery. The legitimacy, we felt, could not be questioned and that was one of the hurdles safely crossed.'

Some outside of Natal were less convinced. Begbie tells the story of McCarthy flooring Mitchell with a quicker one when Natal played Transvaal in the '47/48 Currie Cup season. 'Suddenly Bruce dropped to the floor, it was the funniest thing,' says Begbie. 'When he got up he marched down the wicket and told McCarthy in no uncertain terms that he chucked his quicker one. You didn't often see Bruce on the floor and you had to do something special to get him to talk to you like that because he wasn't a man of many words.'

McCarthy's provincial team-mates were less inclined to see him as a chucker. 'I remember we were travelling up on the train for a game against Transvaal,' says John Watkins, a cornerstone of Jack Cheetham's side to Australia in 1952/3. 'We were working out a few things about their batsmen and, really, he seemed more interested in thinking about his chickens back on the farm. If he had had that nasty attitude of some of our fast bowlers – like [Peter] Heine and [Neil] Adcock, for instance – then he probably would have done far better. He was the quickest I've ever faced: as quick as [Frank] Tyson and quicker than [Keith] Miller and [Ray] Lindwall. But he just didn't have that shithouse attitude. That's what really prevented him from becoming a great bowler.'

As Natal's Currie Cup season progressed, so Nourse asked more and more of McCarthy, increasing the length of his spells. In the game against Eastern Province, McCarthy bowled Eric Norton in the EP second innings with a 'jaffa' – the bail streaking '60 yards' into the distance. But it was only during Natal's penultimate game of the season against Rhodesia that McCarthy served notice. 'His six for 43 and four for 45 found him now a Springbok "prospect",' says Nourse. 'It was comforting to find that he remained just the natural modest youth. He had his leg pulled unmercifully by his team-mates and took it all in good fun. I was watching this carefully and found it a healthy sign.'

In keeping with their status as the previous year's Currie Cup champions, Natal provided the MCC with their stiffest resistance prior to the first Test of the 1948/9 series. The MCC batted first, with Compton scoring a century in the tourists' 391. Of the MCC's nine wickets to fall, five were taken by McCarthy, lending encouragement to those who rightly believed that South Africa needed to replace her limited pace battery prior to the first Test at Kingsmead.

Elsewhere in the country, Tuckett had taken four wickets for Orange Free State against the MCC in Bloemfontein and Begbie (154) and Tony Harris (98) had prospered for Transvaal in a high-scoring game at Ellis Park immediately prior to the first Test. 'After weeks of caution akin to convalescence,' writes Duffus in the City Late edition of *The Star* of December 13, 1948, 'South African cricket comes out of plaster today with the announcement of the team to play in the first Test match in Durban. Here in the Transvaal, the centre of liveliest competition, performances have been over-shadowed by ambitions and in the MCC match international aspects popped up at every turn, like small boys after Compton's autograph. At any rate, it is charitable to believe that the Transvaal batting was unduly influenced by the scrutiny of three official and 18 000 amateur selectors for, apart from Begbie's innings, it was all disappointingly defensive.'

'It belongs to a novel, not Wisden...'

Despite scoring 92 for Transvaal against the tourists, Melville didn't captain the South Africans in the home series against the MCC, that honour falling to Nourse and a just reward for his patience. Melville had sustained a damaged wrist earlier in the season and decided not to risk further injury. The home team included Owen Wynne, the young opening batsman from the Cape who had scored two impressive centuries against the tourists, as well as Begbie and Harris, but otherwise it was the usual array of suspects such as Athol Rowan and his brother Eric, Osie Dawson, Lindsay Tuckett, Billy Wade as 'keeper and Tufty Mann.

Demonstrating an out-of-character recklessness, the selectors chanced their arm on McCarthy, although Duffus made no bones about being a dissenter. 'He [McCarthy] is raw but fast acquiring refinements,' he writes. 'The presence of Dawson and Tuckett in the side should allow a desirable rationing of McCarthy's overs.'

In the event, the major threat to South Africa's chance of going one-nil up was their inability to occupy time at the crease. Batting first they were bowled out for 161, Begbie pinching 37 and his captain wresting 37 precious runs from an attack featuring Alec Bedser and Cliff Gladwin. 'I was always going to prosper against Bedser because his stock ball was the in-swinger, and I got a good look at him in the match against Transvaal,' remembers Begbie. 'I was always very good on the leg-side through mid-on and I picked him up early. He did bowl the cutter that went the other way and he made very good use of the crease but you could spot him because he used the crease differently depending on the delivery.'

Len Hutton and Cyril Washbrook were cruising within 17 runs of the South Africans' total when the ever-modest Mann accepted the invitation to bowl. He finished with six for 59, his best bowling in Tests, and England were all out for 233, Compton eking out 72 – England's top score. Facing a first innings deficit of 92, South Africa lost crucial early wickets (Wynne failing for the second time in the Test) before Begbie and Wade provided a stabilising influence. The two fashioned a partnership of 85 precious runs and South Africa managed to stay in the Test, hanging on for dear life.

Late on the fourth afternoon and in deteriorating light England batted for a second time. They needed to score 128 in 131 minutes to win. Washbrook was dropped off the first ball of the England innings by Wynne, Hutton departed soon afterwards and then new boy McCarthy dropped the England skipper, George Mann. But McCarthy made amends. Bowling quickly in the soupy light he burrowed into the England innings, taking six for 33 in 10 hostile overs.

The last over of the match arrived with England needing eight runs and South Africa two wickets. In the heat of the moment, the Test having barrelled to such a wonderful conclusion, several bowlers seemed reluctant to accept the challenge. 'Last over,' says Arlott in the commentary box, 'and heaven knows who dare bowl it. Lindsay Tuckett looks to me like a man who doesn't want to. And Dudley Nourse is going to decide it and he's going to put Tufty Mann on, which is the wisest thing he's done in this innings. Tufty doesn't want to either. It's Tuckett after all. I think he asked Tufty Mann whether he could take that over or not and Tufty, who is very much out of practice, I think he's only had about two matches apart from this one has, I think, said Lindsay had better bowl for a draw because if Tufty goes on to bowl he's bowling for a win. It's Lindsay Tuckett from the Umgeni end. The last over...'

Bedser, facing Tuckett off the first ball of the final over, scrambled a leg-bye after the ball had looped to second slip. The single brought Cliff Gladwin on to strike: seven balls, seven runs. 'Bad light, steady rain,' narrates Arlott, 'and Tuckett is bowling with only two men near the wicket, a slip and a silly mid-on. Bowls to Gladwin, Gladwin's wiped this up in the long field. It's over the fieldsman's head and it's gone for four. A hundred and twenty-five for eight. One-two-five for eight. Three to win, two wickets to fall, six balls to go. Cliff Gladwin, who hits a catch every ball, and if he goes Doug Wright follows him, and he only hits one ball and hits a certain catch off that. A hundred and twenty-five for eight. The last over, Tuckett to bowl the third ball. Bowls Gladwin a bumper, off Gladwin's wrist to long-leg. A hundred and twenty-six, they daren't take one for the throw. Two to win, that was the third ball. If this goes five balls there will be no commentator left. Bedser touching his toes then, I think for mental relaxation. Tuckett wiping the ball on the towel; the hills of north Durban completely hidden by rain which is falling steadily round the bluffs. And Tuckett bowls to Bedser and Bedser swings and Dudley Nourse has stopped it and he's tried to run him out. And he's hit him and he hasn't run him out.'

Bedser was hit in the stomach by the next ball from Tuckett, the ball passing over the wickets. No run was taken. With three deliveries to go, South Africa needed two wickets, England two runs. The sixth ball of the over was a bumper; Bedser dragged it awkwardly into the covers. Arlott is on the verge of hysteria: 'They're going to run, they'll never make it. They daren't take the overthrow. A hundred-and-twenty seven for eight. They didn't dare the overthrow, I don't think either of them have got sufficient nerve or sufficient wind and I certainly have no wind at all. Two balls, one run, two wickets. And the two wickets could go just as easily as the one run could come.'

At this point it dawns on Arlott that the Test has been tied. England are nearly home and dry. But Tuckett has a trick up his sleeve. He bowls Gladwin a bouncer, ballooning over leg-stump. The tailender flaps. The ball is missed. In an attitude of profound relief, Wade captures the ball and prevents it from being byes. Arlott again: 'Tuckett, from the Umgeni end, to Cliff Gladwin. One run to win and one ball to go. Tuckett to Gladwin… and, he's knuckled it, and they're running, and Bedser isn't run out and they've won on the last ball of the last over.'

After he has gathered his breath and his wits, Arlott sums up: 'If you wanted to put it in a book no-one would ever believed it. It belongs to a novel, not Wisden. Never in all my life have I imagined that I would see such a finish. They're carrying in Gladwin now and anyone else who has got the strength even to be carried. And McCarthy. And this wicket looks even worse now than it did a minute ago because half of Durban is running on it. All juvenile Durban. It's just the most incredible finish.'

There was to be a further twist to the nail-biting saga of the first Test, for South African radio listeners at least. Unable to deal with the fact that the concluding moments of the Test ran across six pm, the news came on promptly as scheduled. Local listeners didn't hear the conclusion of the Test in real time, having to wait until the end of the bulletin before hearing the news of Gladwin's scrambled leg bye.

An achievement with the queerest twist...

Eric Rowan, recalled for the series against George Mann's side after failing to be included in the 1947 tour party, had an unerring instinct for the grand gesture. On the front page of *The Star* on November 13, 1948, he appeared in a photograph, pulling a ball for six. Underneath the photograph, the caption read: 'Eric Rowan, with a mighty swipe to leg, sent up the 100 for the Transvaal in their match against Natal at Ellis Park this afternoon, with a six that sailed into the hands of a spectator who took a brilliant catch. The spectator was none other than Peter van der Bijl, a national selector. Wade, the Natal wicket-keeper, watches as the ball flies over seven rows of benches into Mr Van der Bijl's hands.'

Rowan, Athol's older brother, scored 97 in the match versus Natal before falling leg before to Dawson. Whether it was the innings itself, the calculated bravado of the six into Van der Bijl's hands or his reputation, Rowan insinuated himself into the side for the first Test, playing for South Africa again aged 39 – this after making his Test debut against England in 1935 and playing his previous series during the rubber which included the 'Timeless Test' before the war. But he failed in the first Test against the 1948/9 tourists and failed in the first innings of the second. By the time he batted again in the series, he knew he was surplus to requirements for the third and wouldn't be catching the plane to Cape Town at the conclusion of the second. It was just the provocation he needed.

The second Test was played in temperatures unusually high for even the Rand in midsummer. During the Test, local newspapers carried dire warnings about the imminent withering of the maize crop and Johannesburg householders were prohibited from watering their gardens between noon and 7pm under threat of prosecution. The *Rand Daily Mail*'s agricultural correspondent filed this report from Heilbron: 'With most of the Union's 500-mile-long maize belt suffering from severe drought, it is almost certain that the country's 1949 maize crop will not be sufficient to meet even internal needs.'

Into this dry Highveld heat stepped a hatless and gloveless Eric Rowan. He was 17 not out overnight after the third day's play, Mitchell there with him on seven not out. Having been bowled out for 315 in their first innings in response to England's mammoth 608 all out, the South Africans started play on the fourth morning in grave danger of slipping to an innings defeat and so going two-nil down in the series. But Rowan and Mitchell were not about to hand the Englishmen their wickets on a plate.

The two batsmen knew each other well. They were first introduced to each other while at school and remained friends well into their dotage. Rowan remembered scoring a century and taking a couple of wickets for Jeppe Boys' High against St John's College at under-13 level, with Mitchell doing the same for his school. 'Well I played against Bruce,' says Rowan, speaking to the SABC's Steve de Villiers with Mitchell in March, 1987, 'when we played school cricket, under-13, he was captain of St Johns. I think he scored 132 and took about six wickets. I scored 112 and took two wickets.'

On the fourth morning, they batted together until lunch. At the interval the 'volatile little fellow,' as EW Swanton called Rowan, was 44 not out, with his partner on 37 not out. The match was beginning to tilt if not squarely in South Africa's favour then certainly in the direction of a draw. Mitchell departed after the break and, at tea-time, the threat of defeat having receded almost completely, Rowan was five shy of his debut Test century. 'When the England players took the field for the last 105 minutes of the match,' writes the *Rand Daily Mail's* TD Nelson, 'their playful demeanour suggested they had abandoned all hope of forcing a victory, and they joined in the ovation when, with a powerful pull to the fence off Bedser, Rowan achieved his century. This took him 273 minutes and he had hit 12 fours.'

Alex Bannister, a syndicated columnist for a number of English papers, offered the following: 'One of cricket's strangest stories was unfolded here today when South Africa successfully avoided defeat in the second Test. Eric Rowan, whom the selectors decided yesterday was not good enough for the third Test starting at Cape Town on Saturday, virtually saved South Africa from defeat with his maiden, and undefeated, Test century. Hatless under a remorseless sun, and scorning batting gloves, 39-year-old Rowan, often described as the problem boy of South African cricket, laughed and wisecracked his defiance of the dreadfully tired England attack for five and a half hours today and 38 minutes last evening.'

Writing in the *Daily Telegraph*, Swanton took a still different line. 'South Africa saved the second Test handsomely yesterday, thanks in chief to an innings of great resolution and moral courage by Eric Rowan, who batted through the entire day and took out his bat for an innings of 156 not out. Only three South Africans have made longer scores against England in a Test match, and what, of course, gave the achievement the queerest twist, was the fact that only a day previously the selectors had reluctantly, no doubt, decided to dispense with Rowan's services for the third Test in favour of a younger player. Thus, for the second time, the selectors have been unlucky, if not in the choice, at least in the timing of their meeting. It is as well that they have so firm a reputation as good and experienced judges. There was no ill-humour, surely, in the cry of the barracker shortly before sunset: "Put the selectors' on, they'll get him out".'

Neither Nelson, Bannister nor Swanton found a means to accommodate in their copy what Rowan did when he went to his hundred. According to his nephew, Peter, he shoved an unmistakable up-yours sign in the selectors' direction, a standard item in the Rowan repertoire. 'Well, he was duly called to explain himself afterwards,' says Peter Rowan, 'and after showering he went to the glass house to put his case. They asked him in no uncertain terms what the hell he thought he was doing. He asked the selectors if they hadn't notice the fearful row going on down at Castle corner – or whatever passed for Castle corner in those days – and they were a bit nonplussed, but reluctantly said yes. He told them that because they had been so supportive of his innings through the afternoon he had given them the V for victory sign. The selectors had seen the gesture the wrong way round because they were on the other side of the ground.'

'Teddy, would you really like to play?'

Unlike his good friend Mitchell, who lived in the prestigious suburb of Houghton, Eric Rowan came from a different part of town. Alfred and Jane Rowan, Eric and Athol's parents, lived at a house in Berg Street, Fairview, and then in Eleanor Street in the far less affluent suburb of Troyeville. Later, after their mother's sudden death, their father lived at 14 Katoomba St in Kensington. 'He was brought up on the wrong side of town,' says Di Thompson, Rowan's only daughter from his second marriage. 'Maybe he felt certain people were a little bit spoon-in-the-mouth. He really had to work very hard for everything. He was an altarboy at the Anglican Church in Marshall St and I remember him telling us how, after church, he walked to cricket because the family didn't have a car.'

The brothers were educated at Jeppe Boys', the local high school, although Athol spent a period at the Troyeville intermediate school before matriculating from Jeppe in 1937. Jeppe Boys' drew its students from the suburbs of Jeppe, Kensington, Malvern, Troyeville, Bertrams and Bezuidenhout Valley – working and middle-class suburbs which fan east from the city itself out towards Germiston and the East Rand. Eric, the eldest of five children (other than Athol, the youngest, there was another brother, Basil, and two sisters, Phyllis and Dulcie), was talented enough to be noticed by the Jeppe Old Boy elders while at school but his mother frowned heavily upon Sunday cricket, a definite problem during the early stages of his career. In 1970, Rowan told the SABC's Charles Fortune the following story:

'One of the first times I ever had to play this great game I was 17 and I had to face the great Buster Nupen, who I'm sure Bruce will agree, was without doubt the greatest bowler you ever will see on the mat. When I was told on the Monday night that I was playing I started to get the wind up. And by the time Saturday came I was in such a state that I could hardly keep my knees from knocking. And, I walked in, and he bowled me first ball. And I can remember my old dad was waiting for me at the gate. As I walked out he said to me: "If ever I see you go in frightened again I will give you the hiding of your life." And my old man used to give me one or two occasionally and I didn't relish them. And that, I think, helped me, because in later years I got picked to play Sunday cricket, mainly because I was able to play Buster and I made a lot of runs against him. At first I never played Sunday cricket because my mother wouldn't allow it. I was a Sunday school teacher, a head server of the church and a choir boy and all that sort of thing and the Jeppe Old Boys needed to beat Old Eds [Edwardians] in the last game of the season and they came along to see my mother to see if she would let me play. Well, I was standing in the passage outside the lounge: she gave them such a dressing-down it wasn't true. They weren't to be put off, because the next day they got hold of my old boss, AE Cooper, and he came round. She threw him out on his ear, it was a wonder I wasn't sacked the next day. Then they made up their minds that they'd have one more go, and they got hold of our minister, a chap called Reverend Tomkin. And poor old Reverend Tomkin arrived at our house and by golly, what my mother said to him was a sin and a shame. I can hear her saying: "And you, a man of God, have the audacity to ask me to let my son play cricket on a Sunday?" To cut a long story short, on Thursday night we were walking along Marshall St to the church for choir practice and my mother, she used to call me Teddy, "Teddy," she said, "Teddy, would you really like to play?" I said, "yes, Mum, I'd love to." Well, she said, you can play on one condition – that you teach Sunday school first. Well, we used to teach Sunday school from 10 o'clock in those days. At twenty past ten there was a motor car waiting outside from the Jeppe Old Boys – we only had one car throughout the entire team, it was driven by Len Wittick, and they were waiting for me. I jumped in the back of the car, I should have been had up for public indecency because I got undressed from my ordinary suit into my cricket clothes and when I got to the ground Buster Nupen was creating havoc. They padded me up and sent me in and luckily enough I made a hundred. But Bob Catteral really set the scoreboard on fire and we beat them for the first time in many years.'

Eiulf Peter Nupen, an off-spinner of Norwegian descent, was part of a generation of South African cricketers who struggled to make the transition from matting to turf wickets. A prodigious spinner of the ball, he could be unplayable on matting wickets, so much so that Herbert Sutcliffe was inspired to write: 'I had batted against 'Buster' Nupen when he played for Transvaal, and I have to confess that he made me look like a novice.'

The family's original name was Lillerorde but they changed it to Nupen, the area in Norway from which they hailed, shortly after arriving in South Africa in 1887. Eiulf Peter Nupen (or Buster as he came to be known) was the third of three sons. He was born on the first day of the first month in 1902 and when he was four he was involved in an accident which was to colour the rest of his life. 'At age four,' writes Heinrich Schulze in his book on South African cricketers who have gone on to make careers in the legal profession, 'when hitting two hammers together, a piece of steel flew into his eye. His father took him to a specialist in Germany but nothing could be done to save the eye and he wore a glass eye from then on.'

A gregarious, vital and strong-willed man, Nupen didn't appear to allow his disability to affect him in the slightest. One of his favourite party tricks in later life involved replacing his usual glass eye with an eye that contained a tiny Union Jack, the logic being that the new glass eye would look exactly like Nupen's good eye at that stage of the party.

A fine all-round sportsman and scholar, Nupen cut a swathe through King Edward, his high school, and played his cricket for the club the school fed – Old Edwardians. In a 17-Test career in which he took 50 wickets at 35, his finest moment came against Percy Chapman's MCC side at the Old Wanderers in 1930/1. Needing 240 for victory batting last, the visitors were skittled by Nupen who, in taking six for 87 (adding to his first innings five for 63) gave South Africa the match (and the series) by 28 runs.

'Nupen's "Test match",' writes Duffus, 'would not be complete without the picture that was to be seen at the close of play. Uncooled from the heat of the match he stood smilingly accepting congratulations. He had three stitches in his chin from a flying snick to the slips – hardly the place you would think for a man with one eye. He had an injured knee wrapped in a bandage and an aching strain in his side from just bowling twenty-five overs [he bowled 51.4 overs in the match]. He had just captained his first and possibly only Test match team to victory.'

Nupen, who had been shot in both knees during the 1922 Rand Rebellion, played only one Test after the three-Test series against Chapman's side in 1930/1 – against Vic Richardson's Australians in 1935/6. After that, it was a distinguished career in the law and the occasional party trick involving the midnight replacement of glass eyes.

While the curve of Nupen's career through the thirties suggested gradual decline, Eric Rowan's was moving in the opposite direction. Born six months after Mitchell, on July 20, 1909, Rowan made his Currie Cup debut for Transvaal during the 1929/30 season, playing once and scoring 48 runs in two innings. His debut Currie Cup hundred came the following season when he scored 393 Currie Cup runs at 56.14, and his growing reputation was confirmed in 1933/4 when he scored two centuries in an aggregate of 469 runs at 78.16. Again he averaged over fifty the following year and was chosen to go to England in 1935, scoring just under 2 000 runs while part of a successful, series-capturing team.

But the seasons immediately following the happy tour to England were tough ones for Rowan. He only played three of the five Tests against the 1935/6 Australians, his wretched form against Richardson's side being reflected in his domestic cricket. In 1936/7 he only managed 175 Currie Cup runs but the following year was considerably worse. In 1937/8 he played 13 innings for Transvaal but could only manage 189 runs at an average of 15.75. Rowan's nephew surmises that Rowan's dreadful form coincided with his divorce from his first wife, Gladys. 'I can only hazard a guess at that,' he says, 'and perhaps that was when he was getting divorced from his first wife. He was an inveterate gambler, Eric, always out to parties and going out with the boys. In an effort to keep him in the house – she would never see him, you see – she would lock him up. She once actually locked him in the bathroom. She was that desperate.'

Rowan played four of the five Tests against Wally Hammond's 1938/9 tourists – scoring 89 not out in the drawn second Test in Cape Town and 67 in defeat at Kingsmead in the third – but the shadows of war were looming. More important was the fact that having captained the home side against Hammond's men, Melville was convinced he wanted nothing to do with Rowan. The Troyeville boy was confrontational, belligerent and bumptious. It was decided that South African cricket could do without him. When the 1947 side to England was announced there was place for an 'A Rowan' but no space for 'E Rowan'. According to Athol's son, Peter, a Pietermaritzburg lawyer, the shock for Athol, eleven and a half years Eric's junior, was so extreme that at one point he was on the verge of pulling out of the tour.

With regard to Eric Rowan, Melville was not alone in his view. Daphne Greenwood, Tufty Mann's widow, remembers Rowan as 'thoroughly vulgar'. Begbie found him helpful and attentive in one-on-one situations, but loud and opinionated in a group. Certainly, Rowan was cut from different cloth to many of the South African cricketers who straddled the immediate pre- and post-war period. He was flinty, competitive and hard – a South African in a baggy green cap – and the establishment found him impossible to deal with. 'The mistakes that occur,' says Keith Miller, 'are similar to the Springbok blunder in 1947 when South Africa actually toured England without Eric Rowan, then unquestionably one of the best bats in the world.'

Mr Mars' bar... and a little Lord's on the peninsula

And so hastily to Cape Town for the third Test. Newlands had been the scene of one of the tour's more controversial incidents seven weeks prior to the third Test when Freddie Mills, the English boxer and a colleague of Denis Compton's in the war, had been prevented from entering the members' enclosure to renew acquaintance with his friend. The incident – dubbed the 'Mills Incident' – was widely reported in the English and local press. Many felt it was symptomatic of the pettiness of the Newlands administration at the time, a ground dominated by one Mr Mars, the president of the Western Province Cricket Club.

'Veteran sports writers and some overseas journalists who are following the MCC tour said yesterday that the Mills incident was the culmination of pin-pricks and insults offered pressmen and radio commentators at Newlands,' writes *The Star's* 'Own Correspondent'. 'One well-known writer from the Rand observed that journalists, particularly South African sportswriters, were being treated like "ink-stained urchins" and were not given facilities for talking to players and managers. Two South African radio commentators were ejected from the members' bar recently by Mr Mars while they were interviewing cricketers.

Press photographers complain that they are no longer allowed to take cars carrying heavy equipment into the grounds and cannot keep cars available to rush pictures to the city.'

Mills, who had served with Compton in Burma during the war, dropped by unannounced after his fight against South Africa's Johnny Ralph at Johannesburg's Wembley Arena, two days previously. Ralph, the local favourite, had a weight, reach and a height advantage, but lost the fight nonetheless. He was stunned by a Mills left hook to the jaw in the fifth, knocked to the canvas five times in the sixth and eventually put out of his misery in the eighth, leaving the majority of the 24 000 fans silent and frustrated.

Mills, his wife, his mother-in-law, his manager, Ted Broadribb, and his sparring partner, a Mr Williams, then caught the plane to Cape Town in the hope of catching up with Compton. But Mr Mars was patrolling the members' pavilion with his usual vigilance. Once they were refused entry to the pavilion, Mills and his manager's case was taken up by Brigadier MA Green, the England manager. Green sought an interview with Mars. Mars explained that the Mills entourage hadn't been refused permission to enter the pavilion, they had simply been refused permission to the members' section of the pavilion including the bar. In order to get to Compton, Mills would have needed to have walked through the bar, admission to which was reserved for members, honorary members and their guests. Had they been accompanied by a member, Mills, Broadribb and Williams would have been allowed into the members' bar, but as they were strangers to Mars, he had felt within his rights to refuse them entry. The crowning glory of Mars' argument was yet to come. 'He also pointed out to Brigadier Green,' wrote TD Nelson in the following day's *Rand Daily Mail*, 'that at Lord's cricket ground, no non-members would be allowed in the long bar, but there visitors could enter the dressing-room without passing through the members' bar.'

Life had long been made complicated at Newlands in that the Western Province Cricket Club were the owners of the ground. Traditionally they leased the ground to the Western Province Cricket Union for big games, but reserved right of admission to the pavilion. Hence Mr Mars' disproportionate influence and telling reference to how similar matters were dealt with at Lord's.

Mr Mars appeared to have reined in his martinet tendencies and love of policing by the time the tourists returned because the Test – a drawn one – passed without controversy. As at the Wanderers, the Test was dominated by high temperatures and high scoring, although the wicket gave the South African bowlers some slight help on the first day. At close of play on day one, England were 294 for nine. They were bowled out for 308 early on the second morning, thanks mainly to the one Rowan in the side, who took five for 80.

'It must rank with one of the great performances in Test cricket,' says Rowan's captain, Nourse, 'because Rowan had little in the way of aid from the wicket. He spun the ball just a shade more than made it comfortable for the batsmen. He gave the deliveries a bit of air and he whipped through faster than usual. It was certainly Rowan's day and the critics were already claiming that he was the finest off-spinner in the world.'

By rights, Rowan shouldn't have played in the series at all. While fighting in the desert, he was dreadfully injured by the recoil of a mortar plate, an injury that limited his contribution to a meagre 15 post war Tests. 'He talked occasionally on how he came to damage his knee through the firing of mortar bombs at the Germans whilst in a river-bed swamp,' recalls his son. 'He was holding the base plate when the mortar was fired, this shifted and severely severed the cartilage and ligaments around his knee. As I recall the story he unfortunately had to lie in the river-bed for a few days before they were able to transport him to base camp.' At the end of the war, Rowan aggravated the injury when hurt in a rugby match at King William's Town where he was involved in basic air force training. According to his son, he was playing for an air force team in a scratch game against one of the Army teams and was tackled hard while hurtling down the wing.

Unlike his wiry elder brother Eric, Athol Rowan was powerful and thick-set. 'My father was an immensely strong person,' says Peter. 'And many people commented on his vice-like grip and sheer physical strength. Both Eric and my dad knew the Toweel boxing family pretty well and I am not sure whether it was one of the Toweels who said of my dad when he was young, that had he followed a boxing career, he would have met with much success. As a youngster growing up on the tough back streets of Troyeville I understand he wasn't afraid of becoming embroiled in a fight.'

Allied to his strength and indomitability was an unorthodox but highly effective technique for an off-spinner. It involved cocking the wrist and gripping the ball tightly between thumb and index finger, with the index finger running parallel to the seam. The middle finger was then tucked as far round the other side of the ball as Rowan could manage. Bowling at a pace a shade faster than your average slow bowler, Rowan was a big spinner of the ball whom no-one relished facing.

'At Jeppe [Old Boys] we used to practise on an old concrete tennis court and we would always rather face Neil Adcock than Athol,' remembers Gerald Ritchie, a Jeppe batsman and regular member of the Transvaal team in the mid-fifties. 'If you stood at silly mid-off you could actually hear the ball fizz. It would hit the concrete and, shit, would it bounce! Athol was a big man, 6.2 I would think, and he had a split between his index and middle finger and he would give the ball a real rip. Adcock wouldn't bounce you, and you could rely on the bounce, but Athol was a terror to play in those nets.'

But back to the South African first innings at Newlands, a reply which brought forth a characteristically eccentric episode from Mitchell. At one point he took three quarters of an hour to score two and nearly an hour to score four. By close on the second day, Mitchell had crept to 93 not out and, with him, Dudley Nourse was undefeated on 64, the South African total sitting pretty on 223 for two. Hoping to build a first innings lead on the third day, the South African innings stalled instead. Nourse went to his century before Mitchell went to his, but the middle-order was unable to capitalise when Nourse fell for 112 and Mitchell for 120. The South Africans only managed 133 runs for the loss of eight wickets on the day and their hoped-for initiative was squandered. 'A glorious chance had been lost,' says Nourse.

England clipped along jauntily in reply, declaring their second innings on 276 for three. South Africa had a fraction over two hours to score 229. Wynne and Melville approached their task gamely but the total was beyond them. South Africa ended up on 142 for four. The Test was drawn. Nourse was in no mood for diplomatic niceties and equivocation. 'No, on this occasion our failure was due to the lack of quicker and more runs from our middle batsmen, from whom we might have expected it,' he says. 'It was frustrating cricket to say the least of it. Once again we had missed the boat.' Was this a way of making a veiled plea for Eric Rowan? Given the history of tension between the two, probably not, although Rowan would have been invaluable in both the first innings and during the chase.

Although Eric was back at his brother's side for the fourth Test in Johannesburg, it made little difference to South Africa's chances of levelling the series. After a high-scoring draw in the fourth, Mitchell continued his painful assault on slow-scoring records. He cobbled together 73 runs in a day as South Africa batted first in the fifth Test at Port Elizabeth, a Test which they needed to win if they were to share the series. 'I must confess that while I was batting with Mitchell I felt the security at the opposite end and it did enable me to go for the runs,' says Nourse. 'But 73 in a whole day is slow by any standards and Mitchell found it difficult, as I did to start with, to pierce the off-cordon of fielders. There were seven of them at times to Bedser and Gladwin and with two bowlers as accurate as they are the vacancy on the leg side might be tempting but would be suicidal to attempt to play to from an off-theory.'

After scoring 219 on the first day, South Africa crept their way to 379 on the second, Billy Wade scoring his debut Test century (125), Mitchell 99, and Nourse and Viljoen 73 apiece. All told, the innings took over nine hours. Initially the painful rate of scoring didn't seem to matter because England looked jittery against Athol Rowan on a crumbling pitch, plunging to an unconvincing 168 for five. But George Mann, the England captain, whisked the innings away from danger. He scored 136 not out as England declared on 395, 16 runs on and with no chance of losing the series. His innings prompted the following from RWV Robins, a Middlesex colleague: 'Now I believe in fairies as well.'

South Africa started off unexpectedly well in their second innings At lunch on the final day, Nourse was beginning to flirt with the possibility of a declaration. Knowing that he had to be bold, this he did at tea, leaving England 172 to win in 95 minutes. 'Before Washbrook and Hutton reached the wicket I knew what the answer to my challenge would be,' recalls Nourse. 'I could sense it in the way they strode briskly to the wicket. Hutton took guard, had merely a perfunctory look at the field as though he was merely counting the number of his opponents and then glory broke loose.' Hutton hit the first ball he faced for four, Washbrook hit his for six. The two brought up the fifty within 27 minutes, and although Hutton fell with the total on 57, the hundred was up in less than an hour. Then Nourse received what he had been gambling on. Washbrook was caught slashing and Compton, Bedser and Mann came and went in quick succession. Gladwin and Griffith then fell in the space of three balls and England were suddenly seven wickets down.

'Must I hit it,' asks Watkins, the next batsman.

'Yes,' replies Mann from the players' enclosure, 'have it out.'

Watkins obeyed, the final over of the match bringing England 13 runs. The winning four was struck by Jack Crapp, Watkins' partner. It raised a puff of dust before cannonballing into the rails. 'I did not grudge England their victory,' says Nourse. 'Any side capable of such a feat is worthy of the fruits of their labours.'

South Africa had done marginally better at home than they had managed to do in England 18 months previously. In 1948/9 the Kingsmead Test was narrowly lost, the three middle Tests drawn and fifth Test sacrificed by Nourse as he gambled on the possibility of an unlikely victory. Other factors there might have been, but the South African catching during this period was uniformly poor. They dropped three crucial catches during England's second innings in the first Test and Nourse notes that at least two catches – including a difficult caught and bowled, the culprit isn't named – were squandered as England began their frantic chase at St George's Park.

'Our opportunities were lost "in the air",' says Nourse. 'Since we, in our home country, should be the more accustomed to the light and the air, there can be no reason why we should fail to hold the catches if the players from a different climate can show us the way.' Ritchie, who as a boy worked the Ellis Park scoreboard during the second Test against Mann's men, remembers that holding on to a catch – particularly off the fast bowlers – was the exception rather than the norm. 'McCarthy used to have so many catches dropped off his bowling it wasn't true,' he says. 'There were so many nicks, Ken Viljoen dropped them, Eric, Nourse, they all had a go fielding in the slips. Usually the ball just went for four because they were too busy looking for someone to do the job. The only decent catcher in that position was Bruce Mitchell. He was a good fielder. In the late forties, when the MCC or the Aussies were here, no-one could catch a damn thing.'

Duffus was broadly in agreement. 'It is probably not too much to say that if, in the era of twenty-five Test matches when Melville and Nourse led the sides and the country scored one victory, only half the catches that were missed had been taken, both would have been famous as conquering captains,' he writes in *Springbok Glory*. 'And with them a whole string of bowlers, particularly Cuan McCarthy, Michael Melle, Lindsay Tuckett, Athol Rowan and Tufty Mann would have improved both their reputations and records most significantly.'

CHAPTER 4

Hassett's happy songbirds

'I can't laugh at Lindwall and Miller.'

On January 8, 10 and 11, 1949, an unknown Eastern Province wicket-keeper made a patient 80 in his team's drawn game with the MCC visitors. His name was Johnny Waite. He was 19 years old and destined to play a pivotal role in South African cricket over the next fifteen years. Prior to the MCC's departure for England on the Sterling Castle, Waite had another shot at Mann's men, playing for an SA Student's X1. This time he failed, but his name, while not quite in lights, was beginning to emit a faint glow. And he was being spoken about in circles outside of his home province.

Waite's next big chance against a touring team came shortly before the first Test against Lindsay Hassett's visiting Australians in 1949/50. He was selected to keep wicket and bat for a South African X1 at Kingsmead and it gave him an opportunity to face not only Keith Miller and Bill Johnston but Eric Rowan. 'Anyhow, I got there,' says Waite, 'I was bloody nervous, I hardly knew a soul. I was actually writing exams at Rhodes [University] in Grahamstown at the time and needed to get special permission to play. Anyway, I put my bag down in the change-room, and I sort of looked around, and the next minute, in comes Eric. "Whose bag is this," he says. "It's mine," I said. He picked it up and he threw it out the bloody window onto the street. So I said: "That's my bag." He didn't take any notice. He just said: "Take your bloody bag! This is my place, I change here, and don't you forget it".'

Waite was not to be intimidated, seeing it as Rowan's unique and big-hearted way of breaking the ice. Soon he was asking Rowan how to deal with hostilities from a more likely quarter. 'He told me that he just stood there and toyed with them,' remembers Waite. 'He said that I should imagine that I was a boxer and crouch. "When Miller bowls me a bumper I just look at him and laugh," that's what Eric said. "But shit Eric, I can't laugh at Lindwall and Miller," I replied.'

Grim-faced and without laughter, Waite batted at seven in the South African X1's first innings. He made 37 in a total of 329 all out, Owen Wynne, the young Western Province opener, scoring a slow 138. Early on the second morning, Waite was hit by a Miller bumper. He knelt down, clutching his right shoulder, as Colin McCool moved forward and Hassett and Gil Langley looked vaguely interested behind the stumps.

'It brought up a big lump, I remember that,' says Waite. 'When I got back into the dressing-room Eric just burst out bloody laughing. He was always like that. If you got a duck in the first innings and you went out in the second he would tell everybody that you were on a pair. He wouldn't say, "look, don't worry, I'll back you up and we'll get you off the mark." He'd make you sweat like hell. You'd call for a run and "Go back" he'd say. Then he'd laugh to the bowler and remind him that you were on a pair.'

Waite didn't have much opportunity to cover himself in glory during the Australian innings of 344 for four – with Jack Moroney and Neil Harvey both scoring centuries – but his contribution was neat enough. He stumped Harvey, took two catches and conceded only a single bye. His star was rising, although it wouldn't be until the following season that he was capped by his country, being chosen to tour England in 1951.

The Kingsmead match against Hassett's men was notable for incidents other than three centuries and the wisdom of Eric Rowan. At three minutes before twelve on the opening morning both teams lined up facing the main grandstand, waiting for the peal of noon bells signalling that the doors of the Voortrekker Monument in Pretoria were about to be opened. The monument had been inaugurated at the end of the symbolic ox-wagon trek of 1938, the main event in the festivities celebrating the 100th anniversary of the original Great Trek in 1838.

The anniversary trek was the brainchild of Henning Klopper, a Mossel Bay port captain and a founding member of the nationalist organisation, the Afrikaner Broederbond. The stinkwood ox-wagons, the 'Piet Retief' and the 'Andries Pretorius', started the trek from beneath the shadow of the Jan van Riebeeck statue on Cape Town's foreshore and, over the course of the next few months, meandered northwards, whipping up support wherever they went. The anniversary trek ended at the site earmarked for the monument itself, two foundation stones were laid and Malan, later to become prime minister, exhorted the faithful to ensure that just as the muzzleloader had clashed with the assegai at Blood River, so the Afrikaner should strive to make South Africa 'a white man's land'.

The history and detail of the event might have failed to capture the cricketers' imagination but even they were dimly aware of what the moment meant. Cricket, for so long played in splendid isolation, was being dragged into the political realm. The sport's autonomy was to be eroded through the fifties as cricket became politicised. The reserve of post-war goodwill, particularly but not exclusively from England, would in time subside. The subsidence took a full twenty years but eventually South Africa – and South Africa's cricketers – found themselves in a hole from which there was no escape. As Ron Saggers, the Australian reserve wicketkeeper and insurance manager, said three months after the completion of the 1949/50 tour: 'Give me South Africa now, but I wouldn't care to insure her future at double the rate I'd insure Australia's.'

Under Lindsay Hassett's twinkling eye

Under Hassett's alive and ever twinkling eye, the 1949/50 Australians proved to be remarkably popular tourists. They started their tour in Eshowe against a Zululand X1 and promptly fell in love with the town. (*Catch*, the book by Dick Whitington and Keith Miller, is dedicated to 'Eshowe and the song of wind soughing in the trees'.) A confident, gifted side with no discernible weaknesses, they were spirited, fun loving and made friends wherever they went. 'Ready to sing on the least provocation,' writes Duffus, 'they quickly picked up and parodied Zulu and Afrikaans tunes and left an echo of mixed vocal refrain up and down the land. After he had led the crowded hall of the Eshowe Country Club in Zululand in the "Blackbird Song" at a cocktail party following the preliminary match of the tour, Hassett brought the house down when he thanked the ladies for all they had done and added, "The night is still young".'

Halfway through the tour, after the Australians had scored 418 in a day against Eastern Province – and were two-nil up in the series to boot – Duffus was again, as it were, singing their praises. 'In a town [Port Elizabeth] that is rugby mad, 12 000 spectators came to watch them and to cap the public interest that is proving even more fabulous than last summer's tour by the MCC,' he writes. 'Already the attendances at Australian matches total 284 000, which is 24 000 more than at a comparable stage of the English programme. The gate receipts exceed 50 000 pounds.'

Going into the third Test at Kingsmead, there were three items which, from an Australian point of view, might have struck a worrying note. The first involved Hassett's continuing struggle with tonsillitis, the second concerned Bill Johnston's car accident as he miraculously found himself and his car in a culvert on the Pinetown to Durban Road on the way to a date with a South African nurse. Miller, not an original choice to tour, was sent out as a replacement amidst much acclaim both at home and in South Africa, while Johnston fought his way back to fitness and health. The third item of concern involved their worrying collapse on a sticky wicket against Transvaal when Athol Rowan, bowling in leg-irons as a result of his war injury, mesmerised the Australians in front of nearly 20 000 of the Ellis Park faithful.

'When Jack Moroney arrived at the crease to open the Australian innings, he looked around to see four fielders sitting on his bat and two almost within leaping distance of the wicket,' writes the Southern African cricket historian, Jonty Winch. 'Grinning widely, the powerfully-built Australian schoolteacher looked down the wicket to Dick Ashman and called out, "Mr Umpire, please see that none of these coves picks my pocket".' Moroney's grin didn't last because Rowan, turning the ball appreciably, was soon among him and his mates. Rowan bowled Miller through the gate for one, had Colin McCool caught by Mitchell at backward short-leg and generally played havoc with the tourists. Ken Archer top-scored with 20 not out, while Harvey, Loxton and Ian Johnson failed to reach double figures. Bowling 15.4 overs, Rowan took nine for 19 and the Australians were all out for 84.

Transvaal hardly fared better. They patched together 125 for nine but many felt that as soon as the recognised batsmen had lost their wickets, Eric Rowan should have declared. Whitington was of the opinion that Rowan had been 'scuffed' in the game at Ellis Park and others have pointed out that Miller certainly dropped a sitter in order to prolong Transvaal's stay at the crease in the first innings. In any event, there was something academic about the debate because Australia were again bowled out cheaply. Rowan took six for 49 in the Australians' second innings of 109. But the Transvalers couldn't manage the reply. In being bowled out for 53 they lost the game by 15 runs and in so doing wasted a wonderful opportunity. 'In the forty-seven years of cricket between the two countries never did a provincial team earn so impressively, and squander so submissively, the initiative for winning everlasting renown,' huffs Duffus. 'It should never have happened.'

Arthur Mailey took the less parochial view. 'In years to come old men will fondle their beards meditatively and reflect on the drama of Australia's first match at Ellis Park,' he writes. 'Walker's sixes will have gone far out of the ground into a neighbouring block of flats, the mercurial Miller's hair will be as long as a caveman's, Athol Rowan's spinners will be regarded with as much terror as its contemporary, the atomic bomb, some will clench their teeth and speak of Eric Rowan as a poor leader, others will say that he was a greater strategist than Napoleon, the less critical will say that the beer was good… It is obvious that the most dominating character in the drama was modest Athol Rowan. Not only did he bowl like a champion, he batted as valiantly as a person who had decided to play the game for fun. I felt at the end of the match when Athol Rowan was being carted off to hospital [with an injured knee which precluded him from playing any part in the five Tests against Hassett's men] like somebody who had seen a hero maimed or a dove killed.'

The history of the South African weather

Just after the war South Africa was visited by professor Athelstan Spilhaus of the US Weather Bureau. Spilhaus took a dim view of the locals' *laissez-faire* attitude to meteorological matters and proposed remedial action. 'The establishment of a network of observation stations throughout the Union and the division of the country into six weather forecast regions are to be recommended to the government by Professor Spilhaus, who has just completed investigations into the re-organisation of South Africa's meteorological services,' writes *The Star*. 'Professor Spilhaus told a press representative that South Africans did not seem to appreciate the importance of accurate weather forecasts, which were of enormous importance in warning farmers of impending high winds or frosts, and for aviation and shipping. A reliable service, he said, would also be invaluable for irrigation schemes.'

Spilhaus might conceivably have added sporting events to his list, because come the third Test at Kingsmead and Nourse, the South African captain, desperately needed a weather report he could trust. After losing Wynne, bowled by Johnston for 18 with the total on 32, and Jack Nel, caught and bowled by Johnson for 14 with the total on 75, Nourse might have expected the predictable procession. But on the first morning Eric Rowan, after scoring 18 for a South African X1 and failing twice for Transvaal in their topsy-turvy match against the tourists, finally came good on his advice to Waite in the Kingsmead dressing-room some weeks earlier. He laughed not only at Miller and Lindwall, but also Johnston and Johnson as he set about mending the early damage with his captain. At close, South Africa were 240 for two and handily placed. In retrospect, their caution through the afternoon session was to cost them dearly.

After a torrential overnight downpour which delayed the start of play on the second morning, Hassett's visitors gained the initiative, taking the wickets of Nourse (66) and Rowan (143) quickly before biting into the middle-order and tail. But as they toyed with the South Africans, Hassett was presented with a conundrum – the sooner he bowled South Africa out the sooner he would have to bat. It would be better to prolong the inevitable and hope to both waste time and take wickets in as unobtrusive a manner as possible. Many felt the home team were slow to spot the ruse of a deep-set field and benign bowling but eventually, despite calls for declarations and alterations in the batting order, South Africa were all out for 311, Lindwall taking three for 47 and Johnston four for 74.

After an opening stand of 31 between Morris (25) and Moroney (10), young Hugh Tayfield, a replacement for Athol Rowan who had collapsed during the Transvaal match and was never to play the Australians again, began to do his quietly effective work. Wickets fell at 31, 35, 37, 39, 42, 45, 46, 53 and 63 as the Australians were bowled out for 75 in a trifle more than 28 overs. Tayfield took seven for 23, Tufty Mann three for 31, as Nourse was left to spend Sunday considering the wisdom of enforcing the follow-on.

On the Saturday night, Nourse had visited the weather station at Stamford Hill airport with provincial colleague, John Watkins. The message from the weather office was clear: expect rain. 'On the Monday morning the pitch was hard but in a somewhat corrugated, pock-marked condition,' writes Whitington. 'Nourse inspected it for about twenty minutes before making his decision as to whether he should order Australia to follow on 236 runs behind or whether he would bat again himself. He had received a weather bureau forecast to the effect that heavy rain was almost certain to fall at about 4.30pm. He decided to bat again himself and was later severely and unjustifiably criticised for so deciding. Hassett afterwards averred that he would have made exactly the same decision as Nourse had he been confronted with the same problem.'

Nourse's hand-wringing made little difference. South Africa plunged from 85 for four to 99 all out in their second dig, with only Wynne (29), Nourse (27) and Nel (20) reaching double figures. Then again, from Nourse's perspective, with a first innings lead of 236, Australia needed 336 to win the match and three Aussies – Moroney, Hassett and Miller – were back in the hut for eighty runs scored by close on the third day.

On the final morning, Neil Harvey and Arthur Morris were greeted by a track that had a dry crust but was still damp underneath. The ball was spinning and climbing alarmingly, and when it hit one of the craters or divots left by the three previous days' play, it could do virtually anything. Despite the obstacles of the track, the attack and the partisan crowd, Harvey prevailed. He scored 151 not out and was helped by Sam Loxton (54) and Colin McCool. South Africa only took two wickets on the day as Hassett's team took the Test with 25 minutes to spare and, with it, the series.

For many it was Nourse, the weather-watcher, who needed to be hung and quartered. Going into the rest day, the prevailing view in the South African dressing-room was that Nourse would be mad not to enforce the follow-on, a fact confirmed by at least one of the players still alive who played in the Test. But for Whitington, the villain of the piece was Rowan. The Transvaal opener, he argued, had batted too slowly on the first afternoon. He had failed to notice that, for once, Nourse wasn't hitting the ball cleanly and should've taken the initiative. Then again, the chemistry between Nourse and Rowan was traditionally lacking. Rowan, for instance, swung into the Newlands bar during the second Test against the Aussies, announcing that he would be prepared to be interviewed by anyone who cared to hear his thoughts on Nourse's captaincy.

Miller noted later that Rowan and Nourse's running between wickets indicated a certain lack of empathy between the men. Whitington was of the opinion that Rowan batted at Kingsmead with one eye on his place in the team to tour England in 1951. But Duffus, traditionally no Rowan fan, was more inclined to praise the 40 year-old. 'Eschewing a past in which he had relied upon prods and provocation,' he writes, 'Rowan adopted aggressive tactics against Australia's fast-bowlers and played quite the best cricket of his career.'

Then again, the defeat might've had something to do with the quick-wittedness and streetwise cunning of the Australian captain, qualities he used to good effect in the final innings of the Transvaal game as his fielders implored the umpires to give decisions their way. 'I remember Tayfield bowling from the town end during the Aussies' first innings,' says Dennis Done, a freelancer for SABC radio who watched the entire third Test. 'The umpire from that end was called Marais. He used to wear one of those straw hats, like the ones that girls wear in convents, with the little bit of elastic to go underneath the chin. Anyway, Marais was one of those slow, determined fellows. He took an age to make a decision. The batsman was Hassett and Tayfield caught him on the back foot right in front. But Hassett was so quick and nimble that as the ball hit his pad he jumped away a couple of steps, as if to confuse this Marais. Anyway, Marais took an age and eventually gave Hassett out, because, of course, he was plumb. As he walked back Hassett kept looking at the stumps, implying, you know, that he wasn't really out.'

CHAPTER 5

The draw specialists

'To blazes with good losers' — Dudley Nourse

At the end of the 1950/1 Currie Cup season (won, incidentally, by Transvaal for the first time in 15 years) five national selectors whittled down to 24 their favourites to tour Great Britain later that year. They halved the 24, put them into teams – captained by Dudley Nourse and Eric Rowan – and asked them to battle it out at Kingsmead in a final trial. Those who prospered, such as Jackie McGlew, a young opening batsman from Natal who scored a century before lunch on the opening day, and Clive van Ryneveld, a leg-spinner who took fifteen wickets for Nourse's team, were rewarded with places in the fifteen to tour. So too were Michael Melle, a fast-bowler from the Transvaal who had taken five for 113 in the fourth Test against Australia the previous season, and Roy McLean, a swashbuckling middle-order batsman who scored 68 for Nourse's team in the final innings of the match as he helped them to a three-wicket win in a match dominated by spinners.

When the team was announced after the final day of the trial on Monday, February 19, 1951, it was noticeable that the selectors had plumped for youth. McGlew was 21, Melle 20, Van Ryneveld 22, McLean 20, McCarthy 22. There was also a place in the side for Waite (21), chosen as one of three wicketkeepers in the party along with Russell Endean (26) and George Fullerton (27). Some of the older faces, such as Nourse, the Rowans and Mann were familiar, but, having lost nine Tests in 15 outings since the war, the selectors felt it necessary to invest in the future.

In interview with Leslie Cox, as the Natal contingent sailed from Durban for Cape Town prior to collecting the rest of the team, captain Nourse bemoaned

63

the fact that the South Africans were traditionally so easily satisfied. 'Not since 1935 has South Africa won a Test match and we are naturally set on breaking that sequence. If the MCC could win in Australia after going from 1938 without a victory, then it is not impossible for our team to do the same. And we shall be trying to be good winners instead of good losers. In England, particularly, you never know what luck you may get in the way of the wicket, either, and it is time we had some of that. But if we have to be losers, we'll try and be good losers.' Nourse's quip about trying to be good winners was an allusion with a family history. Apparently his father, Dave, a member of Herby Wade's team to England in 1924, had said that he was sick and tired of being bracketed a good loser. It was time to become a good winner. The words were to prove more prophetic than Nourse junior could know.

The Arundel Castle docked at Southampton on April 20. The rest of the month was spent playing scratch games in the south of England, first in Maidstone, then at Blackheath in London, then Luton. The age divide between fresh young things and irascible old pros such as Nourse manifested itself early.

'Before the first proper match of the tour we had several one-day games,' remembers Waite. 'You would have thought that all the young guys would have been the chaps who would have played in those games but they got to the fifth game and they still hadn't played. I said to Eric, because I was close to him, "What's going on here?" And he said that he would see what he could do. And then Dudley came and asked us at breakfast time if I wanted to play. "Of course I want to play," I told him. "We're playing against the Union Castle team, you can play for them," he told me. So my first game for South Africa was actually against South Africa and for the Union Castle line team. At any rate, I opened the batting with some guy. And I was trying like hell because this was my first game abroad and I had had to wait a long time for my chance. I remember I had got my score up to 25 or 27, slowly, but it was a difficult pitch and we had lost a couple of wickets quickly. And then Dudley came up to me and told me I'd had enough and I was to give my wicket away. "I can't give my wicket away," I told him. "What do you mean," he said. "I want to play, I'm not giving my wicket away," I said. About two overs later I said: "I'll tell you what, I'll retire". So I just walked off and said that I had retired. But that was typical Dudley. He didn't come to you and say, "Look, don't worry that you haven't had a game, we want to give the senior players a chance to acclimatise". He just didn't tell you anything.'

Like the relationships between generations, the weather was slow to thaw.

The game at Luton was abandoned due to snow, and rain throughout the last day of the first official game of the tour against Worcestershire forced a draw. The weather at Bradford on 5, 7 and 8 May for the game against Yorkshire was also poor, as South Africa narrowly avoided losing, with Bob Appleyard and Freddie Trueman rampant with the ball. 'Few of the frozen watchers can have regretted the saving of a game played in conditions which taxed the fortitude of the hardiest Yorkshireman and must have been sheer misery to anyone from a warmer climate,' writes Michael Melford. 'The north wind, often accompanied by sleet, howled through the stand, numbed fingers and relentlessly cut through the thickest sweaters. This, in itself, could provide a genuine excuse for a most moderate display by the South Africans. The exceptional slowness of the wicket was an added torment.'

With squalls tracking the tourists south, a full day's play was lost in the three-day game against Cambridge University at Cambridge, but skies cleared for the game against Glamorgan. McGlew scored a century in the tourists' painful first innings in Cardiff but then Geoff Chubb, and later Athol Rowan, harvested wickets to give the South Africans an innings victory.

And so across the Severn to Bristol for the game against Gloucestershire. Here Nourse suffered a broken left thumb as he attempted to stop a drive from Tom Graveney while fielding at cover-point. At one stage, the South Africans fielded four substitutes, one of those off the field being Athol Rowan. 'From that stage the efficiency and teamwork of the side deteriorated sharply,' writes Duffus, 'until incidents occurred that were to lead to the gravest upheaval and most regrettable chapter in the country's cricket. Tufty Mann, who took a jealous pride in the conduct and accomplishments of South African cricket, felt the decline so keenly that he obtained permission to talk to the younger members of the side. He took them into a hotel room and in the plainest terms condemned their slovenliness in the field, their lack of guts, and the swollen heads that some of them were developing. After that there was a noticeable improvement in their keenness.'

The next three games – against the MCC at Lord's, Oxford University and Essex – were all drawn, the final game in exciting circumstances as Essex sportingly chased 280 in two and a quarter hours and fell just short. Nourse returned for the match against Surrey as the South Africans were bowled out for 209 and declared their second innings on 358 for eight. The official tour captain's contribution at the Oval was 45 and 23. He went into the first Test at Trent Bridge severely handicapped – a steel pin had been inserted into his thumb. To add to his and his team's worries, he hadn't scored a 50 on tour. It was all beginning to look horrifyingly familiar. Nourse's 'we are naturally set on breaking the sequence' quote to Cox at the beginning of April looked gauchely optimistic – and a long way away.

'Next Monday might be a better time to assess yesterday's rate of scoring.' — Louis Duffus

Waite's Test debut was filled with novelties. Alec Bedser bowled to him in the nets prior to the start of play on the first morning and then he found out more about his immediate future from a scorecard than from Nourse.

> 'Dudley was an uncompromising guy. He wasn't the kind of guy who'd say "look, I've got a bunch of kids with me here, and I must encourage them and that." If you went out to a bad shot or something like that he'd come and tell you. I mean, the first Test I played with him and I was run out. To start with, this is just to give you a bit of background, I'd been batting at number three. I'd started off opening the batting a bit and then I went to number three and I was doing very nicely. We came to the first Test and, you know, at a lot of the grounds they sell these scorecards. And you fill them in, you know, it's quite a nice thing. So I thought, well, it's my first Test, I must buy myself a scorecard. So the guy gave me a scorecard, he said, "here, take this," and it had the two teams, England and South Africa written down. And it said: Rowan, Waite, McGlew, Nourse. And I went to Dudley – he hadn't even tossed yet – and I said to him, "Look, I've got this scorecard, just as a memento for my first Test." So Dudley wasn't too impressed with this. And I said, "Look, they haven't even got the bloody batting order right, they've got Rowan, Waite, McGlew instead of Rowan, McGlew, Waite. They've got me down to open." He says: "That's not a mistake, you're opening." He didn't even come and tell me I was opening. And then I got run out for 76 – it was entirely his fault – and he didn't come and say "Well played" or anything. When I came out eventually he said, "You could have got a hundred. You want to keep your bloody mind on the job. Keep in the game, he said, you go fast asleep out there."'

At close on the first day, South Africa were on 239 for three – with Nourse on 76 not out. Waite was out for 76, Rowan for 17 and McGlew 40. At times it was agonising but Duffus felt the means would justify the ends. 'One onlooker remarked sarcastically: "I don't think anyone will have heart-failure from excitement." But here, in my view, was the case – perhaps the only instance of the season – where caution was fully justified. They are playing in five-day cricket. They lost one of their two best batsmen for 17, and the other was forced to play out of character because of his hand injury. And two of their first four batsmen were youngsters appearing in their first Test match. Next Monday might be a better time to assess yesterday's rate of scoring.'

On day two Nourse was joined by a parade of partners. First Jack Cheetham, the not-out batsman overnight, departed for 31; then George Fullerton compiled 54 in a fifth-wicket partnership of 121, and Van Ryneveld 31. Nourse was ninth out for a wonderfully courageous 208, as he declared the innings closed on 483 for nine.

Given that they were strangers to the winning habit, South Africa might have expected to be victorious in the Test, but from such a position it was going to be difficult to lose. England, meanwhile, were not about to gift them the first Test of the rubber. The home team lost Jack Ikin (one) early, but Len Hutton (63), Willie Watson (57), Reg Simpson (137) and Compton (112) moved the home team's innings into safe waters at 382 for five, before rain and a tame lower-order capitulation encouraged Brown to declare England's first innings on 419 for nine. The South Africans, having been captained by Eric Rowan since the start of the England first innings, with Nourse off the field, had a first innings lead of 64, but they couldn't manage Bedser (22.4-8-37-6) in their second knock, caving in hopelessly for 121.

Eric Rowan was perky at the change of innings, gleaning his motivational metaphors from the war. 'We've got 'em. They've got to make 'em. Up and at 'em, boys,' he cried, before the South Africans took the field. Chubb and McCarthy then bowled 14 overs between them before Eric Rowan tossed the ball to his brother and Mann. Athol Rowan dismissed Hutton (11) for the second time in the match via a caught-and-bowled (all in all he dismissed Hutton 11 times in Tests), repeated the trick with Simpson (seven), and Mann arrowed in a yorker to castle Ikin (33). Bailey (11) was the only other batsman in England's broad middle-order to reach double figures as Compton, Watson, Brown and Evans melted away.

Johnny Wardle, batting at nine, decided that attack was the best form of defence. The Yorkshire left-hander hit five fours and a six in four overs, as England passed the hundred and climbed toward the 185 needed for victory. Yet he heaved the long handle once too often. Roy McLean, fielding for Nourse, claimed the catch in the long field (as Arlott might have said). England were all out for 114 and South Africa had won in England for the first time in 16 years. 'McLean had the last one,' writes Duffus, 'a long, lingering hit to the boundary high into the drizzly sky. It was a lifetime coming down. From a distance we could not see the ball but we could see McLean manoeuvring underneath it. Then he had flung it into the wind and a memorable match was won.'

In later years, McLean made light of his own catch. He was more inclined to praise Eric Rowan's captaincy – and a catch taken by a colleague. 'I remember Cuan McCarthy was still pulling his sweater on,' says McLean, 'and, Eric, to get through the overs quickly, had him at leg-slip rather than down at fine-leg. And I don't think that Cuan had even taken a slip catch at practice in that position. But he just put his sweater on at leg-slip and Jack Ikin just hit the ball down his throat off Geoff Chubb. Eric was a very shrewd captain. He was a better captain than Dudley. Very shrewd. But Eric was his own worst enemy. He was always a little bit too loud. He just didn't fit into the pattern as it was at the time.'

For Athol Rowan (27.2-4-68-5) and Mann (24-16-24-4) the victory was just reward for years of post-war pain and disappointment suffered at the hands of England and Australia. Athol struggled valiantly to recapture the strength in his left knee after being hospitalised after Transvaal's game against the 1949/50 Australians, but the 1951 tour to England was his last. In a limited-edition memoir, John Arlott says the following of him and the Trent Bridge Test: 'Something bigger than what news reporting can contain brought Athol Rowan back again for the first Test.' The Test was a similarly splendid occasion for Mann, who fell ill later on during the tour and was to die of testicular cancer on July 31, 1952. This, though, was their finest hour, as they ran through timid England, while a hectoring captain screwed his close packed field ever tighter. For Waite, in his first Test, it was a fairy-tale, and for Eric Rowan, a moment to be savoured as the team gorged themselves on champagne on their way south to Northampton for their next engagement.'

'Years later and the scene shifted to Port Elizabeth,' says Waite. 'It was South Africa's centenary and they'd invited all sorts of people to come out. And it was announced that the former captains of South Africa were going to drive around in a motorcade. They didn't ask Eric to drive around with them because he actually never captained South Africa; he was vice-captain of that team at Nottingham in 1951 but he was never, as such, captain of South Africa. But, as you know, in that first Test Dudley got 208 with a broken thumb and after the first innings Eric took over the captaincy but he wasn't captain of the team. He was very bitter and twisted about that. "Why are you so worried about that," I said to him. "Because it's bloody not right, I captained the side," he said. "But you actually didn't, you didn't captain the side," I replied. "Johnny, you remember what happened, that bloody Dudley Nourse, we saw him for two days and he buggered off. We never saw him. What did he do?" "Shit, he got 208 for one thing," I told Eric. "And who won the game for us," he said, "I did".'

Lancashire hot-spot

The light-headedness inspired by the win at Trent Bridge couldn't last. The latent tensions in the party, between young and old, pro-Nourse and pro-Eric Rowan, were bound to fester, and at Old Trafford, during the game against Lancashire (the last before the second Test), they came to a head. 'Well it was so bloody funny, really, when you think of it, because in that Test match where I batted with Dudley [the first innings of the Trent Bridge Test] there was quite a lot of slow hand-clapping,' says Waite.' And I remember Dudley saying to me: "Look," he said, "if those guys are upsetting you" – this was after the game – "you just step aside and wait until the noise stops." So there I was, a few games later, I think Lancashire were county champions, and Eric and I opened and we did well. We were slow but we were still there at lunch-time and we put on a big score. But then the crowd started slow-handclapping, so I thought: "Well, this is a good time to put old Dudley Nourse's advice into practice." So I sort of stood aside, and it still went on, and the next thing I looked over and it looked as if Eric was having a suntan on the beach. They had a very nice guy called Nigel Howard, who was captain of Lancashire. And Nigel came up. The crowd had started to get bloody restless by this stage and when that happened I sort of got up a bit, I sat on my haunches. Anyway, Nigel came up. "I say," he said to Eric. "What do you want," barked Eric. "I think we should resume," said Nigel. "Go and fuck yourself," said Eric. "If your assholes can't behave properly, then I'm not getting up until they stop. You'd better go and talk to them."'

Shortly after the resumption of play, Rowan touched a delivery from Allen Wharton to first slip to be out for 66. Having reached the pavilion, he was involved in an altercation with a member of the Lancashire committee. Following that, he was reported in the next day's *Sunday Express* as being less than complimentary towards the natives. 'The truth is that the Lancashire bowling is not good enough – so why take it out on me,' the *Express* quotes him as saying. 'The crowd not only insulted me but they insulted their own bowlers. I was upset by the bad manners of the crowd. I'm not going to throw my wicket away for Lancashire or any other team in England. I object to barracking when a bowler is making his run. I won't even give the kids autographs after this.'

Versions of the story diverge at this point. According to one, there was a tabloid reporter lurking in the dressing-room shadows, who, unbeknownst to Eric Rowan, was taking him down verbatim as he poured his heart out to Athol, who was receiving treatment for his knee on the massage table. The other version of the tale – let's call it the Duffus version for convenience's sake – has it that Eric Rowan gave the interview in full knowledge of who the reporter was and what he was doing, this while he, rather than Athol, was on the massage table.

The incident happened after lunch on the Saturday and, in Monday's early edition of *The Star*, Duffus put it in perspective for his South African readers. 'His sitting down at the wicket was not by itself reprehensible, though it was out of character with South African cricket,' writes Duffus. 'But unfortunately he made remarks when entering the pavilion, and a Sunday newspaper reports on its front page under a three column headline, "Bad Manners, Insult", says South African', comment he is alleged to have made while lying on the massage table. When consulted, the newspaper claimed that Rowan was aware there was a reporter present who had called for an interview. His statements, if he knew they were to be made public, were of a nature to call for some disciplinary action.'

The situation was complicated by extenuating circumstances. Eric Rowan had scored 202 not out at Northampton the day before the first day's play in the match against Lancashire at Old Trafford. At that stage of the tour (and with the spate of injuries at Bristol in the match against Gloucestershire), he had played in all but one of the 13 games. He'd also picked up a minor injury against Northants and the Test had so exhausted him that he told the South African press afterwards that it had taken 10 years off his life.

If the occasion allowed Duffus an opportunity to call for disciplinary action, Rowan repaid the compliment by 'leaking' a story to a rival journalist. On the Sunday night of the match against Lancashire (played on 16, 18, 19 of June), Sam Mirwis, the South African Press Association's (SAPA) correspondent on tour, received a call in his room. It was Eric Rowan, tantalising him with a 'scoop'. Having been called to Rowan's room Mirwis arrived to find not only Rowan, but half the side, some of them in their pyjamas. Once there, Mirwis was told by Rowan that Pegler [the SA manager] was about to send him home on the next available ship.

Mirwis took a second or two to regain his composure and then asked Rowan for an opportunity to phone his editor in Johannesburg as well as to visit Pegler. Rowan agreed. Mirwis's editor liked the story and wanted Mirwis to file. But Mirwis managed to persuade his editor to wait until he had visited the manager. Pegler went pale when Mirwis told him that not only did he know about Rowan being sent home but that half of the team were going to join him. By way of reassurance, he added that should the matter be sorted out the story would be suppressed in the interests of South African cricket. Mirwis returned to his room, wondering whether he had done the right thing. After fifteen minutes his phone rang. It was Pegler, asking him to come back to his suite. The tour committee – Nourse, Chubb and Mann – had been woken and as Pegler cleared his throat to give him the news, Eric Rowan winked at Mirwis. Eric Rowan was staying; a crisis had been averted and the story was never published.

Waite believes that if a secret ballot had been held that Sunday night, the team would have voted overwhelmingly in favour of having Rowan sent home. Eric Rowan had his foot soldiers and apologists – among them Athol, Waite, McLean and McCarthy – but Pegler was a Nourse man and so too were Mann and Chubb, two senior members of the team who also sat on the tour committee. McLean remembers that it wasn't only members of the inner sanctum who wanted Rowan sent home. 'It did get to the stage where there was Rowan and his followers and Dudley Nourse and his followers on the '51 trip,' he says. 'Clive van Ryneveld stimulated something I remember. He had just come from Oxford, he was an Oxford blue, and he was the one who tried to get Eric sent home. We had a team meeting at the Grand Hotel in Leicester. I'll never forget it. Athol turned round and told everyone that if Eric was sent home he would go too. Clive just didn't like the way that Eric ate, the way he crossed his knife and fork and maybe the manner of Eric's speech and things of that nature. So he got permission, he wanted a team effort to send Eric home, because he thought it wasn't in the interests of cricket – assumedly – to have Eric around. Not that it lasted for long but the message was soon received that we couldn't do without him – which we couldn't.'

Waite disputes that Van Ryneveld, a junior member of the party on his first overseas tour, would have been brazen enough to call for Rowan to be sent home. Nevertheless, the battle lines had been drawn. The victory at Trent Bridge was the high point of the tour. After that remarkable individual performances predominated, but the team was moving in different directions. Its members were seldom in harmony.

'Evans behind me, passing gentle flatulence...'

After the first Test at Trent Bridge and the public relations nightmare at Old Trafford, there was still the little matter of a cricket tour. The second Test was at Lord's in late June and after that the tour nosed south for a game in Portsmouth against the Combined Services. Thereafter it swung northwards for a second game against Yorkshire (at Sheffield this time), the third Test at Old Trafford and then up to Glasgow for two games against Scotland before hopping across to Ireland (Belfast and Dublin). After the Gaelic turn it headed for the mainland to take in matches at Derby and Leicester, then the fourth Test, this time at Leeds. After Headingley, however, there was still a full two months to go, with the tour taking in the sights of Taunton, Swansea, Birmingham, Hove, London, Southampton, London again, Canterbury, Hastings, Norwich, Scarborough and the Hague, for the game against Holland on September 15 and 16. The team was scheduled to leave Southampton on the Winchester Castle on September 20 and arrive in Cape Town on October 4. The Arundel Castle had left Cape Town on April 6, a full six months before. The tour was less of a tour than a Victorian expedition and, midway through, the itinerary was beginning to look cruel rather than simply daunting.

After being bowled out at Lord's in the second Test for 115 and 211 on a sopping wicket, South Africa had an opportunity to recapture lost momentum at Old Trafford in the third, with the series level at one-one. South Africa made one change from the team they had fielded for Tests one and two. 'I had my 21st birthday on the day I played my first Test match,' remembers Roy McLean. 'Jackie McGlew played the first two Tests and I played the last three – Jackie was twelfth man. We played in a game where Freddie Brown and Dudley disagreed about the wicket, because in those days they covered the run-up, they never covered the wicket. I remember going out to bat to face Alec Bedser. And Godfrey Evans, of course, never stood back, and so you can imagine: Bedser running up to me on a wet wicket, Evans behind me, passing gentle flatulence. So I can tell you, it wasn't an easy time. The first ball I faced I sparred at and it went straight over my head for four byes.'

McLean scored 20 and 19 in a low-scoring Test as the South Africans crumbled, scoring 158 and 191. England batted last needing 139 to win, and a repeat of the Trent Bridge heroics was hanging in the air. But where Brian Statham, Jim Laker and Bedser had managed to use the spite of the wicket to their advantage, the South African bowlers were unable to do the same. The yeoman, Geoff Chubb, was too tired to repeat his six wickets in the England first innings and Hutton batted masterfully for 98 not out as England went two-one up.

Leeds was where South Africa would have to make their last stand. A defeat at Headingley would see the series lurch out of reach and render the Oval Test academic. Thankfully, Nourse won the toss (Brown's record was 11 incorrect calls out of 14) and South Africa batted. Eric Rowan, having turned 42 six days previously, was in the mood for a hearty scrap. Not out on 160 overnight, he exclaimed on the second morning: 'I could fight Dick Turpin this morning, crikey, I'd like to score 365.' In the event, he passed the 208 scored by Nourse in the first Test which, at that stage, was the highest score by a South African against England. He then progressed to 231, the equal highest score by a South African in Tests with Dudley Nourse. After being dropped twice in the early 200s, Rowan eventually lost his wicket on 236. When Bedser caught him in the gully at 3.42 on the second day, he became the oldest player to score a double century in the history of Tests.

With Rowan's help South Africa stockpiled 538 runs. It was a good day for the Rowan family because Eric and Athol's uncle apparently indicated to Eric while he was still batting that he had backed winners in races at 2.30pm and 3.30. Along with the 'young 'uns,' Van Ryneveld (83) and McLean (67) and the slightly older Percy Mansell (90), Rowan had kept the series alive. During their turn, though, England too scored heavily (with a young Peter May making a debut Test century) and the Test was drawn, rain ruining the fifth day. Rowan added to his 236 with 60 not out in the South Africans' second innings, helping South Africa to fight another day.

But the Oval Test was a bridge too far. On a pitch that took spin early and was significantly less welcoming to batsmen than might have been expected, South Africa were beaten by four wickets inside three days. As had happened so often before, the Test turned on a catch. 'True to character Brown swiped at a ball from Athol Rowan,' wrote Duffus. 'It soared straight towards Cheetham who, possibly delayed in picking up its flight because of the background buildings, hesitated a fateful second. The ball was falling a little short when he dived and hugged it to his chest, but he could not prevent himself from falling to the ground with the ball clasped under his body. There was every reason to expect that South Africa would had won had the catch been taken.'

The implications of the dropped catch were not lost on Cheetham. He would make catching and fielding the cornerstone of his assault on Australia, 15 months later. It was an assault that would have to make do without both Nourse and Rowan, team-mates and adversaries. Nourse's broken thumb, age and the stresses of the tour indicated that retirement was in order. For Rowan, his run-getting was not good enough for the South African cricket establishment. On the South Africans' return they summoned him with news he had half been expecting.

'One Thursday morning in October, about 10 days after the 1951 cricket Springboks had returned from Britain, I sat down at my desk in the office of a flourishing Johannesburg printing business, of which I was a representative and am now a director, when the telephonist gave me a message. "Please ring Mr Algy Frames at the Wanderers Club without delay," she said, and I dialled the number of the SA Cricket Association secretary. "Hello, Uncle Algy," I opened. "What can I do for you?" "That you, Eric?" he answered. "I'd like to see you as soon as possible. I've got something from the Board for you." His tone was imperious and not typical of the 'Uncle Algy' with whom I had bantered for so many years. I experienced a spasm of apprehension, but to say that I was not expecting some altercation with South African cricket officialdom would be ludicrous. There had been the 'Manchester incident' on the English tour, which I thought had been dropped entirely until, on our arrival at Cape Town, manager Syd Pegler gave to the South African Press Association a resume of each player's performance, but omitted myself and my brother Athol, and when I reached Johannesburg the attitude of some officials left me in little doubt that something was afoot.'

On the following Monday, according to his unpublished memoirs, Eric Rowan met Frames and Ronnie Grieveson, a former Springbok and one-time provincial colleague of Rowan's who was also a member of the South African Cricket Association. In a situation in which 'the air was blue with tension,' Frames and Grieveson presented Rowan with a letter stating that his international career was at an end. The letter read: 'I am directed by the Board of Control to advise you that whilst appreciating your play for South Africa on various occasions, the Board has decided unanimously that you shall not be considered for selection in the team to tour Australia during 1952/3 – Yours faithfully, Algy Frames.'

After reading the letter, Rowan asked if he would be allowed to refute the allegations contained within it. Grieveson replied that such refutations would need to be tabled before the full executive. 'I left the Wanderers and went straight to my solicitor,' writes Rowan. 'The following Sunday the Johannesburg *Sunday Express* published a story and picture of myself on their front page – Eric Rowan thrown out, he will not go to Australia – and all hell was let loose on South African cricket.'

After his monumental innings at Trent Bridge in the first Test, Nourse played a secondary role on tour. He only scored 673 runs in 28 innings (average, 25.88) while Rowan scored nearly triple that (1 852 runs at 50.05). In playing 26 games, Rowan played the highest number of matches along with George Fullerton of anyone on tour, holding the South African batting together out of sheer bloody-mindedness. Four other South Africans scored over a thousand runs on tour (Fullerton (1 129), Cheetham (1 196), McGlew (1 002) and Waite (1 011), but Rowan scored runs so consistently and in such vast amounts in relation to his colleagues that, in judging him one of their cricketers of the year, *Wisden Cricketers' Almanack* said that he was almost solely responsible for the 17 500 pounds record profit earned by the South Africans.

True, the relationship between Rowan, on the one hand, and Pegler and Nourse, on the other, was not exactly a harmony of minds, but one wonders if the Rowan issue was as terminal as the authorities sought to suggest. It was Pegler, after all, who allowed Rowan to take the team to The Hague for the two-day game against Holland by himself. Nourse, feeling the effects of a long tour, also absented himself from the trip. Stories have since emerged that it was not the 'Manchester incident,' as many have presumed, that finally snapped the establishment's patience with Eric Rowan, but what went on in the Dutch capital, whatever that was.

After breaking the original story, the *Sunday Express* kept on hammering away at the Rowan issue. On Sunday, November 4, 1951, Vivian Granger, their sports editor, wrote the following:

'Mr "Tup" Holmes, who voted for Eric Rowan to captain the Springboks in Britain, has been left off the South African cricket selection committee to choose the team to Australia. Why? If the South African Cricket Board have found the time to elect the selectors for next year's tour of Australia and not the time to issue a statement to the public on the Rowan 'incident,' or reply to inquiries which, I understand Rowan has put to them in letters, then they must resign. The selection committee announced on Friday is Arthur Coy, Syd Pegler, Carl Schawbe, Geoff Chubb and Frank Lambert. The cricket public, particularly that in the Transvaal, is becoming heartily sick of the 'iron curtain' that has been dropped between them and our national cricket administration. The Transvaal Cricket Union are also adopting a 'hush-hush' policy. It is a fortnight since the board announced that Rowan had been thrown out of national cricket and no statement from the SACA has been forthcoming.'

The 1951 tour to England was not only a swansong for Eric and Athol Rowan. By hook or by crook, Rowan senior had managed to keep the English umpires from no-balling McCarthy – at one point Rowan had threatened 'to take the boys off' if umpire Frank Chester called the fast-bowler – but by the time McCarthy returned the South African Cricket Association had seen enough. McCarthy, too, received a letter informing him that he was surplus to requirements. He was no-balled while playing for Cambridge University a year later and quietly disappeared, but the phrasing of his letter remains one of the unsolved mysteries of South African cricket history. The phrase 'for reasons other than cricketing ability,' was used in his case, but the exact nature of McCarthy's indiscretion remains a riddle.

If Eric Rowan and McCarthy fell foul of the authorities, Geoff Chubb, the bespectacled Transvaal accountant, was simply too tired to continue. Described in one of the tour brochures as having a dry wit and a genial disposition, Chubb, like his good friend, Tufty Mann, had spent time as a prisoner-of-war, although Chubb was confined to Bavaria rather than north-eastern Italy. 'He once managed to smuggle out a postcard to a rather naïve relative back in South Africa telling her that he was in the Black Forest,' recalls Michael Chubb, Geoff's nephew. 'She wrote back to the effect that she was pleased he was seeing the sights and enjoying his trip to Germany.'

After spending a brief period in England upon his release, Chubb returned to South Africa. He played five matches for Transvaal in the 1947/8 Currie Cup campaign, taking 16 wickets at 23, but age appeared to be catching up with him – this despite his being a dedicated fitness fanatic. 'He played a great deal of volleyball in Germany and although he may have bowled a little bit before joining the Imperial Light Horse he became stronger in camp and developed his bowling arm. Afterwards he dedicated himself to bowling rather than batting, which is how he started off when playing for Border in the Currie Cup before the war.'

In the 1948/9 season Chubb only played three times, taking nine wickets at 33, and the season after that he didn't play for his province at all – giving rise to speculation that he was a spent force. Michael Chubb thinks his uncle's erratic appearances could have had something to do with the war itself. 'He didn't come out of the war totally unscathed,' he says. 'He used to blame his various stomach ailments on the war. It's the b-b-b-loody G-G-Germans he would say, because he had a stutter. Also, don't forget, he watched his good friend Tufty Mann die. Mann struggled on the '51 tour and it was an ordeal for Geoff.'

The prospect, if not the promise, of a tour place galvanized Chubb into action prior to the 1950/1 season. During the season itself, he took 33 wickets at 14.66 each in six matches and, during the final trial, took four for 38 in 20 overs in the Nourse X1 first innings, bowling his canny away-swing off a not insubstantial run. His wickets included those of Waite, Nourse, Van Ryneveld and Wright, and the selectors saw in his technique and temperament a natural foil to the tearaway McCarthy and the relatively untested Melle. Chubb didn't let them down. He took 21 wickets in the Tests, including four for 146 at Trent Bridge, five for 77 at Lord's and six for 51 at Old Trafford. All told, he took 76 wickets on tour, 17 more than McCarthy, 23 more than Athol Rowan and 26 more than Melle. He was a godsend to South Africa, as important to their attack as Eric Rowan was to the batting order. More than his wicket-taking, his fellowship was a balm to those around him. 'Geoff was pitchforked into opening the bowling,' recalls his nephew. 'He was expecting to bowl at first change but then Cuan injured his back and he was asked to open the bowling. He never used to complain but it was hard work. First it was Hutton and Washbrook; then came Compton and May. After that you had Evans. When he got back to South Africa he was just buggered.'

'The greenness of England hit me between the eyes' — Steve de Villiers

The first time Steve de Villiers met Charles Fortune, then a freelance SABC radio commentator, was at Palmietfontein airport prior to the long, truncated hop to England. After an unscheduled overnight stop at Brazzaville, the flight duly arrived on the fair and green isle – with De Villiers and Fortune by now firm friends. De Villiers, like Fortune, was a radio commentator, but unlike Fortune, commentated in Afrikaans. 'I remember my first commentary spell in 1951,' he says. 'It was during the Worcestershire game and I didn't think that I was doing too well. He [Fortune] was sitting next to me in the booth because we took turns and then he said to me: "Excellent, my boy, I really like your turn of phrase." And, you know, I felt great and then it dawned on me that he hadn't understood a word of it because he didn't understand Afrikaans at all and was only being kind.'

De Villiers had impeccable Afrikaner credentials. Born in Germiston, his father was a minister in the Dutch Reformed Church and his uncle – ML de Villiers – composed *Die Stem*. According to De Villiers, his dad was a keen golfer. 'He remained a golfer for 47 years,' says De Villiers. 'I remember him playing to a six handicap. My mother wasn't very keen on golf – or on sport as such. But she allowed him his golf. She had him confine it to Monday mornings. Otherwise the congregation would start gossiping.' Despite the threat of maternal disapproval, the young De Villiers fell in love with cricket. And, aged 13, he saw Dudley Nourse's 231 against the Australians. 'It left an indelible memory,' he says, 'and he became my first sports hero. And, lo and behold, in 1951 I got to know him intimately.'

In his final year at Voortrekker High in Boksburg, De Villiers played Nuffield cricket for North-Eastern Transvaal. He was the only Afrikaans-speaker in the side. Later, he continued playing cricket at Tukkies, where he became first XI captain, in-between moonlighting as a part-time broadcaster in the early forties. In 1947 the Afrikaans service of SABC radio sent the earthy Dana Niehaus to England to cover Melville's tour, but four years later it was felt that listeners needed a change. 'Dana was very good at getting the ordinary chaps to listen,' says De Villiers. 'He didn't over-indulge in technicalities and so on. "*Hy vat die rooi pampoentjie* (he takes the red pumpkin)," was what he would say, "*en hy bowl hom soos die pitte spat* (and bowls it so its pips burst out)." At one stage Dana had a very big audience. In 1951 when I took over from him I then introduced more technical stuff. I tried to be lively but I also tried to introduce listeners to the essence of cricket.'

Fortune, then himself just a novice, introduced De Villiers not only to the essence of cricket but the essence of England. They buzzed down the English country lanes in a car the Fortunes had left in England before settling in South

Africa. For De Villiers, the experience was mind-expanding. 'Charles was my mentor,' says De Villiers. 'He introduced me not only to many players but to England because he had his wife's car there and we drove all over the place. He took me to the daffodil field and said: "Now watch this." The greenness of England hit me between the eyes.'

Although a mentor to De Villiers, Fortune was in 1951 not yet the institution he was to become. He took long leave from St Andrews in Grahamstown, where he taught as a physics teacher, in order to go on tour and his broadcasting career was hardly established. But soon Fortune, with his distinctive turn of phrase and his command of the language, was beginning to make a name for himself. So too was De Villiers. But he was doing so in a different language, capturing the intimacies of the English game for a new generation of Afrikaans listeners.

CHAPTER 6

The tourists who said they could

'Well good luck, Jack, even though luck can't help you chaps at all.' – a 'fan'

Johnny Waite and Roy McLean fortified themselves with a regular supply of strawberry and chocolate milkshakes on tour in Australia and New Zealand in 1952/3. It was that kind of tour: blissful, innocent and, above all else, fun. Uncharacteristically for a South African cricket tour abroad, it was also sure-footed. 'I don't think they [Cheetham and Viljoen] had an anxious moment on that tour from anybody doing the wrong thing,' says Waite. 'Nobody put a foot out of place, nobody. You just didn't do it.'

Such sure-footedness was largely the result of the endeavours of two men – Cheetham, the tour captain, and his trusted and much-loved manager, Viljoen. It was also the result of circumstance being used by Cheetham and the team as a motivating factor: at one stage the tour was hanging in the balance, the Australian board believing that the South Africans were unworthy visitors and would get trounced. The resultant compromise was an unusual one but eventually the South African Cricket Association agreed to financially underwrite the tour. 'I think the very negative attitude of our press, especially the senior cricket writer, Louis Duffus, became a major motivating factor,' says John Watkins, one of the quiet men of the party. 'He did the press reports on all the matches and we made sure he got some very strong verbal messages whenever we won a game. The negative press certainly strengthened our resolve to do well.'

From a playing and management perspective, the team to Australia was very different to the team that had gone to Britain in 1951. Out went the forty-somethings, Dudley Nourse, Eric Rowan, Tufty Mann and Geoff Chubb; out too went Athol Rowan, unable to continue because of his gammy knee. Clive van

Ryneveld, George Fullerton and Cuan McCarthy also failed to board the Dominion Monarch, as did the long-suffering Syd Pegler, the manager in England in '51. Survivors from England included Jackie McGlew, Cheetham's vice-captain in Australia, Russell Endean, Percy Mansell, Hugh Tayfield, Waite, Melle and McLean, but new faces there were many. Some were on the young side – such as Gerald Innes (20), Eddie Fuller (21) and Headley Keith (24) – but age was not discriminated against in what was essentially a wisely-chosen, pragmatic team. The Eastern Province duo of Anton Murray and Eric Norton were either nudging thirty in Murray's case, or just over it, in the case of Norton. The Rhodesian accounting clerk, Mansell, weighed in at 32. Discrimination based on age could hardly be otherwise: the captain himself was 32.

If Cheetham was beset by doubts on the voyage to Australia, he kept them well hidden. Prior to the five-Test series, he had played nine post-war Tests: one at home against the 1948/9 MCC tourists, three against Hassett's side the following year and the five under Nourse on the '51 tour of England. His Test average after the five 1951 Tests was a modest 24.33, although he fared better outside of the Tests, scoring 1 196 runs (average, 42.71) in the first-class games as a whole. Since captaining the South African College School (SACS) under-14 team, Cheetham had suggested himself as captaincy material but, in later life, was never a batsman to bunk school for. He was obdurate, without having Mitchell's mind-numbing tenacity, and was blessed with neither Melville's grace nor Nourse's power. As much as it was a battle to convince the sceptics about his team, the trip was an opportunity to finally establish himself. As one unnamed local cricket follower told him before the team's departure: 'Well good luck, Jack, even though luck can't help you chaps at all.'

Cheetham's ordinariness with the bat was one thing, his talent for adventure, preparation and motivation quite another. Most of all he had a talent for learning and it is said that as a ten year old he never forgot watching the first Test ever played on a grass wicket in South Africa, the match at Newlands against Percy Chapman's 1930/1 tourists. During the Test, Mitchell and Jack Seidle, the South African openers, put on 260 for the first wicket. Seidle was out for 141, caught by Chapman close to the wicket. Upon making the catch, Chapman quickly tucked the ball in his pocket. Cheetham never forgot the sleight of hand. In the act, it is said, he saw the possibility for making fielding a cornerstone of attack.

Other than realising the importance of fielding and the fact that, with an average age of 25 years and eight months, the South Africans were considerably younger than the long-in-the-tooth Aussies, Cheetham and Viljoen reasoned that they must dispense with the safety-first approach that had dominated South African cricket for so long. With Cheetham it was always thus. After scoring 94 for the Cape Province against George Mann's 1948/9 tourists, he cracked the game open with a bold declaration. The decision backfired and Cheetham was castigated, but boldness would have its day. And Cheetham had been noticed. 'With a little luck yesterday Cape Province might have saved the game,' writes Duffus in *The Star* of 10 November, 1948. 'None made a more admirable attempt to do so than Jack Cheetham, whose time for appearing in international cricket seems rapidly approaching. He is well equipped with strokes for both attack and defence and hooks with power and telling effect. Yesterday, as on some previous occasions, he lost his wicket to a sudden, but pardonable, impetuosity.'

As an engineer Cheetham was no stranger to close detail and his preparation prior to the tour and on board the Dominion Monarch bordered on the obsessive. A constant stream of letters wound their way between Cheetham, Viljoen and Leo Marquard, the president of the SA Cricket Association. Endean and McGlew were approached for their views and Cheetham sought out advice from Herby Wade. Before sailing Viljoen had contacted Danie Craven, then professor of Physical Education at the University of Stellenbosch, and Craven provided the tourists with an exercise programme. It was the duty of every player to be physically fit when they sailed on October 3, 1952.

The physical jerks were continued on board at 11.45am each day and, in addition, all the tourists had to spend half an hour each day devoted to a private regimen of exercise. 'The pull of the team spirit was most apparent when the voyage was nearing its end, and the finals of the deck games were underway,' writes Cheetham. 'All the boys were there to cheer on Anton Murray and his partner, when, in the finals of the mixed doubles deck tennis, they opposed Stan Sismey, the New South Wales wicketkeeper, and his partner. Anton won it, much to our delight – we felt it was an omen.'

'Any atomic bombs in this lot?'

After a bumpy ride across the Indian Ocean, the Dominion Monarch tied up at Fremantle harbour's wooden jetty on Tuesday, 14 October, 1952. Docking at the same time was the pride of the Australian navy fleet, the aircraft carrier, Sydney, which had just returned from a mission to the Monte Bello islands to observe the detonation of an atomic bomb. Jock Leyden, the South African cartoonist, represented the South Africans' arrival in Western Australia with an Australian customs officer (depicted as a kangaroo) asking the South African team: 'Any atomic bombs in this lot?' The South Africans, who were all squashed into a cricket holdall, replied: 'We'll tell you at the end of the tour.'

With the possible exception of Tayfield and Endean, the South Africans' luggage held no atomic weaponry. Instead, they immersed themselves in the hard work of fielding practice, leading Duffus to dub them the 'hardest working team I've ever seen.' In-between the civic receptions and fielding, they played night bowls under floodlights, visited Perth's 'No Smoking' cinemas and even saw the famous hypnotist, Leon van Lowe, once of Benoni, perform his tricks.

Jackie McGlew followed his 88 versus Northam, during the first match on tour, with 182 against Western Australia, scored at the rate of 23 runs an hour. Already the press contingent were braying about negative cricket, although the possible after-effects of Van Lowe's show were never mentioned. 'Don't put all the blame on McGlew for the slow scoring rate,' writes the *Sydney Sun*'s Dick Whitington. 'The main reason was the negative bowling – short of a length, first on the off-side and then according to leg theory – by the Western Australian fast-medium men, Price, Dunn and Puckett.'

From Perth, the team flew to Adelaide aboard a Skymaster, the pilot circling the Adelaide Oval to show a waterlogged field. The South African batting was again slow, and Whitington, having established his terms of reference, indulged in the journalistic equivalent of wagging his finger. 'This won't do, South Africa,' he writes as the tourists laboured to 132 for four in reply to South Australia's 354 all out (Gil Langley 70, Tayfield four for 99). 'The dull, negative chicken-hearted batting display given by Jackie McGlew and Johnny Waite between lunch and tea on the Adelaide Oval today will drive the crowds away from the Springboks' games – and the South African batsmen have got to be told this if they cannot realise it for themselves.'

After being bowled out for 201 in their first innings, South Africa became more chipper in their second. An opening stand of 56 between Waite and McGlew was followed by a stunning middle-order collapse – Norton (three), McLean (one) and Funston (10) – before Cheetham (83), Keith (50) and Murray (47) put the innings back on its feet. 'We were well-pleased to have fought back so well,' writes Cheetham, 'but Dick Whitington, the *Sydney Sun* cricket writer, criticised me for "lack of moral courage." He felt that I should have declared and allowed the state team to chase a victory. But I was quite happy that we had battled through to a draw, and not blotted our copy-book so early on in the tour.'

Tayfield was no A-bomb in flannels but against Victoria in Melbourne for the next game he just kept ticking away. The Natal off-spinner took seven for 71, including a hat-trick, helping to dismiss the Victorians for 159 in their second innings. South Africa needed 185 to win, batting last, and were tottering on 71 for four when rain put an end to play. 'Once again they [South Africa] retained their status,' writes Duffus, 'but were denied the opportunity to improve it.' And so to Sydney by overnight train. On the journey, Cheetham was woken early one morning by a garrulous conductor who was keen to discuss a theory or two – a situation the South African captain could have done without.

Cheetham's mood improved over the days that followed but, after being put in on a green top by Keith Miller, the New South Wales captain, it at first remained dark. With Ray Lindwall experimenting with his new-found in-swinger and Alan Davidson jabbing away at the other end, South Africa were hit hard. 'Even the commentators on the hill were dazed into silence,' writes Duffus. Three for three became four for 17 and seven for 93. Endean, batting at five, followed the example of Ken Funston (31) and went boldly on the counter-attack, a decision Duffus praised as vital in the context of the tour as a whole. With Murray, Endean put together an eighth-wicket partnership of 89 as South Africa just managed to reach respectability on 202 all out. Endean was last out for 77, Murray made 27 and Tayfield 40, as Lindwall eased his way to five for 30.

In front of 12 616 spectators on the Saturday, NSW resumed on 82 for two, with 'Golden Boy,' Cheetham's nickname for Arthur Morris, still there on 50. Morris added five and Richie Benaud 12 to their overnight scores. Tayfield snuffled them both. Had it not been for 71 down the order from Ian Craig, New South Wales wouldn't have reached 289. Tayfield took six for 117 and Watkins two for 29. The next day Endean added to his two spectacular catches (to dismiss Benaud and Keith Miller (30)) with his second fighting innings of the match. He scored 95 as McLean and Funston reached fifties. South Africa totalled 361, leaving NSW 274 to win in 250 minutes. In the event, the South Africans lost the match, but for the South African captain it was a turning point. 'The match was the making of our side,' he writes. 'It was there that the team showed remarkable powers of recovery; the fielding showed a brilliance which was to be sustained through the trials of Brisbane, Melbourne, Sydney and Adelaide.'

After two minor games in Newcastle and Bundaberg, the South Africans moved to Brisbane for their game against Queensland – the last before the first Test. The Queenslanders rattled up 540 in their first innings after Jackie

McGlew, deputising for Cheetham, won the toss. Don Tallon, batting at eight, used the opportunity to score a point or two off Jack Ryder, the Australian selector present at the 'Gabba. Ryder was one of three who left Tallon out of the home side for the first Test and Tallon felt it was time to make a point in capital letters. He duly rattled up 133 in 165 minutes. Batting with Tallon, Colin McCool scored 83, but the South Africans only had themselves to blame. Tallon was dropped on seven and 24 and they couldn't gain any initiative on the second morning as the home side resumed on 308 for six. Russell Endean prospered for the visitors, scoring 181 not out in a total of 362. In the follow-on innings he scored 87 in South Africa's 215 for seven. Waite, too, found useful form in scoring 59 and 35, as did Ken Funston, who scored 47 and 43. South Africa avoided defeat, but it all looked horribly touch and go and not the best possible way to prepare before the crucial first Test.

Cheetham lost the toss on the first morning at the 'Gabba. Against the backdrop of a rising thermometer and simmering local frustration that Tallon was not in the side, Hassett elected to bat. Batting at four, he saw to it that his decision was the correct one, combining with Harvey for the Australians' best partnership of the innings – 155 for the third wicket. Having clipped almost contemptuously to his century, Harvey was undone by the second new ball. He failed to control a glide off Melle and Gerald Innes, lunging at backward square-leg, hung onto an excellent catch. Hassett went soon afterwards for 55 as the home side squandered their early advantage.

Melle grabbed two quick wickets on the second morning and the Australians were all out for 280, with Melle ending on six for 71. Despite taking the wicket of Harvey, Melle was critical of his own contribution. 'I hated left-handers, especially Harvey,' he says. 'He was an absolute murderer and his ability to hit you for four on the leg-side from a ball bowled outside off was incredibly frustrating… I was disappointed with my bowling in the first Test. I mentioned to Ray Lindwall when he congratulated me that the wickets were mainly "nine, ten and jack." He replied that they were in the book and what mattered were the six wickets. The strange thing was that shortly after the Brisbane Test my away-swinger disappeared. How it came back I don't know but for some weeks I bowled very badly.'

Having fought their way back into the Test after the impressive third-wicket partnership between Harvey and Hassett, the South Africans were unable to take a first innings lead – crucial if they were to win the Test because they were batting last. With the exception of McGlew (nine), who opened, and Tayfield (three) and Melle (not out seven) who batted at ten and eleven respectively, eight visiting batsmen reached double figures but none scored more than Waite's 39.

In Waite's case, many runs were scored in front of the wicket against Miller (10-0-46-1) and Lindwall (12-0-48-1), both of whom bowled to attacking fields, with only Harvey in the covers mooching in the wide open spaces. 'I remember the first Test match we played on that Australian tour,' says Waite. 'There was an umpire called Ron Wright who had a terrible game. Hell, he shouldn't have had a name like Ron Wright because all his decisions were wrong. I remember I caught Ray Lindwall twice in one over. Blatantly, I mean they were blatant chances. And at the end of the over – I was quite dumbstruck by this umpire not giving him out – I remember, I didn't know Lindwall then, and I was the opening batsman so I didn't have too much to say. I had to go in and bat against him a couple of overs after that, I remember I said: "Excuse me, didn't you touch that?" "Touch that, I broke my bloody bat on it," he said.'

According to Waite, Wright subsequently apologised. Still, the visitors couldn't manage more than 221, trailing by 59 on the first innings. Wright was at it again in the second innings, as he failed to uphold two appeals against Arthur Morris, both off Melle. Cheetham maintained that Morris' life when he was on eight was the Test's turning point. Waite thinks otherwise, noting that other than the intense heat and Wright, who was suffering from 'flu, the South Africans lost the Test because they lacked self-belief. 'We were very excited going into the final day's play because we had heard that Lindwall wasn't well,' says Waite. 'We were actually doing quite well. We'd bowled them out for about 270 and we needed about 340 to win. Jackie and Ken Funston were not out overnight and we needed less than 200 to win. But our information about Lindwall was wrong. He took wickets on that last day. In retrospect I don't think we actually believed we could do it – that was our problem.'

South Africa's start to the final day was wretched – McGlew (69) going back to a Lindwall scuttler off the eighth ball of the first over to be adjudged leg before. 'Jackie was very figure-minded, a very statistics-oriented kind of guy,' says Funston. 'That night and the following morning he kept on saying to me, "Ken, you must get a century, you'll be one of the few to have made a century on their Test debut." I never would have thought I'd become a Springbok, let alone play in a Test, and it was a struggle just to be there. Anyway, after Jackie went out in the first over I said to him – but said it with a smile – that he was the guy who should have gone to the century.'

Only McLean (38) and Cheetham (18) delayed the inevitable as the Aussies sniffed blood. As the 96-run defeat sank in, Cheetham was reflective: 'After the game, we had a drink with the Australian team in their dressing room. Although happy to have won the game, they were nevertheless very thoughtful. Our innings had shown up their fielding in a very bad light – it had been slovenly, slow and unsafe, and their players had, with a few exceptions, seemed out of condition. We too had much to think over – our policy in the field had paid dividends, and to have dismissed them twice for under 300 runs was a feat in itself. But from the batting angle we had to improve…'

The Christmas Test

Miller, who didn't bowl in the second innings at Brisbane, regained his sweetly menacing touch during the second Test at Melbourne. On the day before Christmas, he harmonised perfectly with Lindwall as the pair took seven of the visitors' ten first innings wickets. Of the South African batsmen, only Anton Murray (51), batting at nine, reached fifty, as the visitors came and went in a sorry procession of ducks (Waite) and single-figure scores from the recognised batsmen (Endean and Funston). Once again, the batting let the South Africans down.

With the Australians 26 without loss at close – and the visitors only 201 on – Cheetham, Viljoen and his team spent much of Christmas day waiting for their dinner. Cheetham timed one interval between courses at 59 minutes, a state of affairs that did nothing to raise the mood. After dinner the players looked forward to the long-delayed chance of speaking to their families back home – but the circuit was out of order and no-one was able to telephone either South Africa or Rhodesia.

Play on the second day was delayed because of a morning shower, but McDonald and Morris shepherded the Australian innings safely to lunch. After the break, Murray pulled up with pain between his shoulder blades and, with Watkins already unable to bowl because of disc problems dating from Brisbane, Cheetham went into the afternoon session with one hand tied behind his back. He had only three bowlers – Melle, Tayfield and Percy Mansell – and Harvey, identified by the South Africans as the crucial Aussie wicket, was licking his lips.

Morris, never fully comfortable, was first to go as Cheetham, fielding at silly mid-off, palmed a sizzling drive skywards and the bowler, Tayfield, flung himself full-length to grasp the rebound. Soon afterwards, Cheetham was in the action again as his right-hand latched onto a screamer from Harvey (11) – 98 for two. Hassett and the free-scoring McDonald pieced together 57 for the third wicket before a tiring Melle was replaced by Mansell, the legspinner. McDonald clubbed a short delivery from Mansell down Eddie Fuller's throat and Hassett failed to punish a Mansell full toss, throttling it straight to Melle at mid-on instead. Hole (13) didn't last long after tea and neither did Benaud (five) or Lindwall (one). Batting at eight, Doug Ring (14), skied a hook off Tayfield to be brilliantly caught by McGlew, and Miller, who had played his normal champagne cricket for a dizzy 52, was out to the most remarkable catch of the summer and one of the most famous catches ever.

'Then came the most amazing catch I have ever seen,' writes Duffus in his match report. 'Miller, who had scored 52 in one and three-quarter hours, with one six and five fours, lofted Tayfield to wide long-on for what clearly was to be another six. As the ball reached the fence Endean leaped in the air and grabbed it almost casually with one hand while the crowd broke into a storm of applause. Two balls later Australia were out for 243.'

While praising McDonald and Morris, Bill O'Reilly's hometown view saw in Miller's dismissal a possible clue to the outcome of the Test. 'He [Miller] was in one of his dangerous moods and it was lucky for the South Africans that their two spinners were able to hold him in check. Miller could have done a lot of damage in a short time if either one of the two bowlers had let up on his concentration. Leading by 16 runs on the first innings with the handicap of batting last on a pitch which is certain to give much more help to the spinners than it has done so far, the Australians are in a fairly sticky situation.'

The situation became progressively stickier. 'With their heads down and their hearts high,' writes Duffus, 'South Africa's batsmen made a superb attempt to win the second Test match today. In front of 36 649 spectators, which is possibly the largest crowd ever to watch a South African Test, they scored 267 for four wickets and lead by 251 runs. A feature of South Africa's determined, great-hearted display was their mastering of Lindwall (none for 40) and Miller (two for 39).'

After McGlew (13) was out early, stumped off Ring's bowling, Waite and Endean played complementary roles in a second-wicket partnership of 111. Endean swung his first ball from Ring to the fine-leg boundary while Waite battened down the hatch. Miller and Johnston pecked away, hoping Waite would pop up a catch to one of three close fielders stuffed into the leg-trap. With the total on 61, the plan came together, Johnston enticing a catch that Lindwall fluffed. After lunch Miller, fielding at slip to Ring, gave Waite another life when he downed a slash.

Having gone to the hundred partnership and his fifty, Waite became Miller's 100th wicket in Tests, caught by Doug Ring in the slips for 62. Funston lived dangerously at first but stayed long enough to face Benaud's arrival in the attack. After tea, with Endean closing in on his hundred, Funston rushed headlong down the wicket as Endean cut to Benaud deep in the gully. Benaud hurled accurately to the non-striker's end and Funston was run out for 26. McLean, new at the crease, galloped along, while Endean lost his bearings in the nineties. The latter used his feet to Ring without success and could do no more than take singles off two Ring full-tosses. From 95, his score rose to 99 and then the coveted hundred – the first by a South African in Australia since Ken Viljoen's 111 in 1931/2. 'I didn't realise you could score a Test century so easily by playing an innings that was not good,' says Endean afterwards.

McLean bubbled to a 55-minute 42 before being trapped by a Miller creeper and Cheetham managed to survive the nine minutes before the close. On the Monday, Endean added 47 of the 121 the South Africans added to their overnight total of 267 for four. Mansell helped with 18, Murray contributed 23 and Tayfield provided 22. South Africa made 388, meaning Australia needed 373 to win. At close on the third day, the home side were 132 for four and South Africa were balancing on the cusp of a famous victory. The man in the way? Miller, not out on 23, after Harvey (60), Morris (one), McDonald (23) and Hassett (21) had already come and gone. Duffus, for one, was not counting his Christmas chickens. 'Miller batted with an ominous sense of responsibility, but so, too, did Harvey,' he writes. 'Many bitter disappointments have taught South Africans not to rejoice prematurely, and their mood tonight is one of realisation that victory is excitingly near but by no means certain.'

The following morning Gil Langley, the night-watchman, was first out, bowled by Tayfield for four. Meanwhile, Miller, according to Cheetham, 'had been walking up the wicket and driving Tayfield's bowling,' a situation which squared with Miller's chirp as he walked through the turnstiles: 'I think I'll catch you boys today – I'm seeing them well.' Cheetham had other plans. 'I had counteracted this [Miller's use of his feet] by dropping the leg-trap back and had reinforced the off-side with an extra cover,' he writes. 'The boys were fielding superbly, and in an effort to break Tayfield's run of maidens, Keith tried to loft a drive over the off fieldsmen's heads. The flight and the turn beat him and the ball knocked the leg stump back – with Miller out six wickets were down for 148 runs, victory was surely in our grasp.'

The Test was to endure still more twists and turns. Hole and Benaud clipped and drove Mansell, as the home team hung on grimly. Tayfield, meanwhile, was winding his way through a wonderland of maidens. With the total on 181, Hole swept to leg off Tayfield, missed, and in Duffus' words, 'was gently bowled.' When Tayfield eventually conceded a run in the session, his figures were 9.3-9-0-3. His final over the previous evening was also a maiden. In it, he had suckered Harvey into a rare indiscretion and so, all told, 10 of his 10.3 overs had been maidens and he had taken four wickets without conceding a run.

The home team took lunch at 207 for seven, with Benaud and Lindwall at the crease. After lunch, the South Africans received a slice of good luck. Lindwall played on to a straight full-toss from Melle and was bowled. Benaud (45) was next to go, well caught by Melle, who darted behind Tayfield to take the catch. After Ring was dropped by Innes close to the boundary when he was on 46, South African hearts sank. Seven runs later and Ring heaved again. The ball flew up and Melle swallowed the catch. Victory for South Africa by 82 runs with Tayfield devouring 13 wickets.

In keeping with their tag as innocents abroad, the team sang 'Jan Pierewiet' – Hassett's favourite South African song – as part of their victory celebrations and then went off to the movies or to visit friends. Sir Robert Menzies dropped by to offer his good wishes. Cheetham, after having endured sleeplessness for much of the previous night, looked back to Perth and the preparation undertaken there as a determining factor in the victory.

For some, such as Jack Fingleton and Duffus, it was an opportunity to eat their words. 'More striking than any single accomplishment was the background setting of their accomplishment,' he writes. 'They came to Australia almost as South Africa's second X1, inexperienced, unsung, with limited skill, their venture opposed at home and their prowess belittled abroad. No one was more strongly opposed to the tour than I myself. If they lose the remaining three Test matches and sustain a sharp financial loss – a prospect which should now diminish – this attainment alone was worth the journey. It would be wrong to say that South Africa's cricket has improved as much as Australia's has declined, but in this matter the closing of the yawning gap which existed between the capabilities of the two teams in 1949/50 was almost incredible.'

Fingleton was more direct. 'A withdrawal and an apology,' he writes. 'I was one of a number who thought and wrote that the Springboks should have postponed this tour for a few years in view of their many losses of the past year. I think so no longer. Though the crowds to this game have been very poor, the Springboks have done Australian cricket the best turn since the war. They have jolted us out of our complacency and smugness and they have shown us that magnificent spirit of fight that never acknowledges defeat – a spirit once inbred in Australian cricket.'

Christmas victory in Melbourne was one thing, New Year suffering in Sydney and Orange quite another. The main bone of contention involved travelling arrangements. These saw the team leave their Melbourne hotel at 6.30am on the day after the second Test en route to Sydney for a second match against New South Wales, in which the visitors came off second best in an uneasy draw. Then it was a flight to Orange for a two-day game against New South Wales Country. The visitors arrived in Orange to find the ground waterlogged. A late start at a nearby ground was proposed but deemed impractical. Instead, the South Africans spent the afternoon writing letters – after their win in the second Test there were 380 replies to wade through. After the match the following day, a group of Australians ferried the team back to Sydney by car, a much appreciated gesture. The original itinerary involved a midnight train journey that would have arrived in Sydney at 5.13am – not an ideal way to prepare for a Test.

The South Africans' punishing schedule prior to the third Test had nothing on the punitive nature of the home team's attack. Lindwall and Miller shared seven sticks between them as the South Africans – after winning the toss – plunged from 83 for three to 173 all out. Funston squared up to the pace battery with 56 but otherwise it was a lame capitulation, McGlew scoring 24, Endean 18 and Waite 32. Harvey then got his revenge. He scored 190 in an Australian total of 443, sharing a fourth-wicket stand of 168 with Miller. Ring bludgeoned his way to 58 at the end and Australia were on by 270. South Africa could only manage 232 in reply, losing the Test by an innings and 38 runs. As Viljoen had said to Cheetham during the tour's early stages: 'We're going to cop it sometime Happy.' And cop it they duly did.

The backwater boy

The 1949/50 domestic season saw Kennie Funston, the young Northern Transvaler, play precious little cricket. But towards the end of the season Funston, the branch manager of Legal and General Insurance in Bloemfontein, was called to the front desk of his office. It was the local provincial selector, 'Plum' Warner. Warner had been told of Funston's recent arrival from Pretoria and wanted him to play in the traditional end-of-season fixture against Transvaal. Funston would hear nothing of it, arguing that he wanted to concentrate on building his career. The more Warner twisted his arm, the more Funston dug in. However,

Funston eventually agreed. Born in 1925, he still had a season or two left and, despite carrying a cruciate ligament injury sustained when playing football aged 18, couldn't resist. The friendly was played at the Ramblers in Bloemfontein and, against a strong Transvaal team, Funston rattled off a polished 164. The innings made him.

The following season and Funston was shadowed by the national selection convenor, Arthur Coy. Not only had Coy heard about Funston's 164, but he'd also heard about several spirited performances against touring sides. 'Against Mann's Englishmen I'd scored 65 and 20-odd in the second innings,' says Funston. 'Denis Compton had seen me during that game and he came into the dressing-room. He was feeling very pleased with himself after scoring that 300 against North-Eastern Transvaal at Willowmoore Park. He told me that he was one of the few players he had seen that used his feet to the spinners and that no matter what, I was to keep doing it. After that Compton singled me out as future international material. I also scored 71 against Hassett's side the following season although it was unheard of for a player from the B-section to be thought of as a possible Springbok.'

Wherever Funston went in 1950/1, Coy was sure to follow. By the time the two of them found their way to Newlands and the final trial, Funston had scored 604 runs at 43.14 and Coy was prepared to leak him a snippet of news. 'Get me thirty and you'll be on that boat,' he promised. But mother nature intervened. Rain chugged across the Peninsula and reduced the scheduled four days to two. 'I played for Jackie [McGlew's] side and was bowled by Melle for 34,' says Funston. 'Afterwards Coy came up to me and said: "I didn't mean just thirty, I meant thirty minimum".'

By the time Cheetham's men arrived in Adelaide for the fourth Test in late January 1953, Funston was a hardy three-Test veteran. Chasing Australia's intimidating 530 (McDonald 154, Hassett 163 in a second-wicket stand of 275), South Africa braved it out to reach 224 for four by close on the third day, with Funston having batted 154 minutes for 71 not out. Come the fourth morning and he and Watkins walked to the wicket with the follow-on target of 380 still 156 runs away. The two pushed the total to 270 before Funston, on 92, rammed a return catch back to Benaud. In so doing, he provided the *Sydney Morning Herald* with one of the photographs of the tour. It shows Funston, head raised, having tossed the bat up into the air. And so it hangs there, as perfectly vertical as the unblemished three stumps behind him. His face wears an expression of such resignation that, behind the stumps, Langley lets out a rueful smile. Even Hassett in the foreground looks strangely silent.

'I must have thrown it [the bat] about twenty feet into the air,' says Funston. 'It was just an expression of complete disappointment. The funny thing was that Ken [Viljoen] had told me there was to be no dancing down the wicket once I got into the nineties. I was to reach my century in singles. I remember it well, I went from 88 to 92 with a four off Benaud. Then he bowled a perfectly normal ball, except it was perhaps a bit slower than usual. My instinct was to hit him over his head as I usually did, except something just clicked in the back of my mind. I hit it firmly but I semi-stopped, I was half holding back. I was never the kind of person who went on. I used to drive Jack and Ken mad. Ken was a marvellous manager, really great, but he was conservative to a fault. I had used my feet to Benaud in the first match against New South Wales and been stumped. I'd also been stumped in the game against Queensland country at Bundaberg. So obviously there was to be no more use of the feet.'

In the end it was close but Cheetham's band avoided the follow-on by seven runs. With the total on 378 for nine, Melle faced a toiling Bill Johnston wretched with fatigue. 'With more luck than skill,' says Cheetham, 'Michael edged the ball between slip and wicketkeeper, and the batsmen ran three – amidst excited cheering of the crowd, and to the obvious delight of both Hassett and Johnston. The latter, in fact, did a little war-dance in his ecstasy – he had bowled 49 overs in the two days and was most pleased at the prospect of a rest.'

Australia crashed their way to 233 for three (Harvey 116) in 47 overs before declaring and South Africa batted out time, losing six wickets in the process. They had salvaged a draw but, at 127 for four, it looked as if the Australians might just render the fifth Test academic. It was not to be and in early February the South Africans returned to the scene of their Christmas pageant – the Melbourne Cricket Ground. Batting first, as they had in the fourth, the Australian innings was an almost perfect replica of what they had achieved at Adelaide. They totalled 520, with Harvey scoring 205 and Morris 99.

After play on the second day, Cheetham delivered a pep talk. 'We always used to meet in his room in the evenings and after their first innings he told us that if we could give him 480 we'd win the Test,' says Funston. 'We all looked at each other as if to say, "This guy's bloody mad." In the end we were shy of that [South Africa scored 435 in their first innings] but he told us that we had scored enough. He was absolutely marvellous in that Test. He never doubted us for a minute. He was exactly the same guy throughout that Test. He never changed one bit.'

South Africa bowled like men possessed in the Australian second innings. Eddie Fuller induced McDonald into a slash off the first ball of his spell, only for

Watkins to put down the catch. Resuming after tea, exactly the same thing happened. This time Watkins held the catch and McDonald was out for 11 – Australia 36 for one. 'The turning point of the innings came in Fuller's next over,' writes Cheetham. 'Bowling to Harvey, he changed his line of attack from the off to the leg stump, and moving the ball off the wicket, bowled Harvey with a ball the batsman tried to glide. I know how I felt when I saw Neil's back moving towards the pavilion, and I can quite appreciate how much of a thrill it was to Eddie. 44 for two, Harvey out for seven, and the fielders clustering round all talking of a win – "It's in the bag, Skip," they said, and I agreed with them.'

Hassett and Morris then hung around before Morris played back to Tayfield once too often, to be adjudged leg before. Ian Craig thrust out his bat to Tayfield as three leg-side fielders – leg-slip, forward short-leg and silly mid-on – breathed down his neck. He and Hassett managed to survive until the close. Australia rested on 89 for three. Despite the best efforts of Fuller and Tayfield, the home batsmen slowly ground out an advantage on the fourth morning. Cheetham replaced Fuller with Mansell and, off the seventh ball of his first over, the leg-spinner gave the ball fractionally more air. Hassett danced out of his crease but the ball faded on him and he could only prod it in the direction of Endean, fielding close to the bat. Australia were 128 for four. Ron Archer had hardly arrived at the crease before he was out and then Benaud joined Craig. Three short of his fifty, Craig skied a short ball from Tayfield into space on the leg-side. Endean darted after it and held a splendid catch running with his back to the ball. Ring was out directly afterwards, providing Tayfield with his thirtieth wicket of the series and, despite an interruption for rain and a rally from Langley and Benaud, Australia were all out for 209. South Africa needed 295 to win the Test and square the series.

Waite and Endean dashed to 29 without loss at tea on the fourth afternoon. With the total on 42, Geoff Noblet, who bowled well after tea, forced Waite into an indiscretion as he chipped a catch to Ring, fielding close on the leg-side. Watkins and Endean watched both ball and clock carefully as the day's play spooled to a close. South Africa faced the prospect of a fifth day needing 201 runs to win with nine wickets in hand.

After the close of the Australian first innings, an Aussie punter had put money on South Africa to win. The odds were long but he thought it worth the gamble. 'He asked us after their first knock what our chances of winning were,' says Watkins. 'He must have thought us quite mad when we told him we would collect.'

The South Africans' hotel in Melbourne wasn't far from the ground and so, after breakfast on the sixth morning, they walked through the Fitzroy Gardens on the way to the stadium. They were dressed in flannels, jackets and ties (no Springbok blazers out of the ground) and Funston remembers that the air was thick with talk of victory. 'The chatter was quite encouraging,' he says. 'We really felt we could do it. Johnny was cracking jokes – Johnny was always cracking jokes – although I think he was out by then so I think he could afford to. The only thing that worried us was that the pitch had crumbled badly on either side of the wicket. Strangely enough, although the wicket was all crumbly on either side of a strip about a foot and a half either side of the stumps, it played quite well.'

Without Miller and Lindwall, a South African win certainly looked like a possibility, although Hassett wasn't about to gift Watkins runs at the start. Noting that Watkins had taken a liking for Ring, Hassett called for a double change, taking the second new ball and tossing the cherry to Johnston and Archer. The multi-talented left-armer yorked Endean for 70 in his first over. Funston then joined Watkins, Archer was replaced by Noblet, and Johnston decided to bowl his slow spin rather than the medium-paced stuff. Before lunch Hassett gave Ring another spell and, shortly after Watkins had gone to his second fifty of the match, Ring slipped one through, Watkins being bowled off the pad. South Africa lunched with 115 runs still to score. Headley Keith, the not-out batsman with Funston, chain-smoked in the dressing-room. A light lunch was served but no-one had any appetite.

'It was unbelievably tense in there,' says Funston. 'Then suddenly Jack jumps into this *tiekie-draai*. He does this little dance for us. We all thought he had gone completely mad. He had this priceless ability to motivate the boys and to do the right thing. The one thing that people don't realise is that he had a great sense of humour. That really made us adore the guy. I don't want to say that he was a father-figure but he was almost like one. He also had this wonderful attribute of making you feel wanted and welcome, especially someone like me.'

After lunch, Benaud bowled Funston with a top-spinner for 35 – and South Africa still needed over a hundred to win. McLean was next man in. 'All my gear was next to McLean's,' remembers Cheetham, 'and I moved over to him to wish him luck, murmuring that it was up to him to play his own game and not throw his wicket away. Roy tugged his cap on and said "Don't worry Pop, I'll get them for you" – and he certainly did – in a manner which I for one, and all who saw the day's play, will never forget.' McLean was dropped first ball by Morris when he drilled a delivery from Benaud to mid-wicket. 'Morris got both hands to the ball, which exploded through them, to bounce on his shoulder and trickle down his back, dropping to the ground,' says Cheetham. 'I shall never forget my reaction to the shot – next man in, I stood up, with an empty feeling in the pit of my stomach, only the crowd's groan and the excited shout from Anton Murray, allowing me to sink gratefully back onto the bench.'

After a dangerous beginning, McLean and Keith slowly got on top of the bowling. Ring's final over brought 18. When Hassett brought himself on the South Africans knew that victory was assured. Three quick boundaries flashed from McLean's bat. The visitors had won by six wickets and so saved the series. Three days after the victory, Whitington summed it all up for the *Sunday Times*. 'Last October three Australian cricket writers – Bill O'Reilly, Percy Beames, who used to captain Victoria, and I – sat together in the George Giffen stand at the Adelaide Oval with our heads well down in our hands. We were completely in despair about the South Africans' prospects in the remaining matches of their tour,' he writes. 'All three of us wished Jack Cheetham's team well. That is why we were in despair. We could not, as we discussed the prospects of the South Africans, help but agree with the cricket-lover of Perth who said, "They will get murdered in the Tests." Yet last Thursday at the Melbourne Cricket Ground, when Roy McLean thundered the way to victory with a brilliant blast of boundaries, the three of us toasted Cheetham and his team. Nor did we forget the inconspicuous, ever faithful, ever self-sacrificing part played by Ken Viljoen, the manager. We knew the magnitude of the achievement. We agreed that every member of the team – including the unlucky and unrewarded Eric Norton – had put more time, more zest, and more devotion to the job in hand than any other cricket team we had followed across Australia.'

Just before dawn in Greytown...

Other than reading the newspapers, many South Africans listened to the radio for news about what was happening in faraway Australia. Mike Shafto, later to become a much-loved feature of South African sports journalism, was at the time offered a room in the back of the Standard Bank's Greytown branch – infinitely superior to the accommodation he rented in the home of the local public prosecutor. The room in Mr Greyling's bank was arranged by Phil Nel, who insisted that Shafto, then farming at Kranskop, 70 kilometres away from Greytown, needed to be closer to the town's fields for rugby practice. Shafto remembers the final day's play well: 'The bank manager had a radio and I got up that morning to listen to the final day's play. The game must've ended in Oz in the early afternoon because it was just before dawn in Greytown when we won. In the still of the morning this line of cars and trucks came down Greytown's main – and only – street, past the bank, hooters blaring; they parked at the Plough Hotel, got the manager out of bed and persuaded him to open the pub. Later, at about 10am, they arrived at the bank and carted off the manager. The respective accountants and shopkeepers shut up shop at midday, balanced the books and by lunch we were in the pub. Drinks were on the house.'

The rest of cricket-loving South Africa was also delighted. Leyden, the cartoonist, was his usual swift self on the draw. Under the question 'Did you McLean your teeth this morning' – a play on the famous McLean's toothpaste advert – his cartoon showed a bleary-eyed, stubble-slapped fan tweaking the dials of his radiogram to be greeted with the news that South Africa needed 201 runs to win. The next image in Leyden's cartoon showed the fan transformed by the news that 'The Springboks have won.' This time round the fan wears a wide smile with the words: 'Roy McLean again' in place of where his teeth should be.

As news of the six-wicket victory seeped into South Africa, so telegrams trickled East. 'The results have completely justified sending this side to Australia,' writes Arthur Coy, the convenor of South African selectors. 'They have proved that there are just as good Springbok cricketers in the South African veld as were ever produced in this country.' There were telegrams too from Dr EG Jansen, the Governor-General, and both Mr Strauss, the leader of the opposition, and Dr Malan, the Prime Minister – the latter's message having been composed by Dr TE Donges, the minister of the interior and a known cricket fan. The best telegram of all came from Jack Cheetham's wife. 'I don't think I will be more excited even when I know Jack is coming home. I have not budged from the wireless this whole match – except when Jack was batting.'

CHAPTER 7

On a roll across the Tasman

The coming of Jackie McGlew...

If a trip to Australia involved an encounter down under, then the passage across the Tasman Sea was literally a journey to the end of the earth. Thankfully for the South Africans, they didn't have to sail to New Zealand. At the conclusion of the Australian tour, they boarded a flying boat at the Qantas Flying Boat Base in Rose Bay and flew to Auckland. The journey took seven and a half hours. Two weeks later, after preliminary games against Otago in Dunedin and Canterbury in Wellington, the South Africans spied their transport home. On the eve of the first Test at Wellington's Basin Reserve, they saw the Dominion Monarch tied up in the harbour, a reminder that the final leg of an exhausting tour was underway.

One member of the squad who was less exhausted than most was Jackie McGlew. The young opener wasn't part of the side that squared the series in Melbourne, having fractured the little finger of his left hand in three places in the match against Victoria. McGlew, the tour vice-captain, missed both preliminary games in New Zealand but such was his importance to the team, as both an opening batsman and fielder, that the claims of others were dismissed and he, rusty but eager for an opportunity, was drafted into the team for the first Test.

Since arriving in New Zealand, McGlew had celebrated his 24th birthday. He had played in six Tests – the first two of the 1951 series against England and the first four of the 1952/3 series against Australia – but had yet to take the game by the scruff of the neck. His workmanlike figures in the Tests against Australia (240 runs in eight innings, with two fifties) suggested a player either learning his art or struggling to impose himself on some of the toughest attacks in the world. By the time he got to the first Test, he was champing at the bit. Cycling down the picturesque lanes and river paths of Christchurch could only take a young Test cricketer so far.

Despite McGlew's slow start to Test cricket, it was always taken for granted that his was a special talent. 'My very first memory of him,' says Shafto, a contemporary and fellow Natalian, 'would have been in 1945 or '46. He is fresh out of 'Maritzburg College and playing for Collegians at the Oval, and fielding at third-man or long-on, where my uncle always parked his old grey Dodge. Anyway, Jackie walks by and raises his cap and says to my uncle, who was a well-known farmer and racehorse owner in the district, "Morning Mr. Cecutt, how are you?" "That's Jackie McGlew," says my uncle, "he'll play for South Africa one day".'

Going into the Wellington Test, McGlew's highest score was 69, scored in the second innings of the first Test in Brisbane. Having regained his touch after Cheetham had elected to bat on a softish track, McGlew sauntered past it and, in partnership with his captain, went to his debut Test hundred. Overnight he was riding high on 151 not out. Records loomed before him like hoardings on the highway. After lunch on the second day, McGlew passed Eric Rowan's 236 scored at Leeds eighteen months previously. 'It was Burtt, the left-arm spinner, who was operating when I sweated it on 235,' says McGlew. 'Then he overpitched, I went forward quickly to make a full toss of it to pull the ball to midfield and that was that. The Kiwis clustered around to offer their congratulations and the crowd was generous. It was two years and some months since I had come into Test cricket, and the road had not been easy. One might possibly be pardoned for feeling that now, with something tangible achieved, it seemed well worth the while.'

At the other end, Anton Murray went to his century (he had already scored one in the match against Canterbury), as the two fashioned a seventh-wicket stand of 246. Murray fell for 109, his one and only Test ton, as McGlew carried his bat for 255. South Africa then bowled New Zealand out for 172 and 172. They had clearly learned a thing or two during their months in Australia – their victory was almost a win the Australian way.

South Africa's performance in the second Test was less spectacular. Again batting first, the South Africans totalled 377, with Endean scoring 116, Waite 72, and Cheetham 54. The home side dragged their innings through a third and fourth day, eventually reaching 245, Tayfield nagging away magnificently with five for 62 in 46.2 overs. Whether out of revenge for the Kiwis' slow scoring or because he was already one-nil up, Cheetham refused to set the New Zealanders a victory target. Although he was criticised for doing so, he batted until 90 minutes before the close on the final afternoon. Predictably, the Test was drawn. Cheetham and his team fell onto the Dominion Monarch. South African cricket was still without A-bombs but their confidence had been primed. They were now armed with self-belief, that most fickle of sporting commodities. As Geoff Rabone's incoming New Zealanders were about to find out.

'Fortified to some extent by Scotland's chief product...'

By his own admission, Funston was the most frustrating of cricketers. Against good sides he played out of his skin – against weak ones he found runs impossible to come by. Neither at home nor away did he manage to score runs against New Zealand, a situation that drove both Viljoen and McGlew apoplectic. Funston thinks that something other than the matter of mind was at work. In Perth, at the start of the 1952/3 tour to Australasia, 'a local physiotherapist cum-chiropractor,' noticed him favouring his left knee. Not wanting to make a fuss of it, he unobtrusively took Funston aside. Funston admitted that he had severely injured cruciate ligaments in his left knee while playing soccer on the left wing for Northern Transvaal and after that he had always struggled. The Australian physiotherapist invited Funston home for dinner and then massaged and rubbed the knee. He repeated the trick before the South Africans flew to Adelaide and even prescribed a regimen of muscle-strengthening exercises. 'I've forgotten the man's name,' says Funston. 'I was afraid that I would be sent home if Ken and Jack found out and so that physio chap was really helpful. He was wonderful really because I stayed free from pain in Australia and New Zealand. The problem was that when I returned I stopped doing the strengthening exercises. I wasn't conscious of it at the time but I think that the knee influenced my cricket from then on.'

While Funston was unable to build on the promise he had shown in Australia, there were other players who used the time when Cheetham's team was away to establish their claims. Two such players were Transvaal bowlers, Wanderers' Dave Ironside and Jeppe Old Boys' Neil Adcock. Ironside's first innings six for 85 for Transvaal against Rabone's 1953/4 New Zealanders at Ellis

Park was the equivalent of giving the selectors a slow wink, yet they couldn't find a place for him in the team that won the first Test at Kingsmead by an innings and 58 runs. Come the second (at Ellis Park on Boxing Day) and the selectors reluctantly gave leave to John Watkins, whose wife was expecting the birth of their first child. Ironside, the injury-prone 28 year old, took his place.

'Dave was a very fine bowler,' says Waite. 'He used to open the bowling for Wanderers and I used to stand up. He was a fantastic bowler in terms of endurance and determination. It wasn't like these chaps today. He used to say to me that his heart was ready to burst but that he just bowl through it anyway and, sure enough, he bowled through the pain. He was an outswing bowler. A clever bowler. We really should have taken him to England in 1955. I think that the selectors were a little concerned that he wouldn't swing the Reader. We bowled with a Kookabura here and they used the Reader over there but that was stupid really.'

The medium-paced Ironside opened the bowling in the Ellis Park Test with Adcock, the liquid tearaway. 'I'd just come up from Port Elizabeth and was play-ing for Wanderers and I'd heard about this young quick from Jeppe Old Boys,' says Waite. 'Of course I'd just faced Lindwall and Miller, who Richie Benaud has gone on to say were a pair of the finest fast bowlers ever. Anyway, I wasn't over-ly bothered. I faced Adcock. And he was sharp. He was every bit as quick as Lindwall and Miller. He was a tall guy, you see. Dave's stock ball was the away-swinger. Neil's standard ball was the in-swinger. He used to get such bounce and then the ball used to follow the right-hander. He was a very dangerous bowler. And nasty. I remember him coming up to play against Transvaal for Natal years later. He phoned me up at the shop. "So who's going to open," he says to me. "Well I think I am Neil," I reply. "That should be good for an early wicket," he says. He was always full of bullshit, Neil, but he was a very fine bowler.'

Batting first on December 26, 1953, South Africa struggled to 259 for eight at close of play on the first day, with Endean (93) and Van Ryneveld (65) domin-ating, as the New Zealanders chipped away on a bowler-friendly wicket. The fol-lowing morning news filtered through from New Zealand that Bob Blair's fiancée had been amongst the 149 killed in the Tangiwai train disaster. It was left to their manager, Jack Kerr, to break the news to the fast bowler.

After taking the final two South African wickets for the addition of only 12 runs on the second morning, the New Zealanders were in immediate trouble in reply. Ironside took a wicket in his very first Test over – that of Rabone for one

– and Adcock picked up his first scalp of the game soon afterwards as he bowled Murray Chapple for eight. Chapple's dismissal brought Bert Sutcliffe, the left-hander, to the wicket. Shortly before lunch, Adcock bowled Sutcliffe a short-pitched delivery which Sutcliffe tried to hook. The New Zealander managed to get bat on ball but only succeeded in helping the ball on its way. The top-edge cannoned into Sutcliffe's left ear and down he crumpled.

'The chunky professional dropped to the ground,' writes the *Sunday Times'* Ray Woodley. 'He lay there without moving. Up rushed the Springboks. Somehow, Sutcliffe managed to get to his feet with the assistance of the first aid men. As he walked out – he refused a stretcher – he turned to shake hands with the Springbok captain, Jack Cheetham. This was a sporting gesture by Sutcliffe, especially as a section of the crowd had started to shout for Adcock to be taken off. Had this happened it would have been most unfair as the Springbok express bowler was keeping a good length. Those deliveries which did rear up alarmingly were not from deliberate bumpers.'

With the New Zealand total on 82 for six, Sutcliffe returned, 'fortified to some extent by Scotland's chief product.' First he unleashed his wrath on Ironside, hitting the debutant for a six off the third ball he faced. He then turned his attention to Tayfield. He hit him for two sixes in an over as he and Frank Mooney scored 56 in 53 minutes. Then Ironside precipitated a minor collapse. First he bowled Mooney for 35 (138 for seven) and then accounted for both Tony MacGibbon (146 for eight) and Guy Overton (154 for nine). Overton's dismissal brought Blair to the wicket. In his book, *Cricket in South Africa*, Jonty Winch quotes from the following 'contemporary account':

'Sympathy for Blair in his sorrow, and admiration for his courage in carrying on, were natural, but somehow the whole vast crowd – normally more matter-of-fact than most – became as one at this poignant moment, a moment the New Zealanders and others will recall with vivid clarity all their lives. He walked out into the sunshine, finding it pathetically difficult to put on his gloves, and the huge crowd stood for him, silent, as he went. Looking down on the scene from the glass windows of the pavilion, the New Zealanders wept openly and without shame; the South Africans were in little better state, and Sutcliffe, walking out to meet his partner, was just as obviously distressed. Before he faced his first ball Blair passed his gloves across his eyes in the heart-wringing gesture of any small boy, anywhere in trouble, but defiant. His was a courage unexcelled in a match which made heavy demands on the New Zealanders. To take physical knocks and come back for more is admirable, but to carry on after one's world has fallen about one's ears surely requires an effort quite out of the ordinary. Then came the most thrilling batting of the series. Sutcliffe swung Tayfield high and dry for six; two balls later another effortless on-drive went for six, and two balls later again he hit another one into a half-demented crowd. Then he took a single to retain the strike, but Blair finished off the over with a tremendous hit far into the seething, cheering spectators at mid-wicket – 25 from Tayfield in an over. A few more were added and then Blair was stumped and the crowd, giving the batsmen a tremendous reception, might have been thought, from the warmth of their applause, to have been cheering a last-minute win in a rugby test. So the batsmen came back, and there was a last little unforgettable gesture. Sutcliffe had hit seven sixes, six off Tayfield, and he had made 80 not out in an hour and a half. With Blair he had scored 33 for the last wicket in ten minutes, he had saved the follow-on, and he was quite entitled to regard the tumult of cheering as a tribute to his skill and daring. But he stood aside at the gate, allowing Blair to pass in first. They went, arms about each other, into the darkness of the tunnel, but behind them they left a light and an inspiration which several thousand lectures on how to play the forward defensive stroke could never kindle.'

By close of play, South Africa were dazed on 35 for three, with McGlew (eight), Endean (one) and Funston (11) all back in the hut. Resuming, South Africa were all out for 148 shortly before tea on the third afternoon. Only McLean (36) and Tayfield (34) provided resistance. The visitors needed 233 to win the Test. Only a pitch still favouring the bowlers and Adcock and Ironside stood between them and a series-squaring win. But the New Zealanders couldn't repeat their Saturday afternoon heroics. On the final morning, they lost seven wickets for 32 runs in an hour and a quarter to be bowled out for 100, losing the Test by 132 runs. Adcock and Ironside took eight wickets apiece in the match and Duffus dubbed it a 'shattering anti-climax'.

Having failed again, Funston was dropped for the third Test at Newlands and South Africa merrily wound their way south. In nine Test matches since Cheetham had taken over the captaincy from Nourse, they had won five, drawn two and lost two. Their win in the first Test at Kingsmead against Rabone's team was their first on home soil since Nupen's team had beaten Percy Chapman's side in December 1930 – 23 years previously.

At Newlands the Springbok juggernaut was temporarily checked. John Reid put a run of bad luck behind him with an attractive 135. John Beck, a surprise choice to tour, made 99, Sutcliffe 66, Rabone 56, Chapple 76 and Matt Poore 44. The New Zealanders reached 505, tamed Adcock (one for 105 in 29 overs, although the Newlands track hardly had Ellis Park's greenish tinge), and watched the return of the ubiquitous South African disease – dropped catches. Despite scoring their highest-ever total in Tests, the New Zealanders, in Duffus' opinion, had taken too long in search of their runs. Although South Africa failed to avoid the follow-on in getting to 326 (Cheetham 89, McGlew 86), he was proved right as the visitors were unable to take more than three South African second innings wickets

After the sun-baked track at Newlands, the New Zealanders returned to Johannesburg via Kimberley, Pietermaritzburg and East London, for the fourth Test. Their captain, Rabone, had broken his foot in East London and Sutcliffe took over the captaincy. Initially Sutcliffe appeared to have erred in sending South Africa in to bat at Ellis Park. McGlew and Dick Westcott carved an opening stand of 104 before the wickets started to tumble. Sutcliffe was vindicated as the home team rested on 200 for seven overnight. They were then bowled out for 243 on the second morning (Waite 52, after McGlew's 61 and Westcott's 43).

The New Zealand opener, Frank Mooney, was hit on the head by Adcock and although he made 23, he received no help from those around him as the visitors bombed to 46 for seven at tea on the second day. 'Hugh Tayfield, the Springbok off-spinner, has broken his Ellis Park Test "hoodoo" with a vengeance,' writes the *Sunday Times*' Ray Woodley. 'Three previous Tests [at the ground] earned him five wickets at a total cost of 337 runs. But yesterday he took six New Zealand first innings wickets for 13 – five of them for three runs in a 40-minute spell before the tea interval.'

The visitors were all out for 79 after tea and had already lost Mooney in the follow-on innings by close. A rain-abbreviated third day saw Cheetham's team take a further five wickets and, with the New Zealanders just passing South Africa's first innings total on the fourth day, it was left to the home team's openers to knock off the runs. South Africa won the Test by nine wickets and so took the series.

While Tayfield created havoc in the first, it was Adcock who did the damage in the New Zealand second innings. He took five for 45, bringing his total in the series to eighteen. In Port Elizabeth he took six more wickets (four for 86 and two for 45) as South Africa cantered home by five wickets in a low-scoring match. 'South Africa romped home to victory so magnanimously in the fifth Test that people whose patience had been tried for three days forgave them their former sins,' writes Duffus. 'Left to score 212 in 225 minutes to win, they made the runs for the loss of five wickets with 40 minutes to spare. The 29 year-old Russell Endean not only carried the side to victory like rolling surf, but at the 11th hour he redeemed the reputation South Africa's batting brought back from Australia. He scored 87 in 94 minutes, hit 14 fours and with John Watkins (45) put on 107 for the fourth wicket. Jackie McGlew started the enterprise with a brisk 38 before he ran himself out with over-eagerness. Why, as so many spectators asked, it should take acute compulsion to make batsmen score quickly and then accomplish it on a wicket at its worst beggars comprehension.'

After the series, both Cheetham and Rabone said what in hindsight looks suspiciously like the things captains say at such times. Except that, in this case, the sentiments were heartfelt, notwithstanding the battering the Kiwis received from Adcock. 'It was quite remarkable,' says Waite. 'It was almost as if 22 guys were playing in the same team. There was a real rapport between the teams. Jack and Rabone became really good friends, it was almost as if they were brothers.' Watkins, dropped after the first Test but recalled for Tests four and five, remembers only one incident in the series – and a minor one at that. 'Rabone had a go at me for running down the track on my follow through at Kingsmead,' he says. 'I was wearing hockey boots at the time, they didn't even have studs, so I couldn't really understand it. We sorted it out pretty amicably though and that was that.'

Along with the quaint, almost chivalrous, gentlemanliness of the series – think of Sutcliffe shaking Cheetham's hand after he had been felled by Adcock in the second Test – there was the strange rise and fall of Ironside. After taking eight wickets in his debut Test, Ironside played at Newlands (46.3-16-117-4) and returned to Ellis Park for the fourth to bring his haul of wickets to 15. But he was injured before the Port Elizabeth Test and never played for South Africa again, failing to make the 1955 side to England, although many felt he should have done so. 'He was a real warhorse,' says McLean. 'He always had this baggy jersey and inevitably he knocked over the bails at the non-striker's end because he bowled so close to the stumps. You'd think the umpire had called no ball and you'd have a heave and you'd be bowled. He used the sun cream effectively too.

He used to plaster it on and of course use it to keep the ball shiny. That was Dave Ironside.'

Harry Shapiro, who played against Ironside when Ironside was in his mid-thirties, remembers one of his earlier Premier League games in the Transvaal particularly well. 'I opened the batting for Old Parktonians,' he says. 'I must have been about 19 or 20. Although Ironside was a Parktown old boy, he played his cricket for Wanderers. Johnny [Waite] was standing up to Ironside and Sid O'Linn was at first slip. He bowled me the away-swinger which I saw late and Johnny wondered aloud to Sid if I should be playing cricket of this standard. He then bowled me the in-swinger which I also saw late and Johnny – who was standing up – wondered if I should be playing for thirds on the field nearby. Johnny was a deluxe windbag. He never stopped talking. Dave didn't play in the fifth Test – I think it was shingles – and then had a shoulder injury. He didn't go to England in 1955 because I think the selectors thought he'd lost the ability to bowl the away-swinger.'

As for Ironside, he was charmed his cricket took him so far. 'I was a trundler and nothing more,' he says. 'I went down to Port Elizabeth [for the fifth Test] but I wrenched my back and I couldn't bowl so I caught the 'plane back up. I was just happy to play when the opportunity presented itself. By the time 1955 came 'round Peter Heine was on the scene. He was a really class bowler. He and Neil Adcock were really class acts. I was the kind of guy who used to hold up an end. I remember Kennie Funston [Ironside's captain at Transvaal] once saying to me that he needed me to bowl from an end. We were in Rhodesia. "Don't look at me like that," he said, "just go out there and bowl".'

CHAPTER 8

One of the best teams to ever leave South Africa's shores

And the sun came out at Lord's...

When John Watkins returned from Australia and New Zealand in 1953, his employers gave him an ultimatum. No more touring, they said, or you're fired. Watkins was the secretary accountant at Forsdicks Motors in Durban and couldn't afford to call their bluff. He played against incoming teams to South Africa after that but never toured abroad again. 'They didn't look on sport the way they do today,' he says. 'They see it as public relations nowadays, as good for the business, but back then that certainly wasn't the case.'

Ken Funston (another who didn't tour) believes that Watkins would have rounded off the perfect side to England in 1955. This is to neglect the role played by Trevor Goddard, the young Natal allrounder, but with or without Watkins, the national selectors – Geoff Chubb, Alan Melville, Dudley Nourse and 'Nobby' Ralph – hammered together a well-rounded side chock-a-block with variety and nous. They were possibly one quality batsman short but bowlers they had aplenty. Adcock had a raw Free Stater called Peter Heine to complement him; Goddard and Eddie Fuller provided less brutal versions of seam and swing, and Percy Mansell, Hugh Tayfield and Ian Smith could rattle off overs of spin.

The batting looked not quite as impressive, with McGlew, Waite, Endean and McLean providing the frame. A rogue element was present in Rhodesia's Chris Duckworth, the reserve 'keeper, and Transvaal's Paul Winslow. Although the latter didn't have a first-class century to his credit, he had spent the previous season playing for Sussex seconds. Whatever their strengths and weaknesses, the South Africans were a side who needed to be at full stretch: England were holders of the Ashes, having beaten Ian Johnson's Australia in Australia three-one in 1954/5.

As important as the composition of the side was the atmosphere that surrounded it. Cheetham – reunited with Viljoen for the 1955 tour – had ushered South African cricket into the modern age with his two-two draw against Australia in 1952/3. Gone for the Australasian tour were the men of the war and, in their place, a collection of near-schoolboys who had cut their teeth on Nuffield cricket and were ready for adventure. Two and a half years later and the youngsters who had been in Australia were less callow and, if not wiser, certainly a little smarter.

For the first time in the history of South African cricket tours abroad, the 1955 team to England flew rather than caught the mailship. The trip, via Salisbury, Lusaka, Nairobi, Khartoum, Cairo, Athens, Rome and Paris, was a 24 hour one but, ever willing to take the opportunity to discuss tactics, Cheetham called an impromptu team meeting on the tarmac at Rome airport – the first of many. Flying from Rome, the team spied Mt Blanc looming below them before landing in Paris. From there, it was a hop across the channel and 12 days of rain, public engagements and training.

In-between net practice and watching the changing of the guard at Buckingham Palace, the team was dragooned off to Alexandra Palace for an appearance on BBC television. A day later and they were trooping off to Pinewood Studios to see the making of a film featuring Norman Wisdom and Diana Dors. 'We were shown around the studio and shown how the cameras worked and saw the clapboard going and that kind of thing,' says Paul Winslow. 'It's still vague but the distinct memory I have is of Tayfield looking up into Diana Dors's eyes and trying to date her.'

Life as a television personality was a whirl, but the tourists still needed to venture outdoors for the odd game of cricket. And deal with the cold. After being rolled by a 21 year old Worcestershire off-spinner called Martin Horton and losing the tour opener by 117 runs, the party encountered such bitter cold against Derbyshire at Derby that Duffus began one of his match reports with the following words: 'Stiffened by a second successive day in the Derbyshire deep freeze…' The big Derbyshire freeze was followed by rain on the third day against Nottinghamshire and rain again against Cambridge University at Fenners.

'We had a great side [to England in '55], we really did,' says Roy McLean. 'It was somewhat spoiled by the weather to begin with because it was desperately cold. We used to wear the two short sweaters and the two long sweaters over them and the only friend that you had was the fire in the dressing-room, it was really cold. And then we played the MCC at Lord's and the sun came out and stayed out for the rest of the tour. That was the last game Sir Leonard Hutton played in. He played on the Friday and the Saturday and then totally disappeared. Jack Cheetham didn't even hear from him.'

The scores for the match against the MCC don't make particularly impressive reading, as the tourists stitched together 185 for nine declared on a damp pitch. They then bowled out the home side for 87, a much-needed fillip. With eight wickets falling to Fred Titmus in the South African second innings, only McLean (85), Cheetham (29) and Waite (27) kept the 'wily Titmouse' (as Waite called him) at bay. Even so, the match was nicely poised, with the MCC needing 283 to win in 300 minutes. In the event, the MCC were bowled out for 189, Ian Smith, the Natal leggie, taking four for 76 and Goddard, Fuller and Tayfield contributing.

The MCC card – with Brian Close, Ken Barrington, Jim Parks, Tom Graveney and Trevor Bailey – was impressive, but the top score was 34 before Peter Loader popped his way to a quickfire 29 not out, batting at nine. 'The South Africans chose a most appropriate place and time to gain their first victory of the tour so far when they beat the MCC decisively at Lord's today by 93 runs with 80 minutes to spare,' writes Duffus. 'This success – coming after an initial period of struggle – in a match generally recognised as the most significant before the opening Test, should not only bring satisfaction but be a welcome stimulant to the team's morale.'

Hutton's disappearance was generally attributed to the lingering after-effects of lumbago. But Winslow suspects that pain in the lower back was the least of Hutton's problems. 'Hutton saw [Peter] Heine and [Neil] Adcock and he retired after that match,' says Winslow. 'There might have been lumbago but he probably had it in Australia as well.'

After their win in the sun at Lord's, the South Africans completed an innings rout of Oxford University at the Christ Church Ground in Oxford. Draws against Glamorgan and Essex followed (due to a rail strike the team were forced to travel between Cardiff and Colchester by bus and only arrived in Colchester at three am on the morning of the match), before a rain-interrupted draw against Lancashire at Old Trafford.

Winslow used the Lancashire match for a bit of bullying, bludgeoning 61 in

43 minutes after a slow start. He hit Jack Ikin, the leg-spinner, for thirty in an over (4,4,6,6,4,6) before Eddie Fuller, not to be intimidated – or, for that matter, inspired – into a flurry of ill-advised strokes, blocked out a maiden. Winslow continued where he left off during the next over, hitting ten more (six, four) off the following two deliveries from Fred Goodwin before being caught by Malcolm Hilton at cover-point.

'"He deserves a stand oop for that," said the Mancunian beside me, as the 4 000 warmly dressed spectators rose to acclaim him as he ran into the members' pavilion,' writes Duffus. 'Apart from the stirring spectacle of Winslow's hitting, it was a triumph of calm temperament. This is a time of tension when several South Africans are worried about their place in the Test team. The usual reaction for batsmen is to tighten up, and when Winslow went in with the total at 80 for five he, too, played circumspectly. It was some time before he scored – with a cover boundary for four off a full-toss from Ikin – and after 28 minutes he had only made eight.'

Winslow's blitz was enough to punt his name in the direction of the final twelve for the first Test at Nottingham. After winning the toss, England crafted 334 (Don Kenyon 87, Peter May, in his first test as England captain, 83) before ripping the heart out of the South African innings in 55 minutes before tea on the second day. At the interval South Africa were punch drunk on 83 for five, with only McGlew (38 not out) and Cheetham (19 not out) offering resolution.

The two were still together when rain halted play 15 minutes before tea on the third day and by then had taken the total to 149 with a sixth-wicket partnership of 94. Thereafter, McGlew was caught behind by Godfrey Evans off Johnny Wardle for a defiant 68. With McGlew out of the way, Cheetham soon followed, as Wardle (32-23-24-4) wrapped up the tail. In the follow-on innings, McGlew (51) again made a nuisance of himself. But after his opening stand of 73 with Trevor Goddard (32) it was all one-way traffic as South Africa were sent packing for 148, losing the Test by an innings and five runs. Winslow, with two and three, was relegated to twelfth man duties for the second Test at Lord's.

The tale of the black cat

The sighting of a black cat as the South Africans were entering Lord's suggested that their luck was turning. Electing to bat on a green pitch, England's first innings lasted a mere 190 minutes – further proof that matters were swinging their way. The home team were undone by Heine (25-7-60-5), the Free State express, and the slinky Goddard (20.2-8-59-4), who plugged away, bowling left-arm round, without appearing to even break sweat. When England took lunch on 68 for four, Goddard hadn't yet taken a wicket. But with the England total on 82, he had Trevor Bailey leg before and, in 70 minutes after the interval, accounted for Titmus, Wardle and Statham. Heine had Evans (20) caught behind by Waite, and England were all out for 133 without having really started.

The South African reply was similarly halting, with wickets falling on 0, 7, 51, 101 and 138. Going into the second day, the visitors' hopes rested with McLean (62 not out) and Headley Keith (nought not out). They didn't disappoint on the Saturday: McLean slashing, cutting and pulling with ferocity and Keith holding up his end. McLean went to 97 with a four off Titmus, took a single to reach 98 and another to reach 99. His century came from a single off Wardle. It was his first against England 'Well I got dropped eight times,' says McLean. 'I was depicted in the *Daily Mail* as a cat with eight tails. All I can remember was that it was a bloody quick wicket. And, yes, maybe at times fortune does favour the bold.'

With a first innings lead of 171, South Africa were unable to hold on to the initiative as the Test unfolded. Peter May (112) and Tom Graveney (60) combined in a crucial second wicket partnership of 132 and, not to be outdone, Compton had the audacity to take liberties with Goddard – the only England batsman to do so, according to one match report – as England bustled their way to 353 and a lead of 182. The match situation had even the headline writers confused. 'Springboks shakily poised for superb victory in second Test,' sung *The Star*'s headline after the third day. But as they must, the headline writers took their cues from the copy. Duffus, no less, was unsure. 'London, Saturday – South Africa stand shakily poised in sight of a superb victory,' he writes. 'With the Lord's gates closed on 30 468 spectators they dismissed England for 353, and to win a match that would set alight the rest of the series. They have the heart and the capabilities to succeed. Brian Statham and rain are two things that might stop them.'

Duffus was spot on. South Africa lost eight wickets for the addition of a mere 94 runs on the final day. When England won the Test at five o'clock, Statham had taken seven for 39 in 29 overs. Cheetham retired hurt after being hit on the elbow by the Lancashire pace bowler and Wardle took the other two wickets to fall. South Africa, so hopeful after their first innings lead, had squandered their chance. The black cat that had run across the South Africans' path as they entered the ground was not a good omen, as Cheetham had hoped, but a bad one. Indeed, the England team photograph prior to the Test shows Denis Compton (flanked by May and Evans) scratching the black cat's back.

Black cats there were at Lord's, but black clouds there were too. 'There could be no doubt that the rest that the stoppage of play [for bad light], lunch interval and tea interval had given Statham, had enabled him to continue his brilliant spell,' writes Cheetham. 'But when one considers that he bowled unchanged from 11.30 – 12.30, 2.30 – 4.15 and 4.35 – 5.0, and at all times commanded respect, no praise can be too high for his sustained brilliance – and no one could cavil at his right for inclusion amongst the great bowlers of modern times.'

'Don't worry lad, tha's won game.'

Batting first in the third Test (Winslow in for the injured Cheetham, McGlew taking over the captaincy), England spluttered to 75 for four before Compton (158) and Bailey (44) yanked the innings back on track. 'It was a typical Compton innings, lots of sweeps,' says Winslow. 'He was an unorthodox player. Wonderful eye. Very slow between the wickets. He was overweight. I ran him out in the Middlesex match as he was taking his third run. I was at second slip and he legglided the ball. I chased it and I ran him out at the bowler's end. It was measured at 110 yards. It was a one bounce throw.'

England eventually reached 284 but the visitors laid out their store early – McGlew, who bagged 'a pair' at Lord's, and Goddard playing impressively in an opening stand of 147. But the middle order were reluctant to build on good foundations. The innings bounced from 147 for one to 179 for three and 182 for four; Waite and Winslow came together on 245 for five. They were still there at lunch on the third day.

'Old Trafford was the only place where we were given hot lunches, funnily enough,' says Winslow. 'Instead of cold meats and salads or cheese and biscuits. I didn't have the roast beef that day, I had fruit salad in the dressing-room. Without talking about it Johnny [Waite] and I decided to play our own game. After lunch he took the brunt of Tyson, I must admit, I didn't face Tyson very often after lunch. Tyson was replaced by Bailey again and when we'd seen him off, and made a few runs, Lock had come on to replace Bedser at the one end and Titmus was brought around about three, quarter past three. I was in the sixties. At that stage Johnny had been given a couple of lives and I was given a life off Titmus. But Tyson didn't even get his hands to it. He was at deepish mid-on, it was in the air but he had to turn awkwardly; he didn't get a hand to it. That was the only time I gave a chance. So he [Titmus] came on and after that I took him for a six and two fours, I think, I hit him for 17 in his first over, trying to not let him get a length. And then he did settle down, but I was milking the odd two or three or four and the same at the other end from Lock – who was spinning it quite a bit and getting a bit of lift. So, after that, we progressed steadily but when we got to roundabout five to four, I knew that the third new ball was due. I was determined that I was going to get it [my century] before the new ball came on, to stop the risk of getting out to the new ball. And so I took a couple of risks against Lock, I swished him against the spin a couple of times, and then hit him into the car park for my six in the over before tea.'

'There was quite a demonstration inside the member's pavilion,' writes Duffus, 'as Winslow, taking the last puff of a cigarette, walked out with Waite after tea. Spectators crowded the stairway and passages clapping, cheering and shouting "keep it up". When he was out lbw soon after the resumption the crowd stood and gave him prolonged applause.' Winslow with 108 and Waite with 113 helped South Africa to 521 for eight declared. Winslow didn't feel overly hard done by, having gone to his first first-class century, but nonetheless had a word about the nature of his dismissal with Viljoen. He was leg before to Bedser, who was bowling inswingers from around the wicket. There were to be more peculiar decisions before the series was done.

After scoring 34 in the first innings, May scored 117 in the second. Compton eased his way to 71 and Colin Cowdrey to a graceful 50. The real fly in the ointment from the South Africans' point of view was Evans, who scored 36. It wasn't so much his runs as the time he took to make them; all of which made the visitors' assault on the 145 in 130 minutes all the more difficult. Joining his Natal colleague, McGlew, at 23 for two, McLean understood the value of the moment – and he wasn't about to let it pass him by. 'I was lucky that day,' says McLean. 'I hit Tyson for three fours in a row. And he was quick. Actually it's quite a funny story. Old Denis Compton said: "Don't bowl bouncers to this fellow, he enjoys them." So Tyson says "Give me the knacker." And, yes, he bowled one, then he bowled another and then he bowled another. Then he packed up.'

Although McGlew (48) and McLean (50) combined for the key partnership of the innings, it was left to Waite to score the winning runs with three minutes to spare. 'Peter Heine was actually walking down the stairs at Old Trafford, because Tyson I think it was, was bowling to Johnny,' says McLean. 'Johnny hit him and it just trickled over the boundary for four – wonderfully exciting after five days. Peter was walking down the stairs and there was this tremendous roar and Peter nearly fell down the stairs. This slightly inebriated Lancastrian said to him: "Don't worry lad, tha's won game".' South Africa were two-one down with two to play.

South Africa came back to earth in the fourth Test at Headingley. Peter Loader, replacing the injured Frank Tyson, took the wickets of four of their top five batsmen in bowling them out for 171 in the first innings. After a 33-run opening stand, they plunged to 34 for four. Only McLean and Endean (41 each) and Tayfield (25) came to terms with Loader and Statham, as their 521 for eight at Old Trafford suddenly looked a long way away. But England also struggled. Heine and Tayfield each took four wickets and the home side were bowled out for 191 – only 20 on.

'England, at 152 for four,' writes Desmond Dimbleby, SAPA's special representative with the South African cricketers, 'with Compton on 61 and Graveney 10, appeared to be on the brink of unleashing a flow of runs. Then Heine struck blow number one, which first saw the innings falter then stutter to a dramatic conclusion in the next hour. Graveney shaped to hook a ball, which should never have encouraged such a stroke, and out he went leg before. With the total unchanged, Compton played a ball from Tayfield on to his pad and it drifted on slowly to give Mansell a simple catch at slip. Next Heine roared again to umpire Bartley as McIntyre was smacked on the pad and an upraised finger made it 161 for seven. Now the plug was out with a vengeance...'

Batting a second time, McGlew and Goddard fashioned an opening stand of 176. After Goddard was out for 74, Keith responded with 73. McGlew, meanwhile, had gone to a deserved century and eventually went to 133. Further down the order, Endean scored a century (116 not out) and South Africa were all out for 500. At close on the penultimate day, England were 115 for two, with May (47) and Doug Insole (30) the not-out batsmen. Goddard effected the breakthrough on the final morning, Keith taking a sharp reflex catch to dismiss Insole for 47. May fell to Tayfield for 97 in the over before lunch and from 204 for four, when May was out, the innings lost all momentum and all semblance of direction.

Chief villain from England's point of view was Goddard. He bowled uninterrupted for four hours, recording figures of 62-37-69-5. At the other end,

Tayfield relieved Mansell after the Rhodesian leg-spinner had bowled 17 overs from the start of play. Tayfield bowled five overs before lunch but then bowled through to the end. In 47.1 overs he too took five wickets, as England were bowled out for 256.

'The Springboks, drenched in sunshine throughout July, rounded off a month of notable successes with a crushing win by 224 runs over England in the fourth Test at Headingley today,' writes Dimbleby. 'Since the beginning of the month the tourists have won four major matches in succession, starting with Yorkshire at Sheffield, England in the third Test at Old Trafford, Surrey, the county champions, at the Oval, and now England again to square the series. England were all out for 256 in their second innings and this series has now flared up into a struggle for supremacy promising an explosive climax in the fifth and last Test at the Oval on August 13.'

While praising the South Africans' 'corporate enthusiasm,' EW Swanton was perplexed by the nature of the home team's capitulation. 'Between lunch and three o'clock the game seemed to descend into a sort of tactical vacuum. The batting in this time defied all rational analysis. During this period we saw the incongruous sight of Bailey defending for dear life at one end and a variety of airy Saturday afternoon strokes at the other. Only at the entry of Lock did reason return to the batting; and by then it was too late…'

Done in the sun... the Oval on August 13

Given the black cat incident at Lord's, the South Africans should have known better, but they went into the Oval Test with a genuine spring in their step. Matters looked even rosier when Ikin, in England's first innings, was brilliant-ly caught down the leg-side by Waite off Heine for 17. Thereafter, May went for three and Close for 32. England finished a rain curtailed first day on 70 for three and Sunday writers were left to reflect on the runs' actual worth. What with rain falling on the rest day, England only scored 81 more runs on the Monday. Compton scored 30, Willie Watson 25 and Lock – batting at ten – a bumptious 18. Goddard, the find of the tour, continued where he left off at Headingley in taking five for 31, and Tayfield picked up his hundredth wicket on tour in taking three for 39.

If Sunday rain had limited England's chances of building on their overnight 70 for three, it played havoc with the tourists. A damp pitch was exactly what Lock and Jim Laker wanted. They bowled 45 of England's 65 overs between them, Lock scooping four wickets and Laker two. Only McGlew, his caricature-friendly chin thrust out defiantly, battled 135 minutes for his 30. Of the others, only Waite (28) and a well-again Cheetham (12 not out) reached double figures as South Africa imploded to 112 all out.

Having picked up his hundredth wicket of the tour, Tayfield picked up his hundredth Test wicket on the third day as England batted for the last time in the series. The man concerned was Graveney, whom Tayfield bowled for 42 with the England total on 95 for three, after Close and Ikin had both fallen cheaply. Tayfield bowled from start of play at 12.30 until lunch and then from lunch through to the close with only the tea interval to gain a breather. His marathon spell helped to restrict England to 195 runs in the day and he finished with remarkable figures of 53.4-29-60-5.

Early on the fourth day, the home team were all out for 204, with May, who carried his bat for 89, the top scorer. But the South Africans were livid. With the total on 39, May, going back, was given the benefit of a confident leg before appeal from Tayfield. Had he been dismissed, the match would have taken on an entirely different complexion. 'We were done in the fifth Test by some very bad umpiring decisions, very, very bad,' says Winslow. 'May was palpably lbw to Tayfield when he had six. And I think he made 89, apart from the runs he made with the other batsmen.'

South Africa were to receive two further rough decisions in their second innings. Both Endean and McLean were given out leg before sweeping to Laker. McGlew – another leg before victim, this time to Lock – followed shortly there-after, and only Waite stood between England and a series winning victory.

'I remember we played Leicester [immediately prior to the fifth Test] and they had a couple of Australians playing for them,' says Waite. 'There was a chap called Jack Walsh, who was a left-arm googly bowler, and another guy called Vic Jackson. And I remember having a beer with them afterwards and they said, "you guys are really playing well and I would make you good things to win the fifth Test. But you've only got one problem; you're playing at the Oval and on that track Laker and Lock are going to give you a tough time." And Laker and Lock got a lot of wickets at the Oval. And there were some very bad decisions. Endean and Jackie were never out. Jack Cheetham will tell you he wasn't out but I think he was. I was at the other end when Jackie was bat-ting. Lock bowled Jackie an arm ball and Jackie went back. It was going down leg – blatantly.'

Not even Waite, who played superbly for 60, could check the rot. South

Africa were bowled out for 151 (Laker five for 56, Lock four for 62), as England took the Test by 92 runs and so the rubber, three-two. All in all, five leg before decisions went against the visitors in their second innings, retribution, perhaps, for the six leg before decisions that had fallen their way during England's first innings of 191 at Headingley.

Whatever the exact cost of dubious umpiring, the tour was a splendid financial success. The South Africans took a profit of 36 000 pounds back to their union and for it were given a bonus of 120 pounds over and above the 500 pounds (100 before, 100 afterwards and 300 during) they received for the five months away. While it didn't quite reach the heights of friendship established between Cheetham and Rabone's teams, the relationship between the teams was cordial enough. And the locals enjoyed themselves. Winslow recounts how during the match against Middlesex at Lords, Anton Murray, the Eastern Province schoolmaster, was cornered by a group of members. He was thanked profusely for his team's contribution to a grand series.

Eighteen months down the line in South Africa and the series was to be equally close. Owing to the teams' mutual respect, though, the cricket was watchful and turgid. Never again would Test cricket between England and South Africa be as consistently exciting.

Highland lassie to marry Winslow...

As far as life away from the cricket was concerned, one relationship on the 1955 tour stands out. Paul Winslow and Moira Lister's paths overlapped at the very beginning of the tour – in sub-zero Derby. She was on the stage, one of 11 women in an agitprop play about single mothers. The South Africans were persuaded to have drinks with the cast and the two tumbled headlong into love. But there was a snag. In echoes of the 1947 tour to England, during which Algy Frames had so irritated Daphne Mann, the '55 tourists were required to sign a document, prior to their departure from South Africa, to the effect that womenfolk were not allowed. Not that this bothered the lovebirds. On Sundays, her day off, Lister travelled to wherever Winslow was playing. Likewise, when he wasn't picked, he met up with her. Eventually their liaison was noticed, although not by the team – some of whom were having flings of their own – or, for that matter, team management.

'Wilfred Isaacs was writing for the *Sunday Express* in South Africa,' says Winslow, 'and late in the tour he had a few drinks too many and he let slip that

Moira and I were engaged.' The next thing the couple knew, they were hauled before an irate Viljoen, the team manager. Isaacs hadn't written about it but, via a cousin in England, had passed on the news to a reporter working for the *Daily Herald*. Winslow and Lister shared the front page with another Scottish lassie, Princess Margaret, who at the time was also considering marriage. 'We were taken in and Ken Viljoen had this article,' says Lister. 'We met this *Herald* man over drinks and I said, "You know, was it you? It was just so disgraceful of you to do a thing like that." We had to swear to Viljoen not to get married. It was like being before the headmaster.'

Winslow and Lister did get married, but only months later, after the team had returned to South Africa. Winslow was a sales representative for a variety of English firms doing business in South Africa and he managed to stay on in England, visiting the factories that produced the files, tiles and toilet equipment he sold back home. After exchanging his return flight for a ticket on the mailship, the two arranged their wedding. It took place in Purley, Surrey, and Compton and Evans were guests. Winslow bought his bride's wedding ring from Evans, who represented a diamond concern in Holland, and the couple celebrated their honeymoon on the Edinburgh Castle as it steamed to Cape Town.

As if matters weren't fraught enough, Lister's father was dying. He died in Edinburgh, her hometown, in June, and the couple were married in October. 'My mother was a very brave, stoic Scottish woman,' says Lister. 'Paul and I drove away from her, all very romantic and dramatic, in a snowstorm, to go back down to England to finish his business and to get the boat to come out here and I left her alone.'

Soon after arriving back in South Africa, the couple headed for Rhodesia, where Winslow was offered a job as a sponsorship manager for South African Breweries. Always a good cricketer with a superb eye – his father won two tennis golds for South Africa in the 1912 Stockholm Olympics – Winslow was soon playing cricket for Rhodesia, his most memorable match coming at the start of Ian Craig's Australian tour to southern Africa in 1957/8. Rhodesia, batting first, scored 210. Winslow rustled up 81 of them in 95 minutes, including a six and 11 fours. Australia, thanks to centuries by Craig, Benaud and Davidson, declared at 520 for six.

'Entering with Rhodesia in desperate stakes at 112 for five in their second innings,' writes Brian Bassano, the South African cricket historian, 'Winslow gave a repeat of his first innings by hitting the bowling all over the ground. His century came up in 157 minutes, and when he was out after batting for

200 minutes he had made 139 with one six and 18 fours. He so dominated the proceedings that David Lewis only contributed 35 to their 109-run part-nership for the sixth wicket, and Winslow scored 57 out of the 75 made for the last four wickets.'

Despite scoring 220 runs in the match against the Australians, Winslow was relegated to drinks-carrying duties for the following match. 'You had to do twice as well as any of the locals to get into that Rhodesian side,' says Winslow. 'Carrying the drinks was the final indignity – it was so public. But also I had a young family and always missed Christmas with them. If we were playing against Western Province over Christmas or New Year you ended up taking three days on the train. In the end I just chucked it in. It wasn't worth it.'

CHAPTER 9

The changing world

Naught for your Comfort

f Winslow was reading the signs correctly, ordinary English people were less tolerant of South Africans in 1955 than they had been in the immediate post-war years. There were no unsavoury incidents, and no demonstrators, but the English were beginning to have definite opinions about the separation of the South African races. He became involved in one awkward incident in which his racial politics were revealed to be less than enlightened, and also noticed that there was a great deal of press and public interest when the South Africans played against Cambridge University: Gamini Goonesena and Swaranjit Singh, a Sinhalese leg-spinner and a Sikh off-spinner, were turning out – as it were – against the tourists. 'As I understood that, it was literally the beginnings of anti-apartheid in sport,' says Winslow, 'and it just grew from there.'

If the South African government was hell-bent on keeping the races apart, the British government in the mid-fifties could only watch the sinking of the colonial sun. On 26 July, 1956, less than three months before England arrived in South Africa, Egypt's President Nasser announced the nationalisation of the Suez Canal. Perturbed by the incident, Britain sent a note to the Egyptians expressing concern that a waterway 'of vital national importance' had fallen into Egyptian hands. Several months of diplomatic initiatives followed and, when they failed, the Israelis invaded Sinai in October, 1956. The Israelis were followed by the French and British, but the gamble misfired. The United Nations erupted and the USA was peeved at her former allies' action. From Britain's point of view the incident came to represent the dwindling of her imperial power. She was no longer capable of sashaying around the globe and enforcing her will on recalcitrant darker nations.

Geopolitics in the faraway Middle East could, of course, be kept at arm's length. But with a tour to South Africa in the offing, precise instructions were given to Peter May's 1956/7 tourists to keep away from political issues at all costs – particularly the one pertaining to 'native affairs'. For the most part, the brief was obeyed, although on the voyage to Cape Town, Freddie Brown, the England manager, was faced with a delicate problem. It concerned a consignment of *Naught for your Comfort*, the best-selling book written by the anti-apartheid campaigner, Bishop Trevor Huddlestone, that had somehow found its way on board. According to the story picked up by the South African newspapers, Brown turfed the entire consignment into the Bay of Biscay – a sure sign of malice. The more likely story is that Brown was under the impression that Huddlestone's book was banned. Fearing an awkward start to the tour when the Edinburgh Castle docked at Cape Town harbour, he simply did what he thought best.

A new ground on the Highveld...

Brown and May, his captain, needn't have worried about delicate matters such as apartheid. From the beginning, their team cut a swathe through southern Africa and were rarely threatened outside the Tests. Against Boland and South Western Districts in Paarl on October 23 and 24, 1956, they scored 385 (Alan Oakman 87, Compton 75) before bowling out the home team for 149 and 109. In Cape Town, a couple of days later, they bowled Western Province out for 129, followed it up with 334, and bowled Western Province out for 129 a second time. For the MCC May scored 162, as they won by an innings and 76 runs.

May's men did even better as they moved along the coast. Against Eastern Province in early November they won by an innings and 201 runs, dismissing the home team for 105 and 59. Against Orange Free State and Basutoland, matters were similarly lop-sided. Batting first, the MCC plundered 420 for four declared. Orange Free State and Basutoland could only reply with a meagre 71 and 181.

Finding themselves in Bulawayo in the middle of November, the innings routs continued. Against Rhodesia they posted 407 for seven declared, bowled out Rhodesia for 192 and wrapped up matters by bowling Rhodesia out cheaply a second time, winning the game by an innings and 86 runs. Match six, in

Salisbury, was equally demeaning for the locals. The visitors casually compiled 501 (Bailey 110, May 206) before Loader crippled Rhodesia with seven for 28. The follow-on was not quite as bad, but still dire, as Rhodesia squeaked to 152, losing by an innings and 292 runs. For Rhodesia, someone called C Bland made 19 and 38, top score in both the first and second innings. Otherwise the two matches were uniformly bleak for the Rhodesians.

It was only during match seven, against Transvaal, that the tourists were tested. The Transvalers were playing at a brand new ground – the Wanderers – having moved from Ellis Park, a temporary venue for approximately ten years. Prior to that, Test and provincial cricket was played in the centre of Johannesburg, at the original Wanderers ground, currently commemorated by a plaque at Park Station. Realising that their inner-city ground was coveted by commerce and government, the far-sighted Victor Kent bought land for the new ground on Corlett Drive, outside the city centre, in 1936. The 200 acres cost the club 47 704 pounds.

In 1946, what Kent had expected came to pass. Jan Smuts expropriated the old Wanderers and, with compensation, the club became half a million pounds richer. Building of the new Wanderers stadium on the land bought in 1936 started on March 15, 1955. 'Grass-planting on the pitch was done in the last week of August, 1955,' writes Charles Fortune. 'It took four days. In South Africa turf is never laid, but the grass put in root by root. The grass used was magennis, and lifted from a green on the adjoining Wanderers golf-course. The outfield was planted between September 1 and 30, 1955. For this a labour squad of about a hundred Africans was used. It was a remarkable sight, for many of the workers were native women, with a tiny babe wrapped into the small of the back with a close-drawn shawl. All day they sang or chattered as in line abreast they worked across the terrain.'

Other than club matches, which started on the new ground in early 1956, the game against the MCC was to be the first international match of significance at the new stadium. It began on the last Friday in November and by the close Transvaal's Endean had batted for three and a half hours for 56 – the home side were 163 for five, having lost 40 minutes' play to a late afternoon shower. A Statham hat-trick early on the second morning, in which he dismissed Gerald Ritchie, Morris Charnas and Heine, condemned the home side to a barely respectable total. Eventually they scratched and poked their way to 212, Endean carrying his bat for 81.

The MCC batted after lunch. Peter Richardson and Colin Cowdrey, their openers, dealt comfortably with Heine and Adcock's wayward opening overs. With the arrival of Charnas, a slow left-arm spinner, the scoring rate plunged and before tea Richardson lost his wicket. Heine picked up Oakman and May shortly after tea and then Cowdrey and Compton combined for the best partnership of the innings – 112 for the fourth wicket. The stand took the visitors virtually past Transvaal's first innings total. 'In the calm of the setting sun Compton played strokes with an easy elegance that were the day's delight,' writes Fortune, 'and perhaps the quiet envy of his partner, Cowdrey.'

With Compton's dismissal early on the third morning (207 for four), the England innings fell flat on its face. They were all out for 279, a lead of 67. Transvaal lost early wickets before close of play and on the Tuesday morning scraped their way to a slight lead. Only Arthur Tayfield (Hugh's brother) showed any passion for the fight against Tyson and Statham. Not out overnight, he chiselled out 38 precious runs in his team's total of 130, the next highest score being Ritchie's 19. When Cowdrey and Richardson went out to bat at ten past three, England needed 64 for victory – an apparently straightforward task. But Heine and Adcock didn't share the idea that a MCC victory was inevitable. The visitors lost two wickets with the total on 10; Oakman was next to go, then Bailey. At 31 for four Compton, having just arrived at the ground after a precautionary X-ray, joined May. The England captain was immediately dropped by Endean in the slips off Heine, a difficult chance as the ball was always falling short of him. May (12) was out shortly afterwards, as 36 for five became 36 for six. With an hour to go, the MCC needed 28 runs to win; Transvaal needed four wickets. Only one recognised batsman – the bruised Compton – stood between the Transvalers and victory. All the more galling, then, that 21 runs of the 28 should fall to Tyson, not one of the recognised batsmen, as the MCC wrapped up the match by three wickets.

The tourists' next engagement was at the Loftus Versveld rugby stadium in Pretoria, where they were scheduled to play against a South African X1. Loftus was chosen because the other available grounds in Pretoria hadn't the necessary crowd capacity, but the pitch was newly laid and the ball either rocketed off the track or plopped and died.

'About six weeks beforehand they laid the pitch in little squares about 35cm by 35cm,' says Funston, who top-scored in the match with a crisp second innings 55. 'The joints never really knit and when the ball hit one of them it tended to scuttle. In the meantime, the middle of the pitch became very green.

Once it hit there, the ball really flew. At one point I remember they wanted to go off. Bailey, I think it was. He was a cantankerous blighter at the best of times. He said it wasn't fit for first-class cricket. They nearly walked off as far as I remember.'

Not surprisingly, the scores by both teams were uniformly poor, the SA X1's 138 in the first innings (McGlew 41, 'Scotch' Taylor 34) proving to be the highest of the match. Other than the condition of the pitch, match eight of the tour was notable for the fact that Hugh Tayfield used it as an opportunity to play himself back into contention for the Test team, after having had a disappointing season in the Lancashire leagues. The SA X1 also demonstrated – taking their cue from Transvaal – that the MCC could be beaten, Tayfield bowling them out for 109 in their second innings as the invitation side won the game by 38 runs.

If the MCC had left scorched earth in places such as Paarl, Cape Town, Port Elizabeth and Bulawayo, their visit to Johannesburg showed them in a different light. In scoring 84 in the England first innings against Transvaal at the Wanderers, Cowdrey batted for nearly six hours. Against Natal, in the penultimate game before the first Test, Oakman and Richardson opened England's innings and again doggedness ruled the day. 'They had the opportunity that comes of a good batting wicket, excellent light, and nothing particularly quick about the bowling,' writes Fortune. 'Together they lasted for ninety minutes, and between them just managed to pick up fifty. It was painstaking stuff, into which Oakman's cover-drive occasionally shot a gleam of joy.'

Richardson was at it again during the first Test on Christmas Eve, cementing the England innings together with single-minded purpose. After eight hours and eight minutes at the wicket, he went to his century just before lunch on Boxing Day (England having spent Christmas having lunch at the Wanderers Club followed by a mellow round of golf). Only Richardson, with 117, and Cowdrey, with 59, scored substantially. 'Four boundary hits helped speed along the compilation of this slowest ever Test match hundred,' writes Fortune. 'The Wanderers' Club had built their new cricket-ground at breakneck pace to have it ready for this Test match. What a reward for their efforts that the first Test century to be scored on it should be the slowest of all time! The Club should erect a monument to Richardson in the car-park. Illuminated each Saturday night, it would serve as a formidable reminder of the dangers of speeding. It could carry this large inscription:

REMEMBER PETER RICHARDSON'S CENTURY
BORING BUT PRICELESS
SO IS LIFE.'

Other than having to deal with the grinding Richardson – and the fact that England took until just before three o'clock on the 26th to be all out for 268 – the South Africans had to deal with the absence of McGlew, their forthright opening bat. McGlew didn't play because of a shoulder injury and Funston, the official 12th man, came down to breakfast on Christmas Eve expecting to play his first Test since the fifth Test against Rabone's New Zealanders two seasons previously. 'So what are you doing here, John,' he asks, noticing Natal's Watkins at the table. 'They flew me up from Durban by light aircraft,' replies Watkins. 'They weren't sure about your knee.'

Watkins was phoned on the afternoon of December 23 and asked to fly to Johannesburg. 'I was disappointed to be left out in the first place,' he recalls. 'Then I was distraught at having to leave the family again over Christmas. The problem was that I just didn't know how to tell the family. Both of our daughters – Carla, the eldest, and Bianca – had been born by that stage and I think that the Christmas tree was actually up and we had the presents all around. At first they thought I was joking. Then the tears started to flow. And here I am feeling a real heel. I told the selectors I couldn't play in the second and third Tests against Rabone's side because my wife was going to have a caesarean and she was already in hospital. After that they told me that if that was my attitude then I wouldn't play again. I said that the wife was more important. Anyway, we sorted it all out in the end but the call [on the 23rd] came as a real surprise.'

Watkins made nine batting at six, as the South African lower middle-order buckled after a reasonable start (Goddard 49, Keith 42). The home side were all out for 215 but heaved themselves back into contention late on the third afternoon. With the pitch betraying its benign appearance, Heine and Adcock got the ball to climb. After Richardson's early dismissal, both Bailey and Compton took a pummelling. After being cracked on the hand, Bailey was caught by Endean off Heine for 10; Johnny Wardle, the night-watchman, was strafed with a straight one and England closed the day on 42 for three, 95 runs ahead.

On the fourth morning, England marched stolidly ahead. The hundred came up in three and three quarter hours for the loss of Compton (34) and Insole (29). But the afternoon belonged to South Africa. Only Evans, with 30, stopped the rot. England were bowled out for 150, their last five batsmen contributing 50 among them. The South African bowling was good but the turning point in the innings came as a result of Endean. When May was on 14, the England captain whipped Heine to square-leg and, making ground to his left, Endean shot out his hand to a ball that was travelling at waist height. The catch stuck.

Tea was taken and, just afterwards, South Africa started their second knock: they had four sessions in which to score 204. In the end they fluffed it completely. By close on the fourth afternoon, they had dug their own grave, faltering to 40 for seven. 'Six of the seven batsmen procured their own downfall,' says Duffus. 'Most of them were lured to destruction by balls outside the stumps given excessive lift off a wicket on which England had struggled for five and a half hours to score 150. The triumph for England's famed bowling inflicted on South African cricket the most severe setback it has suffered since the 11 were dismissed for 30 at Edgbaston on a good wicket 32 years ago. It would be uncharitable not to give every credit to Bailey, and to Statham, who took two for 20, but in a dispassionate analysis the fact is inescapable that the South Africans revealed woeful lack of the technical requirements demanded by the situation... The innings throughout was invested with unjustified risk – as if there were urgency to score the 204 runs for which they were allowed eight hours. Here was an instance where the country's prevailing characteristic of possessing many useful batsmen but none of top international class was ruthlessly exposed.'

Watkins remembers that complacency was the key to the South Africans' failure. 'The problem was that we went in [to our second innings] thinking that it was a piece of cake,' he says. 'We batted really badly and then we discussed it afterwards. It was really a case of counting your chickens.'

Having lost the first Test by 131 runs, South Africa tossed away the second with even greater abandon, losing this time by 312 runs. Batting first on the Newlands featherbed, England fretted their way to 214 for four, Cowdrey taking two and a half odd hours for 43 by close on the first of January, 1957. Sharing a sixth wicket stand of 93 with Evans (62) Cowdrey nearly ran out of partners but eventually went to his hundred after lunch on the second day. Adcock bowled tidily on day two and Tayfield bowled 53 overs in the innings, taking five for 130 with 21 maidens. Tayfield was required to do further duty before the day's play was over. Shortly before the end he came in as night-watchman for the departed Keith. South Africa reached 51 for three at the close, with McGlew and Goddard the other batsmen out.

For forty minutes the following morning, Tayfield and Clive van Ryneveld held up the England attack. With Bailey coming off in lieu of Jim Laker, Van Ryneveld clipped Laker's very first delivery down to long-leg. Tayfield, the non-striker, barrelled down the pitch for the single and then refused to budge. Van Ryneveld, thinking that a two was in the offing, found himself face-to-face with Tayfield at Evans' end. By this time the ball, having been returned by Statham, was in Evans' gloves. He calmly rolled it towards Laker: the hit was a direct one and South Africa were 63 for four.

McLean replaced Tayfield at the crease and at lunch he and Van Ryneveld had taken the total to 105 for four. Van Ryneveld was out for 25 soon afterwards, then McLean (42), mis-timing a pull. Other than Waite (49) and a couple of sizzling strikes from Adcock, the life was strangled out of the South Africans in the afternoon. They were bowled out for 205, taking 452 minutes to score their runs. 'Where the England players spend long hours at the crease,' writes Cyril Medworth, 'they do at least show worthy returns for their patience. This Test match, like its predecessor, has signally failed to capture the public's hearts. Eventually this snail's pace of batting will sound the death knell of Test cricket or five-day matches.'

Batting again, England scored their 220 for six declared comparatively quickly in the context of the slow-scoring series. They faced just under 64 overs, Compton grabbing 64 and Cowdrey 61. With a first innings lead of 164 they set the home team 385 to win. It was by no means impossible, but unlikely, given the depth of the bowling resources at England's disposal. The fifth day rendered all equations academic. Resuming on 41 for two, South Africa lost their third wicket one run later and their fourth on 56. With the total on 67, they lost four wickets and, shortly afterwards, were bowled out by Wardle for 72. England had won the Test by 312 runs.

Kingsmead: the beginning of the big turnaround...

Kingsmead, the venue for the third Test, was the only ground in the series thus far on which South Africa gained a first innings lead. Batting first, England ground out 218. Their openers, Richardson and Bailey, compiled 115 for the first wicket, but after that Compton (16), May (two), Cowdrey (six) and Insole (13) all melted away under the sustained barrage from Adcock (four for 39), Heine (two for 65) and Goddard (one for 42).

In reply, South Africa opened with Tony Pithey, the new cap, and Goddard.

A Rhodesian, but qualifying to play for South Africa via a residence qualification, Pithey had recently scored a century for Rhodesia against Transvaal and
came into the team because of McGlew's continuing shoulder problems. The
University of Cape Town student contributed 25 in an opening stand of 65. 'I
found batting with Trevor a great experience,' says Pithey. 'He was a fine judge
of a run and could always be relied upon to call decisively. At that stage of his
career he had a great deal of Test experience compared to me and his technique
against fast-bowling was excellent.'

After Pithey's dismissal, the South African innings hit turbulence, losing
wickets at 76 and 81. First to fall after Pithey was Keith, then Endean. Endean's
dismissal brought McLean to the wicket. He was about to play one of the
innings of the series and Goddard (69) gave him bold support. 'It was an
absolutely magnificent innings,' says Funston, who batted with McLean some
of the way. 'He played some incredible shots. The one that I really remember
was a shot off Loader. Roy played a tennis shot to a short ball that bounced
above his head. His bat was absolutely perpendicular, I'm not exaggerating. He
hit it for six, straight into the sightscreen. Loader was quite a handful. He used
to throw his quicker one. But Roy just smashed it back past him.'

Not out on 35 on the rest day, McLean resumed on the Monday morning.
While at the crease, he lost Goddard, Funston and Waite before going out for
100 exactly. He was particularly severe on Laker (12-1-47-0) but, whenever
carnage threatened, May reverted to Bailey or Wardle or both. After McLean's
departure, South Africa limped to 283, a lead of 65.

In their second innings, England relied almost entirely on Doug Insole.
The vice-captain scored 110 out of 254, the next highest score being
Richardson's 32. Although Bailey and Compton were the not-out batsmen
overnight on the third day, Bailey had been struck on the little finger by Heine
before close and didn't come out to bat on the fourth morning, the honour
falling to Insole. With several interruptions due to rain, batting was awkward
for England, Adcock, in particular, making life interesting for Insole. But he
survived. Partners came and went at the other end: first an exhausted Cowdrey,
suffering, so one commentator surmised, from 'apricot sickness' – whatever
that was – caught in the Cape. The mighty Evans only scored 10 before being
caught by Waite off Tayfield, his departure bringing Bailey – with swollen and
bandaged hand – to the crease.

With precious little time left on the fourth afternoon, Clive van Ryneveld,
the South African captain, decided to put the squeeze on. He surrounded

Bailey's bat with close fielders and told Tayfield to drop the ball on the prover-bial tickey. The Kingsmead crowd, noticing the drama, started to roar and cat-call. Bailey withdrew until silence descended. Facing the second ball of Tayfield's over, Bailey thrust out his bat; the ball shivered to Van Ryneveld at leg-slip. The captain hurtled forward, catching the ball just before it hit the turf. 'Why aren't you walking Trevor, you got a touch,' asks one of the close fielders. 'I know,' replies Bailey, 'the question is: did the ball hit my bat or go from pad onto bat.' 'It doesn't matter Trevor,' says the fielder, 'you're still out.' 'One does like to get these little things right,' replies Bailey. 'Shit Trevor, let's go in,' comes the reply.

Doubtless aware that he might run out of partners, Insole resumed on 77 not out on the fifth morning. England were 192 for six – 127 on. They added 62 more runs in 100 minutes, Insole cadging 33 of them to carry his bat for 110. Tayfield continued where he left off on the fourth afternoon, taking the last four wickets to fall. On his 29th birthday, he recorded his best figures in Tests; eight for 69 in one ball short of 38 overs. Despite the haul, praise for his performance was muted. Several journalists believed that his seven wickets for 23 against Hassett's Australians was the better spell of bowling.

South Africa's target was 190 to be made in 250 minutes. This required a scoring rate of 46 to the hour and most pundits – Charles Fortune and Cyril Medworth for instance – were of the opinion that the equation was beyond the South Africans, particularly with the ultra-cautious Pithey opening the batting. In fact, only 50 runs were added during the first 120 minutes, Laker and Wardle giving nothing away. Laker's figures were particularly impressive in the middle session: he bowled five maidens in his ten overs, taking one for eight.

A further ten runs were added in the fifteen minutes after tea. Then, some-what belatedly, Funston started to attack. 'Russell [Endean] came up to me and suggested that we have one last wild canter,' says Funston. 'He said that he wasn't capable of hitting out, so I was to have a go. Don't forget that the Kingsmead pitch was a bit of a problem by that stage. It was keeping really low. Anyway, I had a go, but May was ultra defensive with his field placings and the accuracy of that England attack was something else.' Funston carved 11 from Wardle's second post-tea over. Bowling from the other end, Statham was start-ing to tire. The hundred was reached after 180 minutes of batting with four wickets down. The equation? Ninety runs in seventy minutes and, with Funston still at the crease, anything was possible. But shortly after 4.30 drinks,

Funston was bowled by Loader for 44. Laker caught and bowled Endean for 26 the very next over and suddenly England glimpsed the outside chance of an unlikely victory. It was not to be. Waite and Van Ryneveld batted out time as South Africa fell 48 runs short.

Winter woollies to vodka, lumbago liniment to hair-lotion...

Reading his copy of *The Star* on the morning of February 15, 1957, Fortune was quietly taken aback. 'For weeks past some knowledgeable advertising agent had succeeded in making MCC players the big draw for the purchase of everything from winter woollies to vodka, lumbago liniment to hair-lotion, and brier pipes to cigarettes. Suddenly all had vanished: no longer from my paper gleamed forth the bright smiles or the grim 'into-action' faces of the MCC. Instead there were mere artists' impressions of elegant but anonymous cricketers.'

By the time the fourth Test wound round, lack of South African success combined with both teams' slow scoring had rendered the series commercially unattractive. Rather than being a magnetic bunch who were asked to lend their name to virtually anything, the MCC were now just a band of anonymous visitors with thick accents and white flannels. Indeed, the fans of the first morning of the fourth Test voted with their feet. Hardly anyone was in the Wanderers to see Wardle catch Pithey off Bailey for 10, the first South African wicket falling on 22.

While local fans would have happily missed the fall of the first South African wicket, they would have been less pleased to miss the rest of the day's play. After Pithey's early departure, Goddard and Waite banged together a second-wicket partnership of 112. After a cheeky 61, Waite was next to go, caught by Evans off Statham. Funston replaced him and at tea the home side were 146 for two. Goddard, not out at tea, fell in the over directly after it and Funston shortly after that, being dismissed rather unluckily after glancing Bailey fine, only for Evans to dive full-length and take a marvellous catch. South Africa 172 for four.

McLean started dangerously, nearly losing his wicket on 19 when he edged Statham into the slips. On 26 he was nearly run out by a throw from May, but after that he started to flay the English attack (at 5.30pm on the first evening Statham left the field feeling unwell) as he and Chris Duckworth posted 62 runs before close – 53 scored in a stirring last hour.

If South Africa had had a good first day, England had a fine second. Resuming on 234 for four, South Africa were all out for 340 at 2.30, McLean being run out for a belligerent 93. And, being a Saturday, the crowds drifted back. 'The magic of McLean and South Africa's favourable position drew 10 000 to the ground for the first ball,' writes Duffus. 'A fair wind tempered the heat.' The turning point in the innings came 10 minutes after lunch. Flicking a delivery from Wardle to Laker at square-leg, McLean called for a quick single. Noticing that Van Ryneveld, the non-striker, had hesitated, he halted, then rushed further down the pitch. By this stage Van Ryneveld had sent him back. But he was too far to scramble back in time and was run out by a significant margin.

At close on the second day, England were 87 for two, the obdurate Richardson (11) and the grim Bailey (13) already having departed. 'From the moment of his coming,' writes Fortune, 'May lifted the whole character of the batting. Cable-boys in the press-box put aside their comics, and the Indian youths in the non-European stand halted the intermittent fisticuffs that had enlivened their afternoon. He had been in no more than a few minutes when Heine bowled him a bumper that the umpire called "no-ball." With the merest quick flick of the forearms, May sent it sailing away down to deep fine-leg and into the crowd for six. The crowd roared its pleasure. When May's cover-drive got working his audience purred its delight… May did more than merely make runs: he established as fact a reputation that hitherto most Transvalers had had to accept on hearsay. In so doing he sent his crowd happily on its homeward way, and gave England firm hopes of a big total on the Monday.'

On the third morning, Insole was first to go, doing a 'McLean.' Playing forward to Tayfield, he dived down the wicket, possibly to divert the umpire from the bowler's appeal for leg before. Unfortunately, he lost sight of the ball and Goddard, standing at first slip, gathered before breaking the stumps with Insole (47) stranded short. May was bowled by an Adcock snorter just before lunch (England, 141 for four, Compton and Cowdrey both three not out), as England's hopes of first innings parity evaporated. First Cowdrey (eight), then Evans (seven) were on their way. Thereafter, Wardle heaved Tayfield over the square-leg ropes for six and, off the next delivery, achieved the same result with a lofted drive. 'Then tentatively,' writes Fortune, 'almost timidly, and as though abashed at his own audacity, he reached inquiringly for a ball that Tayfield spun slowly and amply away.' Tayfield got his man.

Despite Compton's uncharacteristically dull 42 and double-figure scores by the tailenders – Laker (17), Loader (13) and Statham (12 not out) – England's 251 was disappointing as they caved in to the second new ball. Even more so was the home team's second innings reply although, in mitigation, they were batting under Van Ryneveld's and Ken Viljoen's orders to hurry things along. Had it not been for Goddard's patient 49 and Funston's 23, they would have surrendered their first innings advantage completely. As it was their 142 all out meant that England needed to score only 232 to put the series out of South Africa's reach.

The South Africans weren't sure whether to hope for victory or pray for rain. 'I can't say we thought we'd win it,' says Funston. 'Although we took the singles and forced May to bring in his field, we weren't sure that we'd given ourselves enough time to bowl them out. Bowling them out in a day and a bit was a tall order. We just decided to hang in there because we knew we had a damn fine attack.'

England resumed their second innings at 3.10 on the fourth day. Heine and Adcock wasted the new ball by bowling too short but, off his second ball, Tayfield had 'Barnacle' Bailey caught by Endean at forward short leg. England reached the close without further loss. They needed 213 to win the following day; South Africa needed nine wickets. The pitch was true enough for England to attempt the win, although it was becoming increasingly slow and thus difficult to work off the square. Under clear skies, the fifth day would deliver a remarkable conclusion.

Richardson and Insole threw down the gauntlet on the fifth morning, scoring 45 in the first hour. Tayfield, the bowler from whom many of the early runs were taken, was first to break through, bowling a sweeping Richardson (39) with the total on 65. Next in was Cowdrey. He and Insole shovelled the total towards lunch and beyond. They were both severe on Tayfield, so much so that Van Ryneveld was forced to drop a fielder to deep backward-square. With runs after lunch flowing at a dangerous rate, Van Ryneveld turned to Goddard. Bowling left-arm round the wicket to a predominantly off-side field, Goddard caused Insole immediate problems. A lucky snick for four through the slips was followed by another. This time Tayfield was there to gobble it up – England 147 for three. One run later and May was caught by Endean off the bowling of Tayfield; nine runs later and Compton was excellently caught in the slips by Goddard off Tayfield for one and England were wobbling.

Even if the end was nigh, Wardle chose to ignore the inevitable. He had been severe on Tayfield in the first innings and, in expectation of similar treatment, Van Ryneveld was forced to spread his field. Pithey, the new boy, remembers being petrified that his fear would attract a catch. 'Wardle really started wading into

Tayfield,' he remembers. 'Sweeping and everything. He hit him frequently to the mid-wicket boundary, which is exactly where I was fielding. I was looking east, towards the slatted wooden stands where the scoreboard is today, and it was very, very difficult to pick up the flight of the ball. Thankfully Wardle's timing was so good that the ball sailed right over my head.'

Van Ryneveld persisted with Tayfield, but counter-attacked from the other end, bringing on Adcock for Goddard. Cowdrey, in turn, saw to it that Wardle was prevented from having to face the South African opening bowler. After a flurry of runs, Wardle lunged at a slightly wider one from Tayfield. The left-hander couldn't resist slashing and Waite, standing almost two feet from the stumps, pocketed the catch. Evans, often dangerous against South Africa through the years, was next man in. He contented himself with dabs to third man against the spin. Tayfield indulged him. Soon enough Evans was in difficulty: attempting his dab yet again, he misjudged the flight and was bowled.

The next batsman to lose his wicket was Cowdrey. The Kent right-hander had been in since Richardson's dismissal and his innings was the frame into which the other England batsmen dabbed their ones and twos. With the total on 199, he darted down the pitch to Tayfield and gave the ball a fearful hammering. But he was unable to get sufficiently under it to heave it past the bowler. Instead, the ball rocketed into Tayfield's midriff, whereupon it disappeared. 'Hugh folded up and a couple of seconds later he pulled it out of his stomach,' says Funston. 'That was the turning point, without a doubt. If Tayfield hadn't caught that one and Cowdrey had gone to a century we would have lost, that's for sure. I think they were a bit stranded at that stage because they didn't know whether to go for a win or bat it out for a draw. Wardle had a go but he always played like that. I think Cowdrey was a bit unsure, although he always played the same kind of game.'

With Cowdrey's departure for a stern and patient 55, so went England's chances. Laker was soon caught, heaving Tayfield to long-on and, appropriately, Arthur Tayfield, the twelfth man, took the final catch. As Loader sprung the ball into the deep, Arthur wheeled round, composed himself and, knees slightly bent, gathered the catch. 'I was fielding at long-on,' remembers Arthur, who was substituting for Funston. 'I didn't mind where I fielded really. The closest guy next to me was Eddie Fuller, fielding at deep mid-wicket. Both of us were out on the fence, looking for catches. Then Hugh waved me in. He wanted me to come off the fence about 15 yards. One of the first balls he faced after Hugh had brought me in Loader popped it over my head. It rolled to the boundary and I picked it up just before it reached. A few balls later and I dropped back again – without Hugh knowing. The thing was it was difficult to see the ball. It would suddenly pop out of the crowd, if I can say that. Fortunately Loader hit it high and hard and I had a chance to pick it up. I had lots of time to get a sighter and there we were.'

South Africa won the Test by 17 runs. And the series was still alive. 'The remarkable feat of Tayfield,' writes Duffus, 'who bowled unchanged for five hours in blazing heat to take nine wickets for 113 runs – a success unequalled in South African cricket – and 13 for 192 in the match, also unsurpassed against England, eventually overshadowed the most enterprising batting that England has produced in the present series. Tayfield's tenacity on a pitch that gave nothing like the response to spin one saw Laker relish on England's soft wickets last summer, was a quality to marvel over. He was thrashed for nine fours and a six by Richardson, Insole and Cowdrey in the early stages and took his last four wickets for 17 runs. In his five series he has taken 135 wickets and with 31 this summer needs only six more to exceed the record of 36 for a season by AE Vogler. On all types of pitch Tayfield must rank as the finest off-spin bowler of modern cricket.'

The South Africans believed they had received their just desserts. They were angry for days after Insole had been given not out before scoring in the third Test at Kingsmead. (He carried his bat for 110.) Had Adcock's appeal been upheld, they argued, they would have won the third Test at a canter. As it was, they were now back in the series. And the psychological scales were beginning to tilt their way.

People came up after the match and took away chunks of the pitch

Scorecards seldom tell a subtle tale but it is nonetheless tempting to see in the card for the fifth Test at St George's Park the story of the match. The highest total in the Test was South Africa's first innings 164; the highest individual total in the match was Endean's first innings 70. No player on either team, other than Endean, exceeded 50; the highest score for England being Bailey's first innings 41. For England there were three ducks in the match and (excluding the ducks) eight single-figure innings; South Africa scored no ducks but 11 of their batsman scored single figures. Unsurprisingly in all of this, the villain of the piece was the Port Elizabeth pitch. 'They top-dressed it and then rolled it and it had the consistency of clay,' remembers Pithey. 'It was quite damp to begin with. Then it dried out and started to crack. By the end of the game spectators were wandering out to the middle and taking home chunks of the pitch for a souvenir.'

Pithey opened the batting with Goddard and stuck around until Endean arrived. 'Russell had a short backlift and a good eye,' says Pithey. 'I don't think he gave any chances in that 70 of his. We definitely got the best of the pitch. It was damp – I remember one rising off a length and nearly taking my cap off – and unpredictable. You couldn't hook or anything. Then it started to dry out and became really dangerous, mostly because it kept so low.'

After South Africa's first innings 164, England snatched 110. Tyson, bowling off a shortened run-up, then wrecked the home side, taking six for 40 in bowling them out for 134 (Goddard 30, Funston 24). Given South Africa's first innings lead of 54, England needed 189 to win. They didn't come close. Tyson, batting at number nine, top scored with 23 as England bombed to a 58-run defeat. Tayfield took six for 78 in the England second innings, but it wasn't nearly as impressive as his nine for 113 at the Wanderers. 'I can't remember any complaints from England,' says Pithey. 'In those days you went to India and played on those kinds of tracks and just sort of managed. Look, people did come in for censure, but it wasn't as if there was any formal complaint to any kind of international body or anything.'

In squaring the series, South Africa were able to put some of the contentious umpiring of 1955 behind them. Not only that, but they were being talked about in glowing terms by people other than South Africans. The respect didn't last for long. Ian Craig's Australians would see to that.

CHAPTER 10

A series of rude awakenings

Winning (and losing) the toss

I f Eric Rowan had a well-developed sense of the dramatic, so too did Roy McLean. It was McLean who took the final catch of the 1956/7 series against May's England, waiting nonchalantly for a skier from Loader to fall from the sky. 'Some say McLean half misjudged his catch,' says Fortune. 'These are they who know not their McLean, have not had opportunity to see the hundreds of such catches that in practice McLean has taken. Roy McLean has a nice sense of the dramatic, and as Loader's hit came tumbling from the skies he moved in right under its path. Hands high, thumbs locked and right back in line with the crown of his head, he held his catch, let forearms drop on to the back of his neck, and then, with a two-handed flick, sent the ball into the skies again.'

A year later and McLean the showman, so crucial against England, couldn't come up with sufficient tricks to tame the Aussie left-arm seamer, Alan Davidson. By contrast, Davidson and his chief accomplice, Richie Benaud, regularly supplied the goods when young Ian Craig needed them most. Unfortunately for South Africa, McLean and friends were seldom able to block their way.

This might be unfair on McLean because, as had happened in the past, the South Africans and their board didn't quite get matters right. From the start they erred in only making Clive van Ryneveld the captain for the first two Tests – a situation that fuelled uncertainty in the team and the cricket-following public at large. There were also misgivings expressed about Van Ryneveld's activities off the field. A liberal advocate with an Oxford education, Van Ryneveld contested an East London by-election in September 1957 and won himself and the United Party a seat in parliament. Some were piqued at having politics and sport coalesce so visibly in one man. Sport and politics, they argued, should never mix, let alone in the form of the South African cricket captain.

Van Ryneveld's four years at Oxford directly after the war broadened his mind and exposed him to students and cricketers from elsewhere in the Commonwealth, such as the young Pakistani, Abdul Kardar (formerly Abdul Hafeez). Upon his return home, and unusually for a South African cricketer at the time, he also found himself moved by the plight of those who couldn't vote. 'I suppose one was a bit idealistic,' says Van Ryneveld. 'I'd always been friendly with [the liberal politician] Zach de Beer. I helped in '53 in his campaign for the Liberal Party. Then [Sir De Villiers] Graaff invited me to contest a by-election in East London – much to my father's dismay.'

As it happened, Van Ryneveld wasn't fit for the first Test at the Wanderers anyway – he split the webbing between the forefinger and thumb of his left hand while captaining WP against the Australians – and so Jackie McGlew took over the captaincy. But the genie was out of the bottle. 'Playing for his place from match to match was not very easy for Van Ryneveld,' says McLean. 'Inevitably it led to speculation and, from the team point of view, left vague feelings of uncertainty. It was not until after the third Test that Van Ryneveld was appointed for the remainder of the series.'

After winning the toss and electing to bat at the Wanderers, the South Africans got off to a flier, McGlew (108) and Goddard (90) hammering an opening stand of 176 before Jack Nel, batting at three, walked to the wicket late on a rain-interrupted first day. Nel, who had played in all five Tests against Hassett's 1949/50 Australians was named as 12th man for the Wanderers, but with Van Ryneveld's injury found himself playing his first Test in eight years.

'Dudley was my captain for the Hassett series and he was a national selector by the time Craig's side visited,' says Nel. 'He was very chuffed for me and all of that, but I wasn't actually expecting to play. I'd done reasonably well in the game for Western Province against the Craig side – reasonably well but nothing more than that. I was a quantity surveyor with my own practice at that stage and certainly wasn't expecting to play Test cricket again. I was working in the garage when my wife shouted to me that she'd just heard on the radio that I'd been selected.'

Nel, who had been called back to the wicket at Kingsmead in 1949/50 after Hassett blocked his way as he was attempting a second run, didn't have a happy match in the Wanderers Test of 1957/8, scoring four and seven. But he has no doubt as to where the Test turned away from South Africa after they compiled

470 for nine declared late on the second afternoon (Waite 115, Endean and McLean both scoring 50 exactly). 'Things were going really well for us because Peter Heine took the early wickets [Australia were 62 for four and 151 for five],' he says. 'But Adcock and Heine ran out of steam through the afternoon and we just didn't have the bowlers to back them up. Smith and Tayfield played, but neither was a big spinner of the ball and Hugh just nagged away. Richie [Benaud] came in at seven and rescued them with a fine hundred. They avoided the follow-on and that was it.'

Eighty not out on Christmas Eve, Benaud spent Christmas Day trying not to think of his impending milestone. He duly went to it on Boxing Day, being helped by Heine's strapped ankle and McGlew's attacking fields. His innings of 122 was characterised by a flagrant disregard for Goddard (who conceded 25 runs in two overs on the third afternoon), the only South African bowler who had consistently stymied the Englishmen in previous series.

Davidson, in the South African second innings, clearly enjoyed his Christmas Day as he shattered their batting with six for 34 – McLean, caught Grout, bowled Davidson nought. Other than McLean, Davidson also accounted for Goddard, Endean, Heine, Adcock and Nel. 'Davidson was an absolutely tremendous bowler,' says the South African number three, discarded in favour of Dick Westcott for the second Test. 'He could bring it back to the right-hander which was one thing, but what people don't realise is that he was a very fine old-ball bowler. He had a very good seam position and that meant he could do things with even the old ball. He was a bit of a hypochondriac. He'd bowl his ten overs and then he'd shoot off for the massage table. He'd come back completely and miraculously revived and be at you again.'

A first innings advantage of 102 combined with their second innings 201 (Waite 59, Endean 77) meant that the South Africans were always safe. The problem was that they had probably batted too long on the second afternoon. It was a familiar scenario: they weren't going to lose but hadn't left themselves enough time to win.

If South Africa had made the most of winning the toss and batting at the Wanderers, Craig and his team did exactly the same at Newlands in the second Test as they poached 449, built on an impressive opening stand of 190 by Jim Burke (189) and Colin McDonald (99). The difference from the Aussies' point of view was that they had big spinners of the ball to counter-attack a South African surge – should it materialise – when the home side batted last.

In the event, there was no fourth innings. Replying to Australia's big first innings total, South Africa slid ignominiously from 209 all out in their first to 99 all out in their second. Not even Van Ryneveld's return on his home ground could inspire them sufficiently: only Goddard kept the visitors' attack from capturing his wicket, carrying his bat with a brave second innings 56. 'To be factual,' writes Dick Whitington, as he indulges in his usual feast of subjectivities, 'most of the South African batsmen fell because they forgot the fundamentals, as Australian batsmen forgot them against Tyson and Statham in Australia three summers ago and against Laker in England last year. With the exception of Goddard in the second innings and Waite, Endean and Van Ryneveld and Tayfield in the first, they also forgot how to fight.'

South Africa's second innings collapse was so quick that there was no champagne in the Australian dressing room when Lindsay Kline took the final wicket of his hat-trick, dismissing Neil Adcock who was caught by Bobby Simpson for nought. Instead, they munched cake and reflected on a job well done. 'In the reversed roles at the Wanderers the Australians had shown wonderful fighting qualities,' says McLean. 'I wonder whether they would have fared as well if the roles had been reversed on the Newlands wicket which was far from being the good batting wicket the Australians had found at the Wanderers. The Australians, in their first Test recovery, had not been faced by a wicket of uncertain height and varied spin. I firmly believe that we helped to defeat ourselves when we saw on the first day that the pitch was 'doing a bit.' Subconsciously we worried about the probable deterioration and looked for greater dangers than were actually presented.'

'We were too generous' — Clive van Ryneveld on Neil Harvey's run out in the third Test

After their innings and 141 run defeat at Newlands, South Africa reverted to form at Kingsmead. Accumulating runs so slowly that they put the painful scoring of their home series against May's men to shame, McGlew chiselled out 105 in a third-wicket stand of 231 with Johnny Waite, this after Adcock (six for 43) had skittled the visitors for 163 on the second morning. 'Although the pitch was pretty lively,' says Waite. 'It wasn't a snake-pit or anything. You know, people were telling us all about how we were going to beat the Aussies and all that but they were a damn fine team. And they had the two fine all-rounders [Benaud and Davidson] who were really a damn nuisance. They were more than a damn nuisance actually. They had a pair of fine opening batsmen and Neil Harvey and then they had really underrated players like Slasher Mackay. He was the Trevor Bailey of the Australian team. No-one ever mentions his bowling, either. He bowled these medium-pacers. He was awfully difficult to get away. No-one really got hold of him.'

At close on the second day, South Africa were 150 for two, 13 runs behind Australia's first innings total. The unshackled merriment continued well into day three, when a paltry forty runs were scored in two hours of brilliant sunshine before lunch. 'I counted 10 full-tosses and long-hops that were hit directly back to fielders,' mutters McLean testily. 'The Australians would have had 40 runs off those gifts.' After tea, first Waite and then McGlew went to their centuries. As well as reaching three figures, McGlew had the dubious honour of passing Peter Richardson's record of scoring the slowest ever Test century – posted at the Wanderers the previous season. McGlew's century took him nine hours and five minutes. When the two eclipsed the best third wicket partnership for South Africa's Tests against Australia, Wally Grout, the Australian wicketkeeper, asked Waite what the clapping was for. Waite replied that it was for a record. Must be a long-playing one, Grout is said to have replied.

Shortly after McGlew was bowled by Ron Gaunt off the very first delivery with the second new ball, Waite was done by a big-swinging delivery from Davidson. Before close on the third day, Funston too had lost his wicket – but the home side were 155 on, with five first innings wickets in hand. They were out ten minutes before lunch on the fourth day – a lead of 221. Benaud ripped through them on the fourth morning and they had precious few answers to either the larger-than-life legspinner nor Craig's deeply set defensive fields. Batting a second time and Australia were on cruise control at the close – 117 for one and not bothered in the slightest.

Van Ryneveld's men had to wait until noon on the fifth day to capture their first wicket of the session. Goddard fiddled one through the slightest of gaps between Burke's bat and pad and the South Africans were in the money. 'We batted so slowly in our first innings because we just didn't want a repeat of Newlands,' says Waite. 'I said to the guys at Kingsmead that all we needed was to be 150 on and Hughie [Tayfield] would do the rest. The pitch was beginning to turn and I sensed that Hugh could do it. But we hadn't bargained with the enigma that was Slasher Mackay. I was in England in '56 and I saw how Mackay's efforts were derided. It also happened with us. At team meetings Hugh would always say: "Leave him to me." After a while we'd say to Hugh that we'd left him Mackay and Mackay was still with us – we just had to look in the book.'

After Burke's dismissal came a tantalising flurry of Australian wickets – Craig falling for a duck on 179 and Bobby Simpson for four on 221 – but, reliable as a dreadnought, Mackay then stepped forward. He fidgeted his way to an unattractive but priceless 52 not out, although he and Harvey were not without a slice of good luck. Just after lunch, Mackay tickled the ball fine on the leg-side and, just before it reached the Kingsmead pickets, Tayfield stuck out a despairing foot. Tayfield picked it up and hurled it in, shouting to the fielders that it hadn't touched the fence as the batsmen had presumed. 'The umpires didn't actually signal a four,' remembers Van Ryneveld. 'The throw found its way to Waite who could have taken off the bails. Instead he heard Funston's shout and tossed to the non-striker's end where I ran Harvey out. We could have insisted on the decision because at no time had the umpires signalled a boundary. Craig came into the dressing room afterwards to register his thanks, but we were too generous.'

The Australians were seven down for 292 at the close but they had successfully salvaged the draw, Harvey making 68. 'The Australian innings had taken nine and a half hours to reach 292,' says a morose McLean, 'the same time it had taken McGlew to reach 105. It had been a thoroughly frustrating Test match. One which I fear I did not in the least enjoy. It lacked any sort of real sparkle and was much too dour a contest from the second day onward.'

In summing up, Duffus was his usual trenchant self. 'This was probably the crucial test of the series,' he writes. 'Australia not only enter the fourth game at the Wanderers on February 7 one up with two to play, but with the prospect of strengthening their attack by the inclusion of either Meckiff or Drennan. For South Africa's tragedy of timid tactics, the best that can be said is that they did not possess the technical ability of forceful strokeplay to put into practice an obvious policy. Nor, perhaps, did they expect the pitch to retain its good condition on the final day. They had all the luck. Even losing the toss proved good fortune. They had several important catches dropped, and they faced an attack weakened by injury. Indeed, they did not deserve to win, for victory would have vindicated methods that are an indictment of the spirit of cricket.'

One nil down with two to play was soon revealed to be an artificial state of affairs. Australia batted first at the Wanderers in Test number four, and before lunch Adcock had slipped from the field with suspected influenza. With

Harvey's departure for five, Benaud, batting at number four, came to the wicket. The all-rounder scored 100 exactly in a third-wicket stand of 158 with Burke and by the time he walked back to the pavilion, Australia were 210 for three. In the meantime, Heine had hurt his heel and Benaud had reopened the hand wound which had necessitated Van Ryneveld missing the first Test. The South Africans always sniffed blood when Craig came to the crease and, although he was out before close, the day belonged to the visitors. 'In 45 minutes [on the second morning] Burke, Grout and Simpson fell, giving Heine his fiftieth Test wicket,' writes McLean. 'Adcock's two scalps he had justly deserved, and South Africa again had a sporting chance.'

It was not to be. Mackay stuck around long enough to collect a character-istically awkward 83 not out and Davidson (62) and Meckiff (26) made nui-sances of themselves to take the Australian total to an imposing 401 (Heine, 37.5-6-96-6). By close on the second day and the South Africans had already lost McGlew (one), caught behind by Grout off Meckiff. They retreated to lick their wounds on the Sunday.

By Monday morning, Van Ryneveld's hand was still painful, McLean had caught Adcock's cold and one of Waite's thumbs was tender and swollen. Of the walking wounded, only Funston remained chipper. He darted to a price-less 70 before slamming a skier to Craig at mid-on off Kline. Besides the odd twenty here and there the South Africans capitulated tamely. Davidson snuffled McLean, Waite struggled for his nine and Van Ryneveld, with five stitches in his hand, was nil not out batting at eleven.

The follow-on again showed Funston in fine fettle. He and McGlew stonewalled their way through the fourth day with a third-wicket partnership of 69 before McGlew (70) departed early on the fifth morning. Although Funston was still there, the innings around him vanished into thin air. From 147 for three, when McGlew departed, the home team subsided to 198 all out. McDonald took a single off the fourth ball of McLean's over to give the Australians the one run they needed for victory.

With the prod came the Test and the rubber. For South Africa, it had been a series of rude awakenings. 'After having seen what Laker did to the Australians at Manchester we fondly believed that we had a good chance,' says Van Ryneveld. 'That painted too rosy a picture. One of the small things people forget about the series was that Trevor [Goddard] hurt his back. It meant he lost that extra bit of pace. He was so important to us in the previous series against May's side. I think we really missed him against Australia.'

Having lost the series, South Africa lost the final Test at Port Elizabeth as 19 year-old Peter Carlstein replaced McLean, who was dropped. It made no discernible difference in a low-scoring match in which Mackay again made a vital contribution – 77 not out in Australia's first innings 291, a first innings lead of 77. In their second innings, South Africa could only scrape together a meagre 144, and the Australians won the Test by eight wickets.

CHAPTER 11

A most challenging tour

So along Griffin came

The free world was by no means drifting to the left in 1960 – the USA, for instance, was governed by Harry Truman's Republicans, Britain by Harold Macmillan's Tories – but, nonetheless, South Africa and her policies were being identified as being significantly out of step with civilized values. Nationalist Party members of parliament got the fright of their lives when, fondly assuming that he was in Cape Town to praise them, Macmillan delivered his famous 'Wind of Change' address on February 3, 1960. In a heady, politically significant summer, two weeks after Macmillan's speech, the National Party caucus adopted a resolution for South Africa to turn her back on Britain and become a republic, a decision that took the official opposition as completely by surprise as Macmillan's speech had taken them. Several weeks later and the prophetic tone of Macmillan's warning appeared to come to life. On March 21, 1960, the Pan African Congress (PAC) launched an anti-pass demonstration in Sharpeville, a township outside of Vereeniging. A group of trigger-happy policemen opened fire on the protestors, killing 69 of them. Most of the dead were killed as they ran away from the spray of bullets – with wounds to the back.

Into such a vortex flew Jackie McGlew and his team of 14 on April 16, 1960. At Heathrow, they were met by their shadows for the rest of the tour – a group of anti-apartheid demonstrators. From the beginning, McGlew had his hands full. Although he was supported by a group of able lieutenants, such as Waite, McLean and Goddard, the vice-captain, there were three significant areas of concern. First, Peter Carlstein, blooded in the final Test against Craig's tourists in 1957/8, Colin Wesley and Jon Fellows-Smith were all young and essentially untried. Secondly, in picking fast-bowler, Geoff Griffin, a player who had been no-balled for chucking in South Africa, the national selectors had gambled to the point of foolishness. Finally, in appointing Dudley Nourse as manager of the tour, the authorities had inadvertently increased McGlew's workload rather than eased it.

Despite strains both within and without, the team started the tour with a good win against Worcestershire. McLean scored a splendid 204 after an unimpressive start by South Africa and, on the final day, McGlew threw down the gauntlet, setting Worcestershire 275 in 215 minutes. The challenge was accepted but in the end the home side fell short – losing by 133 runs as Athol McKinnon took seven for 42. Although comfortable wins against Derbyshire and Essex were interspersed with less a comfortable win against Cambridge University, the South Africans were still unbeaten when they arrived at Lord's. Unfortunately the trip to the spiritual home of cricket was to signal a change in fortune.

In their match against Derbyshire, the South Africans noticed that Harold 'Dusty' Rhodes was no-balled for chucking six times in their second innings. Griffin, their man, wasn't no-balled in the Derbyshire match at all, but this changed at Lord's. Both umpires, Frank Lee and John Langridge, no-balled the Natal fast-bowler, setting in motion a worrying trend. After a loss against Northants (McLean scoring a dizzy 185), the South Africans ran into further trouble at Trent Bridge, venue of their match against Nottinghamshire. Griffin was no-balled eight times and afterwards Nourse sent him directly to Alf Gover's coaching school in London for remedial action.

'One must remember that at that stage England was on the purge,' says Wesley. 'They were calling all sorts of bowlers for throwing because it was getting out of hand. They were calling their own bowlers. They were calling a guy called 'Butch' White, who had an almost classical action. And Dusty Rhodes, from Derbyshire, he got called. And there were a couple of others they were looking suspiciously at. You know, not everybody remembers this, but Geoff had been called for throwing in South Africa. I can remember when we played Border, I think it was, one of the Schoof brothers called him for throwing. He was called for throwing in a club game – Des Fell called him for throwing. There is no question in my mind, as my understanding of the law was, that if there is doubt, the man is not allowed to bowl. Now if two umpires disagree, there's got to be doubt – by definition... But we needed him [Griffin]. He had got so many wickets in the Currie Cup tournament prior to that [35 wickets in the 1959/60

Currie Cup at 12.23]. And we needed a partner for Neil Adcock. The bowlers who were at the trials were Graham Bunyard, 'Goofy' Lawrence and Jimmy Pothecary. So there were no other really fast bowlers and Geoff had such a great season. So along he came.'

The Czech factor... and the leg-cutter

After a good look at Griffin, Gover tweaked and tinkered. But the changes robbed Griffin of pace. This became especially evident in the penultimate match before the first Test at Edgbaston – against Glamorgan at Cardiff Arms Park. Despite anxiety about Griffin's lack of pace as well as the threat that he might be no-balled, the South Africans persisted. Griffin was chosen for the first Test.

Their insistence that Griffin should play was motivated in part by their pre-tour anxiety about Griffin's new-ball partner, Adcock. 'No, it was our bowling that worried us most,' says Waite. 'Neil Adcock had shown little of his 1953-4 form or even his 1957-8 form during the summers of 1958-9 and 1959-60. He had been good for a few fast overs and that was all. He also had been most prone to injury. Altogether in the last two South African summers Neil had taken less than 20 wickets in first-class matches.'

Waite and the men who counted needn't have worried. Adcock himself was less than satisfied with his performances in England in 1955, and months before his departure for England five years later, he started a radical regimen of fitness and strengthening exercises. 'Beau Skarda, who had coached the Czechoslovakian football team before the war, used to coach me at Jeppe Quondam on winter mornings before we left,' says Adcock. 'I told him that I didn't want to become an Olympic athlete but he told me: "I'll get you so fit for cricket that you won't recognise yourself..." I'd also torn muscles in my right shoulder and the muscles had calcified. I used to go to Sam Busa – another Czech – and his gym in Fox Street in the Johannesburg city centre. The gym work and running were tremendously helpful because I found that when I arrived in England I could do anything I wanted. I'd always been able to bowl the delivery that bounced and came back to the right-hander but I'd also learnt to bowl the leg-cutter. The pity was that I got so much movement sometimes that it more often than not completely beat the bat. I'd read about bowling the leg-cutter in a book by Bill Bowes. He told you where to put your feet and what to do, so by the time I got to England I had the full repertoire.'

Adcock bowled superbly at Edgbaston. Batting first, England lost only three wickets on the first day, but Adcock helped transform South Africa's fortunes on the second, reducing the home team from 175 for three overnight to 292 all out. Adcock was wonderfully supported by Tayfield (three for 93) and finished with five for 62 in 41.5 overs. Having ploughed to 61 for five, O'Linn and Waite puzzled it out until close on the second day. Their sixth-wicket stand of 85 was eventually broken on the third morning (O'Linn, 42) and Waite went on to top score with 58. The visitors trailed by 106 on the first innings.

Batting for a second time, England were hot and bothered, bumping to 118 for seven. The tail wagged via Peter Walker (37), Fred Trueman (25) and Brian Statham (22), as England inched past 200. Needing 310 to win with over a day to play, South Africa were handily placed with McLean and Waite due to resume on the final morning. But off the second ball of the day, McLean (68) played a rash shot. At 120 for four South Africa were always struggling. 'We panicked on the last day, that was our problem,' says Adcock, who picked up a further three wickets in the England second innings. 'Roy went out to a bad shot. It was very sad. Johnny stuck around but that was it. We had worked hard to get ourselves into that position.'

Farce at Lord's

Griffin bowled 42 overs at Edgbaston and took four wickets for 105 runs. He was not called for throwing and the South Africans, although having lost the first Test by 100 runs, breathed a collective sigh of relief. It didn't last long. In the match against Hampshire at Southampton, he was called six times in all. It was agreed by the tour committee as well as Geoff Chubb, the South African Cricket Association president who arrived in England six days prior to the start of the second Test, that Griffin was to go flat out. Lord's then, was to be a crossroads.

A rain-interrupted first day at Lord's saw Colin Cowdrey win the toss and elect to bat, England finishing the day on 114 for two. 'Griffin was called by [umpire] Lee on his 18th, 19th, 44th, 66th and 68th deliveries,' says Waite. 'Five in the first seventy was a much higher ratio of infringement than had been 17 out of 1 390 in the matches that preceded the second Test. The writing was on the wall now and only Persian King Balthazar would have been blind enough to overlook it.'

On day two, both Raman Sabba Row and Mike Smith nosed into the nineties, Smith falling on 99 to the last ball of a Griffin over. Off the first two balls of his following over Griffin captured the wickets of Peter Walker and Fred

Trueman, becoming the first player to take a hat-trick at Lords. 'I tell you what,' says Wesley. 'Trueman didn't realise that it was a hat-trick because he forgot about Smith's wicket in the final ball of Griffin's previous over. He forgot. He was just a fast bowler. He just had a swing at the ball. If he'd remembered he would have stuck everything in the way and taken his chance on a leg before or getting a nick or something like that. He wouldn't have just had a slap at the ball. Never, he was too fierce a competitor for that.'

Cowdrey declared the England innings closed overnight on 362 for eight. Batting for the first time in the match, the South Africans groped their way to 152 (Fellows-Smith 29) as Brian Statham and Alan Moss shared ten wickets between them. Following on, South Africa's second innings was even worse. Bamboozled yet again by Statham, they lurched to 137 all out, only Goddard, Wesley and Fellows-Smith offering resistance.

In the exhibition match that followed the early conclusion of the Test, Griffin was again no-balled. Although bowling at half pace off a shortened run, Griffin was called four times for chucking. In a final indignity, he was no-balled one more time – for failing to alert the umpire and batsman that he was bowling the last ball of the over underarm. Although he continued to bat, it was the final ball he bowled on tour.

Griffin responded to the Lord's debacle with an equanimity bordering on saintliness. He was fully aware that as the result of falling off his bicycle as a boy, he had broken his arm, fracturing his elbow in three places. His parents lived in Eshowe at the time and there was no sophisticated medical equipment to check that the bones had been correctly set. Griffin also knew that English cricket was still smarting from their four-nil pasting at the hands of Benaud's men in 1959, and were particularly concerned about Meckiff – 17 wickets in the series at 17.17. Meckiff was allegedly a chucker and the theory was that if Griffin was singled out for special treatment, the Australians would be unlikely to pick Meckiff (or, for that matter, Gordon Rorke, another alleged chucker) when touring Britain in 1961. This is exactly what came to pass, a situation which inspired Norman Preston to write the following in *Wisden Cricketers' Almanack* of 1962: 'Indeed, the tour which marked the passage of one hundred years since the first English party visited Australia, went through without adverse incident and was most pleasant and entertaining for everyone.'

Griffin insists, though, that Gover had told him that there was 'a witch-hunt for specific fast-bowlers and that it would be wrong of him to make a public statement as England coach. He did say that there was nothing wrong with my action though he did admit that it was unusual.' Conspiracy or not, Griffin has no regrets. 'People say to me: "you must have been distraught and upset." Not at all,' says Griffin. 'I always see the lighter side of life and I was a really good and talented sportsman. I played rugby for Natal under-19; I was chosen for the 1964 hockey side for the Tokyo Olympics and I was a fine athlete. In those days you played for pleasure, not for gain. I had a good job and a wonderful family. If it had been my livelihood it might have been different.'

One other factor remains. It is too easy to point the finger of blame at the English cricket establishment. John Arlott saw which way the wind of change was blowing and wrote that the South African Cricket Association had cynically failed to respond to any number of his hints to the effect that there was a good chance of Griffin being snagged on Law 26 – which stated that if the arm is bent and straightens immediately prior to delivery then the delivery is an unfair one – if chosen to tour. Later, Arlott went further, accusing the SACA of being 'utterly unsympathetic towards the game of cricket and towards Griffin as a human being.'

After the Test, Chubb, the SACA president, read the following statement: 'It has been decided that Griffin will continue as a member of the South African touring team. But for reasons obvious to all, he will not bowl any more in this country. The touring committee has requested that no additional player be sent from South Africa, and this request has been acceded to.' The truth was not quite as simple. The touring committee, comprising of McGlew, Waite and Goddard, asked for Peter Heine, but the board refused. When their original request was rejected, the tour committee, in their wisdom, decided not to pursue the matter.

'My understanding of that, and, again, I wasn't in the hierarchy of the team, but my understanding was that the South African board asked the team whether they wanted a replacement and the team – whoever made the judgment – said, "yes, we want Peter Heine",' says Wesley. 'And they said, "No, no, no, you can't tell us who you want. You can only say whether you want a replacement bowler or not." And, subsequently, I was led to believe that [Graham] Bunyard had been told to stand by. Graham told me that. I've seen him over the years through various activities, and he was evidently standing by to go. But the team in their wisdom said: "No, if we can't have Heine, we won't have anybody. We'll just carry on."'

The stalemate between players and the SACA had been a long time in coming. 'Part of the problem with the 1960 tour was that we had a completely ridiculous administration,' says Adcock. 'They were completely detached from the players. No-one ever said a word to us. To tell you how stupid they were, we weren't allowed to wear floppy hats. Never mind that we were cutting these cancers out of our ears and noses. They said to us that it was either caps or nothing. And they had us over a barrel too. All we had was our tour fee to look forward to. They treated us like kids. You had to be in bed by 10.30pm. We were adults. The senior players would see to it that if the younger players stayed up late and didn't perform they'd be sorted out.'

How Sid O'Linn trumped the selectors

Born in 1927, Sid O'Linn went to Sea Point Boys' High in Cape Town. A far better soccer player than cricketer, O'Linn was offered a contract by Charlton Athletic Football Club in south London at the age of 20. A skilful inside right, he jumped at the chance. 'I was there [at Charlton] for ten years,' says O'Linn. 'I came back in 1957 and then moved up to Johannesburg from Cape Town where I had a clerical job at British Petroleum [BP]. The job was arranged for me by Dudley Forbes. Dudley and I had gone to Australia in 1947 with the soccer Springboks and later played for Charlton together. Anyway, when I came up to the Transvaal I started playing cricket here and, a few years later, was chosen for the final trial for the team to England in 1960.'

Waite, a good friend of O'Linn's, takes up the story.

'Sid was quite an interesting case in 1960. If you'd have given him marks for style he'd have got none. But he was a fighter, Sid, he did bloody well on that tour, really. He played in every Test and it was never in doubt that he'd be in the team – he did well. But the selectors didn't want to pick Sid. He was awkward; he had a funny backlift and he just didn't look good. Anyhow, we had a Test trial before the team was chosen. We had a trial match at Durban. And I remember they put Sid in the weaker side. He had all the best bowlers against him, but he made a century and a ninety in the two innings. So now they were in a predicament because you have a Test trial and a guy gets a hundred and a ninety and you can't not pick him, otherwise don't bring him to the Test trial. And then they had a brainwave because Sid wasn't divorced, he was living apart from his wife, and she was living in England. And they found that out. And they went to Sid and said: "Look, we can't pick you, because no wives are allowed in the British Isles during the tour." So, anyhow, Sid, now he's in a tight spot. So typically with Sid he decides that he's going to get divorced. He thereupon got divorced and trumped the selectors. He got hold of me one day, it was a Sunday, and he said to me that he wanted to go and see his in-laws, won't I come with him. And we went out, I forget where it was, but I know we went off on this mission to go and see his in-laws. They were bloody bitter and twisted when he told them. They kicked us out.'

O'Linn came to the fore in the third Test, scoring a second innings 98 after South Africa had been bowled out for 88 in reply to England's 287. South Africa resumed their follow-on innings at 34 for three on the third morning before McGlew was accidentally obstructed by the bowler, Moss, which led to his run out. 'A most nonsensical interpretation of Law 46 by Test umpire Charlie Elliott, supported later by his colleague, Frank Lee, resulted in the dismissal of the Springbok captain when South Africa were 91 for three,' writes Whitington. 'McGlew was heavily but undeliberately obstructed while dashing for a run for a tap towards cover by O'Linn. Moss, with his back to McGlew, swerved in front of him and the Springbok captain, who was bumped off balance, lost at least five yards to be run out by two yards when Statham's throw struck the middle stump. Despite the clear obstruction in mid-pitch Elliott gave McGlew out from square-leg.'

After a brief consultation with some of his players, Cowdrey recalled McGlew. It was to no avail. Elliott, supported by Lee, stuck to his decision. Despite catcalls and boos from the Trent Bridge crowd, McGlew was forced to walk back to the pavilion. Carlstein and Wesley didn't last for long after their captain's departure, and it was left to Waite and O'Linn to restore a semblance of South African pride. This they managed to do for most of the third day, as their partnership forced England to bat again. In the end, neither O'Linn's innings nor Waite's 60 was quite enough, as South Africa were bowled out for 247. England lost two second innings wickets in gliding to an eight wicket win. With it they wrapped up the series emphatically. It had been a disrupted and dispirited tour – and it showed.

'Dudley didn't use to suffer fools gladly,' says Adcock. 'He was not a compassionate man. If you dropped a catch or didn't perform well he just didn't understand it because he was such a great player. Jackie was a diplomat. All the speaking duties fell to him during and after the Griffin affair. And Dudley wouldn't even speak to the press. Even that fell to Jackie. It was a crying shame that Jackie didn't win the series and because of that he received no accolades. But as a captain he was better than Ali Bacher and Peter van der Merwe. He could have beaten them with one hand tied behind his back.'

Hughie Tayfield's final fling...

The *Rand Daily Mail* of July 27, 1960, ran a snippet in its news pages about Hugh Tayfield. Headed 'Tayfield: a slow bowler and payer,' the article detailed a minor matter between Tayfield and Jill Adams, a London actress.

'A London court yesterday ordered Hugh Tayfield, the South African Test spin bowler, to appear in the court for allegedly failing to comply with a High Court order. Mr Justice HJ Herbert granted an application on behalf of the actress, Jill Adams. The order, for repayment of a loan of 230 pounds, was made in May. Neither of the parties were in court yesterday Mr Denis Henry, for Miss Adams, said Tayfield would not appear because he was taking part in the cricket Test at Old Trafford in Manchester. "He was a slow bowler and an even slower payer," he said. The debt was in respect of a loan made four years ago, and no effort had been made to repay it, Mr Henry added.'

Charming and irresponsible by turns, Tayfield was the closest South African post-war cricket came to having a playboy. His notoriety, both in his pursuit of women and his legendary inability to manage his money, meant that his private life was frequently chaotic. All of this was left behind when he tied up his boots. Tiger Lance, for instance, tells the story of playing alongside Tayfield for Southern Suburbs, shortly after he arrived in Johannesburg. Tayfield, according to Lance, broadened his cricketing brain. Once they were playing against Old Edwardians and Tayfield suggested to Lance that he ask to see the batsman's gloves. Slightly non-plussed, Lance agreed. He started chatting to the batsman between overs, this while looking at his batting gloves. When they had returned to their respective fielding positions, Tayfield asked Lance what he had seen. Lance replied that they gloves were made by Slazenger, were in good condition and probably cost around R30. Tayfield swore at him in reply, telling him that he'd completely missed the point. The batsman's right-hand glove, said Tayfield, was far more worn than the left-hand glove, suggesting a bottom-handed player who worked the ball to the leg-side.

The 1960 tour to England was Tayfield's last. He took 123 wickets in the county games but was significantly less successful in the Tests, only managing

12. Unusually for Tayfield, they were also expensive, costing him 38 runs apiece. After the fifth Test (Tests four and five were drawn), Tayfield never played for South Africa again. Since making his debut in 1949/50, he had played 37 consecutive Tests for South Africa.

Born in late January, 1929, Tayfield was not one of those players immediately destined for greatness. He didn't, for instance, play for the SA Schools team while at Durban High School, although he made his provincial debut for Natal at a relatively young age in 1945/6. During the following season, he played six Currie Cup matches for Natal, gleaning a good haul, including a hat-trick in a match against Transvaal. The following season and he transferred briefly to Rhodesia, spending time in the Rhodesian Army, and playing five matches for his adopted province. It was in the game against Border that he really caused tongues to wag – taking nine wickets for 94 runs. However, with Athol Rowan the Test incumbent, the analysis didn't have the pundits writing him up. But, like the good spinner he was, Tayfield was patiently making his move from left field.

'The thing about Hugh was that he was so subtle,' says Cyril Mitchley who, like Lance, played with Tayfield at Southern Suburbs. 'Sometimes I didn't even notice what he was doing. And I was keeping to him! He'd bowl three identical balls that the batsman would hit into the covers. Then the fourth he'd hold back just a fraction; the guy wouldn't get properly over it and suddenly you had a catch.' When Rowan's knee gave way in the Transvaal game against Hassett's Australians in 1949/50, Tayfield found himself in possession of the Springbok cap he was later dutifully to kiss at the beginning of every over. His figures during the first Two Tests were ordinary – five wickets for 234 runs – but a damp track at Kingsmead in the third was his making.

A master of flight without being a big turner of the ball, the years slung across the middle fifties were Tayfield's best, but in the latter part of the decade his aura began to dim. This had partly to do with the fact that he didn't bowl well to left-handers – in particular, 'Slasher' Mackay – or so went the theory. There were other theories. 'What you must remember here is that this is the old days, when everyone played straight,' says Mitchley. 'Anyway, Tom Graveney, I think it was, started sweeping Hughie and hitting across the line. Graveney was playing here for the Cavaliers, you see, it must've been in 1960/1. This filters down to provincial and club cricket. And, suddenly, everyone is doing it. Everyone is sweeping. Hugh became very unpleasant to play cricket with. He would eyeball guys and virtually go chest-to-chest with them. It all became a bit much. He went off the rails cricket wise.'

Given his habits with women and other people's money, Tayfield was never as far as he might have liked from the disapproving eye of public scrutiny. Although his fine cricket brain was recognised belatedly in his career when he was occasionally made captain of Transvaal, Tayfield was not one to go into coaching, umpiring or administration. 'Temperamentally umpiring just wasn't for him,' says Arthur, his younger brother. 'It just wouldn't have suited him.'

Divorced twice, first from an Australian then from a British wife, and a loner to the very end, Tayfield died penniless and forgotten in a Durban hospice in 1994. 'When my wife and I went to Durban we always used to pay him a visit,' says Mitchley. 'It was about a kilometre from [Test umpire] Dave Orchard's place. If memory serves, he was in Ward seven, which I think is the terminal ward – they're just waiting there, there's not that much they can do for you. I always thought it was cancer of the oesophagus, although I wasn't sure. He couldn't talk when we went to see him. Other than family and his girlfriend, we were the only people who came to visit and I don't think they saw him very often. When he saw us, all I remember was seeing tears sliding down his cheek. He couldn't speak so he wrote 'chocolate' on a piece of paper and I popped out to get some slabs. It just dribbled down his chin, he couldn't swallow. We went to see him later and he was managing to eat sandwiches, so I thought: "Here we go, he must be improving".'

Questioning 100 Van der Merwes from various walks of life...

As the tour to England was drawing to a close, the *Rand Daily Mail* ran a fascinating story on its front page. Compiled by the paper's staff reporters, the article detailed how the Rand's largest family, the Van der Merwes, were likely to vote in the fast-approaching October 5 referendum on whether South Africa should become a republic.

'Just over half the members of the Rand's biggest Afrikaans family – the Van der Merwes – will vote for a republic according to an opinion poll conducted by the *Rand Daily Mail*. But 69 percent of them wanted to stay in the Commonwealth. The result of the poll, which was obtained by questioning 100 Van der Merwes from various walks of life, showed that: 57 percent will vote for a republic; 26 percent are against a republic; 15 percent are still undecided. Two percent would not answer the questions put two them. Only eight of the 100 people questioned stated that, in their view, South Africa should leave the Commonwealth.'

The Rand Van der Merwes were a reasonable microcosm of the country at large because after the referendum it emerged that 52 percent of voters had voted for South Africa to become a republic. Despite the voters' republican intentions, the Prime Minister, Hendrik Verwoerd, wanted to remain in the Commonwealth, if at all possible. But at a Commonwealth Conference in March of the following year, he and South Africa's apartheid policies were so criticised that he withdrew South Africa's request for continued membership. In a sense, it was the logical conclusion of utterances made by Prime Minister Malan fifteen years previously. Bridges of feeling and emotion between South Africa and Britain there might still have been, but formal ties were few.

From a cricketing perspective, South Africa's departure from the Commonwealth meant that she left the Imperial Cricket Conference, of which she was a founder member. As a result, there was temporary uncertainty that South Africa's Test future was in the balance. It wasn't, as John Reid brought a successful and well-liked New Zealand side to South Africa in 1961/2. As for the 1960 tour to Britain, it brought particular success to McLean and Adcock, both of whom were named as *Wisden Cricketers' Almanack*'s cricketers of the year, but for McGlew, Goddard and Tayfield, the tour did little to further their reputations. South Africa salvaged some self-respect in not losing Tests four and five after being three down after three. Then again, South Africa had lost six times in ten Tests since the start of the home series against Craig's men. The last time she had won a Test was back in early March, 1957, when she had beaten May's team by 58 runs to square the series at two-two.

CHAPTER 12

John Reid's big-hearted
New Zealanders...

'The Fezela, in Zulu, means sting of the wasp.'

N on-representative teams of first-class standard or close to it were all the
rage in the late fifties and early sixties. Three Commonwealth Cavaliers
teams visited South Africa during the period, the last of them in 1963,
under Richie Benaud. In the South African winter of 1961, shortly before the
arrival of Reid's team, a generous benefactor called Stanley Murphy raised the
10 000 pounds needed to send a team of young hopefuls to Britain. The team,
dubbed the Fezelas, was captained by Roy McLean.

'It was all stimulated by Murphy, a very successful Zululand farmer,' says
McLean. 'And the Fezela, in Zulu, means sting of the wasp. He was friendly with
me but we'd just got back from England and Barbara had our third child just
after we'd got back. Now he wants me to go back to England for six weeks with
the Fezelas. So I spoke to her and her father happened to be in aviation. Kim
Elgie was my vice-captain and I managed to see to it that Barbara and Kim's wife,
Jill, came over for the last two weeks so it somewhat appeased them. My parents, who were still alive, looked after the three girls. It was left to me to pick
the side and it gave me the opportunity to do pretty much what I liked. David
Pithey was originally in the side, but his dean wouldn't let him go and so I
picked Eddie Barlow instead. There was Eddie, Colin Bland, Denis Lindsay,
Jackie Botten, Colin Rushmere, Graham Bunyard. We had a very useful side. We
had three first-class games along the way. The fellows really learned to hit the
ball. I gave them free rein. Of course it set a pattern. They hit the ball. They were
the dominant ones in the field. There was none of this push and prod. And that

set the pattern for the whole of the sixties. They stuck to that.'

The transition from Fezela to Springbok wasn't seamless. But one player in particular used the arrival of John Reid's 1961/2 New Zealanders as an opportunity to render the national selectors frisky with the possibility of handing out a fresh Springbok cap. His name was Colin Bland. Recently out of Milton in Bulawayo, Bland played against Reid's team in match one and three of the tour – the second was played against a Rhodesian Country Districts X1 at Que-Que – and his runs positively glowed in an otherwise uniformly drab home team effort. He scored 91 (out of 311) and 45 in the first match, and 67 and 58 in the second. The Milton schoolboy, who as a fullback had reputedly been able to punt a rugby ball the length of the rugby field, was finding senior cricket to his liking.

'Bland invariably represented his province when on vacation [from Rhodes University in Grahamstown] and was invited to tour England as a member of the Fezelas,' writes Geoffrey Chettle in the 1961/2 SA Cricket Annual. 'He returned as a giant refreshed; much more assured in his batting he proceeded to score 261 in the first two matches against the New Zealanders. This put him in the running for a place in the Test team and it came as no surprise when he was awarded his Springbok cap and retained his place throughout the series.'

Bland enjoyed the two matches against Reid's New Zealanders, but others were not as convinced. By the time the Kiwis arrived in Rhodesia in late October, 1961, Geoff Griffin had moved northwards to take up a post with South African Breweries in Rhodesia. According to Griffin, Reid wasn't interested in playing ball. Immediately prior to their two matches against the tourists, Rhodesia played against North-Eastern Transvaal in Salisbury. In the game Griffin was no-balled by umpire Howard Fletcher, the express purpose of which, believes Griffin, was to prevent him from not only playing for Rhodesia against the tourists but also to prevent him from playing for the South African Test side. 'The funny thing was that I played under an assumed name before the game against North-Eastern Transvaal and Fletcher was umpire,' says Griffin. 'He didn't once no-ball me. I don't think he even knew who I was.'

Word got around in Rhodesian cricket circles at the time that Reid had put his foot down about Griffin. If Griffin was chosen to play against the New Zealanders, the visitors would simply not honour the fixture. In actual fact, Griffin did play against Reid's team, although Griffin was unable to use it as a springboard to higher honours. 'The way they [the SACA] did it was very underhand,' says Griffin. 'That left a very bad taste in my mouth.'

TESTING TIMES

ve van Ryneveld: Oxford educated and a liberal member of parliament for East London. Van
neveld replaced McGlew as captain for the 1957/8 home series against Ian Craig's Australians.

Unassuming Russell Endean: a string of fine performances for 'Cheetham's Babes' in Australia in 1952/3.

ove: South Africa went into the Oval Test of the 1955 series against England all-square with
e to play. In the end the series victory eluded them, several dubious umpiring decisions
twithstanding. Here Jack Cheetham (left) and Peter May toss the coin.

low: England's Willie Watson clips to leg during the 1951 series. Waite is behind the stumps and
c Rowan is at silly mid-off.

Fit as a Czechoslovakian athlete: Neil Adcock had a superb series against England in 1960.

iends and openers: Johnny Waite and Sid O'Linn open the batting during the unhappy tour of
gland in 1960. A former inside right with Charlton Athletic, O'Linn was an unattractive,
g-hearted batsman. He missed his debut Test century by two runs in the third Test.

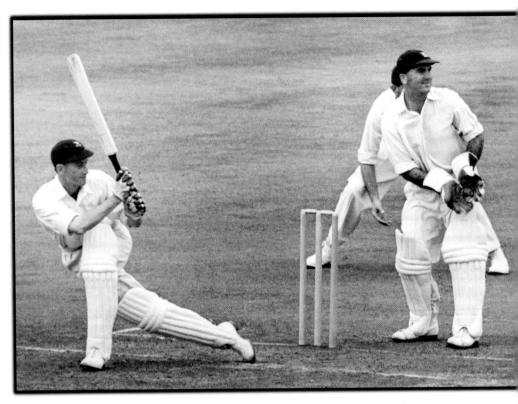

Above: The shot Hugh Tayfield couldn't resist — here he goes on a trademark sweep.

Below: The youngsters who all made it happen in the middle and late sixties: from left to right: Mike Procter, Graeme Pollock, Denis Lindsay, Colin Bland, Eddie Barlow, Barry Richards. (Note the bruise under Richards's right eye.)

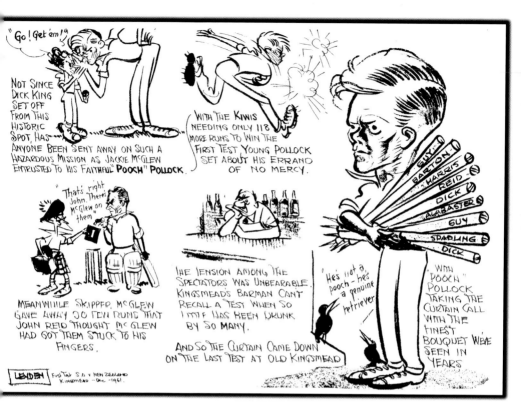

above: Peter Pollock terrorised John Reid's 1961/2 New Zealanders. He took nine wickets in his debut Test at Kingsmead, including six for 38 in the Kiwis' second innings. Pollock's performance certainly gave Jock Leyden food for thought.

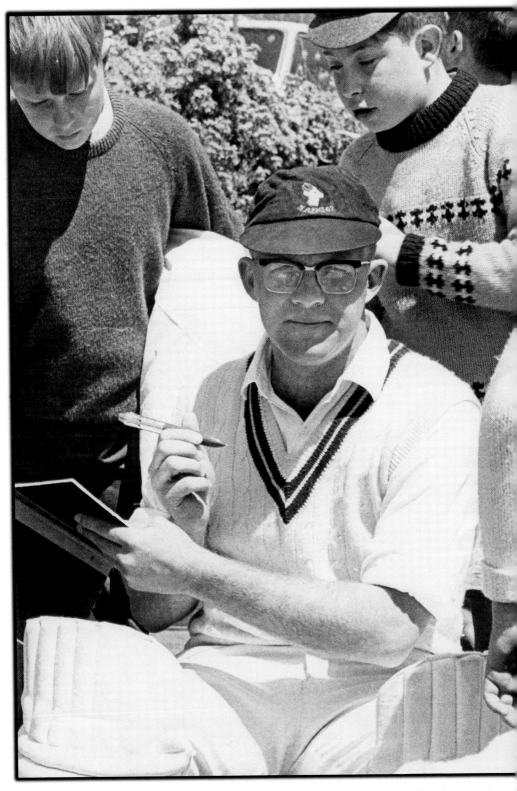

Another who made his debut against Reid's New Zealanders was Eddie Barlow. Here he gets down the serious business of signing autographs.

Beneath smooth Gordon Leggatt's charm...

Nearly ten years previously, Rabone's team had made South African friends but lost the series. By the time John Reid's 1961/2 New Zealanders arrived in South Africa, they were determined to learn history's lesson. Without being confrontational, they were hard-nosed and professional. And the Griffin incident wasn't the only one. Shortly before the first Test at Kingsmead, their manager, Gordon Leggatt, expressed reservations about the umpires chosen for the match, Gordon Draper and Peter A'Bear. 'Imagine the surprise when rumour filtered through that the New Zealand tour management had apparently objected to these two men following Reid's disagreement with their no-balling interpretation during the New Zealand-Natal match a month earlier,' says Hayward Kidson, the former Test umpire. 'Draper and A'Bear had been firm and unyielding on the issue and their attitude had, I suppose, rubbed the tourists up the wrong way.'

In the end, Des Fell and Pat Anderson were appointed by the SACA with the New Zealanders' approval. It made no great difference. Their interpretation of the no-ball rule was such that, between them, they called 53 no-balls in the Test (22 bowled by the visitors and 31 by the home side). Indeed, no-balls might have made all the difference because the Test was a low-scoring one. Batting first with seven new caps in the side – Bland, Eddie Barlow, Harry Bromfield, Kim Elgie, 'Goofy' Lawrence, Peter Pollock and Ken Walter, four of whom had been Fezelas – the home side bungled it slightly to be all out for 292. McGlew signalled an impressive return to form after the disappointments of England by carrying his bat for 132. Had it not been for him and McLean, who pasted together a third wicket stand of 103, the South Africans would have been in early trouble. As it was, Bland (five), Elgie (one), O'Linn (eight) and, batting at eight, Pollock (nought), only rustled up 14 between them. Barlow made 15, Waite 25 and Lawrence 16, as a young side struggled to come to terms with both their nerves and the dogged New Zealand attack.

Zin Harris (74) and Gary Bartlett (40) starred in the visitors' reply of 245, Walter taking four for 63, Pollock three for 61 and Lawrence three for 63. With a handy lead of 47, the South Africans were in immediate trouble in their second dig. Slipping to 38 for three, Waite stabilised the innings with a timely 63. With the exception of Bland (30), precious few offered him any help and the home team sleep-walked to 149 all out – meaning that the New Zealanders needed to score 197 to win. The match situation couldn't have been skewed more firmly in their favour. They had over nine hours in which to make the runs and the pitch held no demons or genies whatsoever. Enter Peter Pollock. The fast bowler took six for 38 as the South Africans mercilessly squeezed the life out of the tourists. (They bowled 25 maidens in their 79.3 overs and Bromfield, with his off-spinners, chipped in with three for 37.) Reid's men fell 30 runs short.

The second Test fell between Boxing Day and New Year at the Wanderers. South Africa retained the side that had won at Kingsmead and, after McGlew's early departure for five, Barlow and Waite got down to business with a second innings partnership of 74. The innings went into a spin with McLean and Bland both falling with the total on 102 as South Africa looked vulnerable on 102 for four. All the while Waite was there, this after having been dropped without scoring. Having cantered to 98, Waite tickled the ball fine down the leg-side for a certain two. The two was duly taken but umpire Hayward Kidson chose the moment to be seized by cramp. Involuntarily he lifted his leg and rubbed it vigorously. The act was interpreted as leg byes and instead of progressing to his century Waite remained on 98. Waite remembers asking Kidson why, when he'd hit the ball, had the umpire signalled leg-byes. Kidson initially missed the point but apologised when he realised Waite had yet to reach his century.

Waite was out for 101 as the South Africans muscled their way to 322. Other than Graham Dowling's 74, Reid's 39 and Bartlett's 31, the Kiwis were unimpressive. No-one came to terms with tall 'Goofy' Lawrence, as the Rhodesian confined them to 223 and took eight for 53 in 30.3 overs with twelve maidens. Dowling was run out and Bromfield took the other wicket.

Along with several others, such as Eddie Fuller and Graham Bunyard, Lawrence had been mentioned as a possible replacement to Griffin on the tour of England in 1960. Like the others, he never made the trip, his lack of explosive pace finally counting against him. Yet the selectors should have known better. The gangly Rhodesian was able to make the ball rear off a length and, like Dave Ironside in the series against Rabone's New Zealanders, was always able to dart it around. The delivery with which he trapped Reid, the Kiwi skipper, in the first innings was preceded by a couple of artful away-duckers. Then suddenly he bowled a delivery which arrowed back off a length, trapping him in front.

Building on their first innings lead of 99, South Africa chugged to 178 for six declared, McGlew, Barlow and McLean all getting 45 runs apiece. McGlew's declaration left Reid, already one-nil down, 278 to get in exactly four hours. 'We've lost so many Tests that losing won't matter now,' quipped Reid. His batsmen were unable to match either his optimism or his casual destruction of the South African attack. He carved 75 not out in a total of 165 for four. Dowling helped him with a patient 58 but otherwise the tourists never came close.

The third Test at Newlands in early January was to show the men in black caps in an altogether more positive light. Batting first, they survived the odd early hiccup before progressing painlessly to 357 for five, Harris scoring 101, Reid 92 and Murray Chapple 69. All the South Africans bowled tidily but the home attack missed Pollock's aggression. Syd Burke, on debut, might have lacked Pollock's raw pace but made up for it with a consistently nagging line and length. He bowled 53.5 overs and took six for 128.

Burke was an anomaly in South African cricket of the period – a B-section cricketer who successfully made the transition to Tests. He commuted to Virginia, Bloemfontein, Viljoenskroon, Kroonstad and as far afield as Bethlehem in order to play his cricket. In the late fifties, he played club crick- et in Welkom for Rovers but, by the time he was selected for his country, his work as a quantity surveyor had taken him back to the Department of Public Works in Pretoria and he was playing his cricket for North Eastern Transvaal. 'I never knew anything about Newlands because we never played there as a B-section province,' says Burke. 'I don't really remember much about the match except that Jackie McGlew gave you what for if you deviated from bowl- ing line and length. He was quite a fearsome captain, so you had to be careful where you put it.'

South Africa contrived to fudge their reply, only Barlow (51), Waite (33) and Bland (32) standing tall as the final five batsmen could only muster 20 between them, this as the home team imploded for 190. Burke again rescued the South Africans, taking five for 68, but with a first innings lead of 195 the New Zealanders' second innings 212 was always going to be competitive. The South Africans made a dash for victory, their 335 being built around a careering 113 from McLean and 63 from their captain, McGlew. The two put on a healthy fourth-wicket partnership of 101 but it wasn't a partnership of quite the magni- tude the South Africans needed in order to take the match. Indeed, they lost it by 72 runs.

Burke was promptly relegated to drinks-carrying duties for the fourth Test. 'I had no expectations of being selected in the first place so it wasn't that much of a disappointment when I was dropped,' he says. 'You must remember that you just weren't in consideration if you played for a province like Free State or North Eastern Transvaal. The thing was I didn't even consider moving to one of the bigger provinces. I had my job to think of and I couldn't just go to my boss and ask for a transfer or anything like that.'

Enter John Reid

The *Rand Daily Mail*'s Dick Whitington maintained that Reid was the best batsman in the world when he arrived in South Africa in late 1961. Clearly, Whitington enjoyed the lusty joy Reid brought to his cricket. Of Reid's 165 against a SA Colt's X1 in East London, Whitington wrote: 'One of the lofted on-drives off Cole landed at least 30 yards beyond the 75-yard boundary. The other merely cleared a deluxe model Cadillac parked perilously close to the boundary line. Obviously its owner had not heard of John Reid.'

Whitington may have been stretching hyperbole when claiming that Reid was the best batsman in the world, but the statistics are certainly compelling: he scored 1 915 runs in the first-class games at 68.39 and 546 runs in the four Tests at 60.64. 'There was something about the country which helped me produce my best,' says Reid. 'The light was really clear, the pitches true. I was able to concentrate on my cricket and play to my best form.'

Despite picking up an injury in the game against Western Australia on the way to South Africa, Reid's magnificent summer didn't end with his batting – he also had the uncanny knack of rooting out South African batsmen. No haul was more vital than the four for 44 in 45 overs he recorded in the South African second innings of the fifth Test, a Test the visitors won to draw the series.

'I didn't miss any games [as a result of the cartilage injury] and it wasn't diagnosed as a cartilage complaint at the time. The attitude back then was that you battled through as best you could. It was never right on the tour. I was given cortisone injections with a huge needle, a case of the remedy being worse than the complaint. Throughout the tour I bowled only when I had to.'

Going into the fourth Test at the Wanderers, Reid had yet to score a century in the series. He compiled a characteristically pugnacious 60 in New Zealand's first innings 164 all out before being miraculously caught by Bland in the covers. 'Bland was in the covers and like all good cover fieldsmen, he edged to his left, because generally that's where the ball is sliced. I really got onto a drive and hit it between mid-off and cover. Bland, who was going left, stopped, and dived to his right and took it with two hands about six inches off the ground. Even I applauded that one. I knew how hard I had hit it.'

Bland refined his catching and throwing for hours as a schoolboy, a situation no doubt helped by his father's inducement of a shilling for every single stump Bland could hit with a throw. 'Two [of Bland's] fielding experiences stand out,' says Peter Muzzell, a Bland contemporary. 'We were playing for SA Universities together and the first instance was against North Eastern Transvaal in Pretoria. Once in both innings he ran out batsmen with direct hits from cover-point. On congratulating him on the "fluke" throw, he told me that he could do exactly the same thing with at least two out of three throws at practice. It should be remembered that we weren't encouraged to throw directly at the stumps in those days because of overthrows. The second experience was also playing for SA Universities against Transvaal at the Wanderers. We played against players of the calibre of Waite and Endean and Bland fielded at cover-point and was the only fielder in front on the off-side. No-one took singles, with Bland leaving skid marks on the turf as he turned from virtually running in with the bowler to give chase to anything that passed him.'

A possibly apocryphal story about Bland was that he had such a reputation in Bulawayo that every girl had his name etched on her desk. Legend or not, one aspect of Bland's single-mindedness stood out: no-one could keep up with his training routine. Muzzell attests to the fact that even as a 'varsity student he was in a league of his own. 'Somehow we viewed him as extraordinary,' he says, 'and far too far ahead to bother trying to emulate.'

South Africa's first innings reply in the fourth Test was a healthy collective effort, with virtually everyone contributing around McGlew's 120. Barlow made 67, McLean 78, Buster Farrer 40 and Heine and Lawrence 30s. South Africa were all out exactly 300 runs on and had it not been for Reid's second innings 142 (next highest score Zin Harris's 46), New Zealand wouldn't even have scraped to 249. As it was, they lost the Test by an innings and 51 runs. 'John, or Bogo as we called him, carried the whole New Zealand team,' says McLean. 'He had some useful cricketers backing him up, but he was the real menace. We all knew that. Our problem was that we didn't know how to attack him. He got right into line and played pace bowling very well, and we did have Adcock, Heine and Pollock, after all. And he really punished spin bowling. He would use his feet and dictate to the bowlers. The trouble was we couldn't keep him quiet.'

Reid took his side to Port Elizabeth in the middle of February with the express intention of squaring the series. In order to do so, the New Zealanders gambled. Barton, who dislocated his shoulder in the fourth Test, was chosen to play. He obliged with a first innings century, scoring 109 out of the Kiwis' 275. Opening with the strange combination of Lawrence and Barlow, the South

Africans then made a hash of their reply. No-one scored more than Lawrence's 43 as they faded to 190 all out. Late on the second afternoon, Adcock and Pollock let rip at Graham Dowling and Harris. Pollock had been left out of the team for the third Test at Newlands for expressly this reason, but with a 85-run first innings deficit the South African opening bowlers were in no mood for generosity. The following morning the Kiwis gutsed it out and set South Africa 314 to win. The home side fell 40 runs short in a brave dash to put the rubber beyond the visitors' reach. Reid's four wickets were priceless but Dick Motz and John (Jack) Alabaster played their part. Indeed, Reid's all-round contribution in the series suggests that Whitington could almost have been right.

Arguably, the two-two all result flattered the visitors. At the same time, the outline of a gifted young South African team was emerging from the late fifties' gloom. Not all of these young players played in the Tests against New Zealand, but many of them had played for the Fezelas or were beginning to make their mark on provincial cricket. A trip to Australia in 1963/4 was the perfect opportunity to demonstrate whether they were as good as everyone suspected or simply one-season wonders. The tour to Aussie would also show that the ethos of politeness and respect for authority that had for so long characterised South African cricket was beginning to fray. Under the general slackening of the permissive age, loyalty and bonds of affiliation were beginning to disintegrate fast.

CHAPTER 13

'Perhaps the most important tour ever taken...'

'It is freely being suggested abroad that South Africa should be reduced to junior status...'

The waters through which South African cricket was navigating during the early sixties were choppy without being gale buffeted. At a farewell function in Johannesburg for Trevor Goddard's team to tour Australia and New Zealand during the summer of 1963/4, Boon Wallace, the South African Cricket Association president, decided that the barometer of international cricketing events was worth reading in full:

'It is generally accepted that this tour of Australia and New Zealand, on which you are about to embark, is perhaps the most important ever taken by a Springbok cricket team. It is important for a variety of reasons but primarily because, since South Africa left the Commonwealth, the SA Cricket Association automatically ceased to be a member of the Imperial Cricket Conference, which controls international cricket. Despite the fact that SA has been given a fair participation in the schedule of tours with Australia and England during the immediate future, it is being freely suggested abroad that South Africa should nonetheless be reduced to junior status in international cricket and enjoy only "shared" tours to England. I am convinced that our success this summer will transcend whatever prejudice and preference that might exist in the minds of the Australian Board. It is with deep appreciation that my Board welcomed the joint statement made by your manager and captain that while they accept the importance of results to be achieved on this tour, they are firmly resolved that the team would at all times endeavour to play bright and entertaining cricket. If you produce positive, attacking and match-winning cricket, I am sure that South Africa will maintain its friends and loyal supporters and Australia and England will be only too keen to fulfil its programme of tours with us as arranged.'

Armed with a telegram of support from Prime Minister Verwoerd, the South Africans slid east, enduring a 14-hour stopover in Mauritius and a refuelling break on the Cocos Islands before landing in Perth. Officially, mild-mannered Trevor Goddard captained the team. In actual fact, team matters, both on and off the field, were controlled to an incredible degree by the team's manager, Ken Viljoen. While in Tasmania Goddard was recorded as saying that he'd have been lost without Viljoen – and from Goddard's actions there was nothing to suggest this wasn't true. 'Goddard was consistently loyal to Viljoen,' writes Whitington. 'But I have reason to believe that Viljoen even settled Test batting orders and had a profound influence on Goddard's tactics when South Africa was in the field. What an extraordinary and, in the case of other countries, unprecedented situation.'

A man who, according to his daughter, Carol, had two haircuts as a player during the 'Timeless Test,' Viljoen was petit bourgeois down to the shine of his shoes. The Gauteng Cricket Board's Derrick High grew up on the West Rand of Johannesburg, where Viljoen became sports manager and chief paymaster of Rand Consolidated Mines just after the war. High well remembers his first encounter with the old Springbok. 'He turned to me and said: "Well played, next time you must look like a cricketer",' recalls High. 'I had tucked my trousers into my socks. That taught me so much. From that I learned so much about what discipline was about. He taught me sober habits. Ken didn't smoke, he didn't drink; he was thoroughly dedicated to cricket.'

A confirmed royalist, Viljoen was neat, punctual and suspicious of the fourth estate. In Adelaide, he famously refused Charles Fortune access to the showers after they had been used by the players during Cheetham's tour in 1952/3. By 1963/4, in a scene that played itself out across Australia, he was trapped in a running battle with Dick Whitington. The scribe sprayed off rounds of invective – he dubbed Viljoen's fielding practices in Perth 'white slavery' – as Viljoen ducked into hotels and dressing rooms as verbal bullets pock-marked the walls. It became so bad that upon his return to South Africa, Viljoen was advised by many to pursue legal action against the journalist. Viljoen demurred, maintains his daughter. For all his tendencies toward control, he wasn't one to hold grudges.

Viljoen had been the manager at home throughout the late fifties. He missed the 1960 tour to England (which was managed by Nourse), but returned to the post with the arrival of Reid's side. Although he was selected to manage Goddard's young team, he thought twice before accepting. 'He had a few tricky times [in Australia and New Zealand],' says Carol Viljoen. 'Some of the speeches in some of the places were very stressful. He had to be very diplomatic. You couldn't be seen to say anything too critical. There was a lot of soul-searching done beforehand with my mom because he wasn't sure he wanted to get into all of that again.'

Other than politics both within and without, Viljoen had a young, hot blooded side to deal with. Since McGlew and McLean made themselves unavailable to tour, the national selectors had no alternative but to look towards youth. And so they did, with Bland, Barlow, Buster Farrer and Peter Carlstein all selected along with two sets of brothers – the Pollocks and the Pitheys. Thrown into the mix, too, were bowlers such as Clive Halse, Joe Partridge, the ageing workhorse, and Western Province's Kelly Seymour. Rounding off the party of fifteen, were Peter van der Merwe, Waite and a pugnacious reserve 'keeper, Denis Lindsay (whose dad, Johnny, had toured England in 1947). In analysing the South Africans' chances, the scribes tended to sit heavily on the fence. Lots of promise, they said, but aren't they a little wet behind the ears?

Muhammad Ali — in glasses

One young man didn't give a precious continental about any of this. A product of Pretoria Boys' High and Wits University, Eddie Barlow was lucky – or so some thought – to have a seat reserved in his name for the flight to Perth. Not that Barlow gave any indication about being bothered by the words that were being uttered behind cupped hands. 'It can fairly safely be said,' writes Whitington, 'that had the Springbok team been announced at the end of February instead of April 1, Eddie Barlow, the team's inspirational pilot, and Tony Pithey, must have been omitted. Barlow was a borderline selection, even after his century against the Cavaliers at the Wanderers.'

Barlow had always been a man with a sense of himself as different.

According to Tiger Lance, a cricketer who played against Barlow when they were growing up in Pretoria in the fifties, 'Eddie, when he was nine or ten years of age, thought he was Muhammad Ali. Nobody was as good as him in anything he did.'

Barlow did nothing in the first two games of the tour to suggest that he had a particular liking for run-scoring in Australia, taking a combined two innings total of 26 runs off Western Australia in the traditional opening match of the tour. During the third game of the tour against a Combined X1 (the second having been played against a Western Australian Country Districts team at Cunderlin), he failed yet again, as South Africa were squashed for 207, with only Farrer making 50. Peter Pollock then came to the party, taking three wickets for five runs as the strong Combined X1 buckled to be 161 all out.

With a first innings lead of 46, Barlow and Tony Pithey proceeded to make Saturday, 2 November, 1963, an important day in the annals of South African cricket. Against an attack that included three Test bowlers – 'Garth' McKenzie, Benaud and Simpson – the South Africans finished the day on 222 without loss. Admiring the action was Sir Donald Bradman, the chairman of the Australian selectors. 'The tour is made,' he tells all and sundry. 'I am tremendously pleased that your players have done so well with bat and ball and in the field so early on in the tour. We are going to see a wonderful Test series which will do immense good for cricket.'

Not out on 129 on the Saturday, Barlow was also happy to share his thoughts with the waiting microphones. 'Don't write this down as my best score,' he says. 'I'm going to get a lot more on Monday.'

And so he did. He added a further 80 runs on the Monday, eventually being out for 209. Graeme Pollock joined in the carnival atmosphere, savaging a century in 88 minutes. He was not out 127 when the declaration arrived with the total on 532 for three. Batting last, the Combined X1 made a brave stab at the 579 needed to win. Simpson weighed in with 246 and Benaud scored a century. In the end the Combined X1 were 529 for nine – just 50 runs short.

Against South Australia in Adelaide, Barlow was at it again – scoring 79, as South Africa limped to 194 for eight batting first. But a priceless century from Lindsay, well supported by Seymour, inflated the South African total to 375. The South Australians – with 155 from their resident professional, Garry Sobers – racked up an impressive 573 in reply. Although Carlstein's 123 stood out for the tourists in their second innings, the home team were able to pass the South Africans' combined total for the loss of only two second innings wickets. 'Maybe more good than harm will come from this defeat,' writes Whitington. 'The Springboks, naturally enough, were a little complacent following their near-victory over a combined side that included Simpson, Benaud, Norm O'Neill and McKenzie. They should have learned much from this game.'

Whether they learned anything or not is a moot point, because Viljoen imposed the infamous curfew after a rash of dropped catches. 'Maybe the young guys did party a bit too much [before Adelaide],' says Lindsay. 'Then the curfew was loaded and it was a joke. It was a joke because the guys were in bed and saying goodnight, up to their chins with bedclothes, and underneath they had their full togs on. We stayed in motels and we would go out and we would tip Mitchie [baggage master and scorer, Mitch McLennan] because he was the guy who would look out for the boss. But it wasn't a case of open rebellion. It was just a case of stupidity on the part of the management to treat adults in that way. You know, a guy like Eddie was married; I was married, my second kid was on the way; Clive Halse was married; Peter Carlstein had four kids at that stage. Now how do you treat adults by telling them that they've got to be in bed by ten o'clock? That's pre-war housekeeping.'

After a match against a Country X1 at Whyalla, the South Africans moved on to Melbourne for a game against a strong Australian X1. The invitation team batted first, totalling 318 after Peter Pollock was forced to leave the field with an injury after only having bowled 12 overs. In reply, the South Africans collapsed to 210 all out, but snapped back and flattened the Australian X1 for 160 in their second innings. Batting last, the visitors started well. Goddard, the South African captain, scored 51 in an opening stand of 82 with Barlow. The man compared to the Louisville Lip by Lance then went to 112 in four and a half hours, as South Africa trooped to a three wicket win.

Although priceless, Barlow's century was not without mishap. He ran out Goddard and later did the same to Carlstein. At lunch-time on the final afternoon, the South Africans sent a message to him which read: 'Would you care to have your lunch served to you on the pitch?' Even Bradman was impressed. 'Eddie has taught Australians something,' he quips, 'how to run out your captain, going for a single from a no-ball.'

After Melbourne there were only two games of importance before the first Test at the Woolloongabba in early December – against New South Wales in Sydney and Queensland at the 'Gabba. South Africa batted first at the Sydney Cricket Ground and blasted their way to 460, with centuries from Pollock (120, 103 of them scored between lunch and tea) and Van der Merwe (114), and 85 from Barlow. The redoubtable Rhodesian seamer, Joe Partridge, then set upon New South Wales. He took five first innings wickets and in so doing, condemned them to the follow-on. Batting again, they crumbled to 23 for five, restored matters somewhat, but eventually succumbed to 147 all out. South Africa won by an innings, a tremendous boost before the first Test.

'When I was chosen to tour Australia I realised that a genuine outswinger, as distinct from an out-cutter, was essential if I was to have a chance of being successful,' says Partridge. 'I read in the newspapers that England never send their inswing bowlers to Australia anymore because conditions in Australia don't favour inswing bowlers. My leg-cutter used to get me by on the grassier, softer wickets of Rhodesia. I had been told that there wasn't much grass on Australian pitches. I had been trying to bowl a genuine out-swinger for about three years. I began trying with the Salisbury Stragglers team in Kenya three years ago. We were in Kenya for six weeks. The wickets in Kenya are matting wickets and my out-swinger worked well on them while the ball was new. When I returned to turf pitches I couldn't make the ball swing away from the bat nearly as well. So last winter I really went to work on my outswinger in the nets, and in eight country games. Former Springbok, Len Brown, who had played a lot of cricket in the north of England, helped me no end, and taught me how to use the bowling crease. Len said that I must learn to bowl the outswinger from close in beside the stumps and from further out along the bowling crease. Then the batsman wouldn't be able to tell which ball was coming unless they could detect it from my fingers.'

'Barlow would have been relished on a country green in Naboomspruit...'

If South Africa were on a high after recent wins in Melbourne and Sydney, they were brought rudely back to earth after the first day's play against Queensland at the 'Gabba. At close on day one, Queensland had raced to 322 for four (Peter Burge 129). On the second morning and through the middle of the day, Tom Veivers took his overnight nine not out to 87. The Queenslanders were eventually skittled for 480 – scored in only 139.4 overs (Seymour four for 104). At close on day two there were no hints of the trouble to follow, with Barlow (42) and Tony Pithey (nought) the not out batsmen. But on the third morning Veivers, the off-spinnner, bowled Barlow for his overnight score. He took the next three wickets to fall and, with the innings on crutches, caught and bowled David Pithey (eight) to condemn the tourists to 167. His figures: 27-9-75-5.

South Africa's follow-on was only a marginal improvement. Goddard (48), Graeme Pollock (43) and Van der Merwe (40) all posted forties and Barlow swaggered to 31. It wasn't enough. The loss of wickets was too regular, the lack of defining partnerships crippling. South Africa were all out for 240, spiralling to an innings and 73-run defeat. It was exactly what Goddard and Viljoen didn't want.

The South Africans were always playing their cricket in the shadows of the Australians mammoth 435 batting first in the first Test at Brisbane. Missing from the match against Queensland, Peter Pollock was back for the visitors. But even his six wickets (22.6-0-95-6) weren't enough, as he received precious little support from his colleagues. Partridge and David Pithey were both expensive and wicketless and Barlow (9-0-71-1), despite his effervescence and boundless self-belief, was a complete disaster. 'Bowling like millionaire philanthropists with the second new ball,' spits Whitington, 'South Africa's Peter Pollock, Partridge and Barlow squandered 86 runs from 10 overs for the reward of Norm O'Neill's wicket after tea in the first Test here yesterday. Pollock, who dismissed O'Neill for 82 with a beautifully pitched outswinger at 208 for four, grew obsessed with knocking Benaud's block off and chose the wrong man for such tactics. Partridge, bowling with a "wooden leg", jettisoned 22 runs from two overs and Barlow would have been relished on a country green in Naboomspruit.'

Thankfully, Barlow had a trick up his sleeve – this despite the unsettling effects of Meckiff's departure from Test cricket for chucking after having bowled only one over. He scored 114 out of 346, as South Africa navigated towards comparative safety. With South Africa batting until shortly before the close on the fourth afternoon, Goddard scored 52, Waite 66 and Graeme Pollock 25. 'South Africa's fight back was led by Barlow, whose century set a magnificent example for his teammates,' writes Bill O'Reilly. 'The stocky right-handed opener is endowed with a batting temperament specially developed for Test matches. When he defends on front foot or back, his bat seems so much wider than others. In this he reminded me of Bill Ponsford and Herbert Sutcliffe. No bowler, not even Benaud at his best in earlier stages of the innings, gave Barlow much worry. He played every forcing shot that is worth seeing and took all the pains that the situation demanded. He scored one of the most valuable centuries yet listed in Test cricket.'

Batting a second time, Australia posted 144 for one declared, thus setting South Africa 234 to win in four hours. In the event, rain imposed a natural solution to what looked like an intriguing Test. South Africa finished up on 13 for one, Barlow following up his debut Test century with a duck. 'It could have been quite an interesting afternoon's cricket,' says Benaud, shortly after the abandonment.

While Benaud nudged gentle understatement in the direction of the reporters, Whitington was frothing. 'Australia had scored 119 at a run-a-minute in the morning on a mushroom patch of a pitch for the loss of Simpson to a glorious catch by Bland at midwicket,' he writes. 'They were all out for victory. It was different with the Springboks. Even on Monday night they were praying for rain – influenced, as I know, by manager Viljoen's extremely defensive thinking on the game he almost always played defensively himself... I am mentioning Viljoen's way of thinking on cricket now purely because if South Africa get another chance to score 234 runs in 240 minutes in this series, they would be highly advised to go for these runs. Viljoen's task as manager of this team should end with his excellent managership. How this team plays is Goddard's job.'

South Africa were to pay for being timorous in Brisbane. They were bowled out before the close of play on day one in the second Test at Melbourne and from then on could only follow the rapidly disappearing home team. Not that Barlow gave any impression of reading from the same page as his colleagues. He batted just over four-and-a-half hours for 109, top score for the visitors by some way. Bland scored 50 on the dot but otherwise the middle-order batted wretchedly, Tony Pithey scoring 21, Graeme Pollock 16 and Waite and Van der Merwe 14 apiece.

Other than failing to start off the new year on a high note, South Africa could take satisfaction from the fact that their 274 was scored unusually quickly – at nearly 3.5 runs per over. Unfortunately it also had the disadvantage of funnelling the Test to an ever more rapid conclusion. At the end of play on day two, Australia had already passed South Africa's first innings total by 34 runs with five second innings wickets standing. They ground out the advantage on day three, their commanding 447 being packed around Bill Lawry's 157 (scored in 329 minutes) and nineties from Barry Shepherd and Ian Redpath. For the visitors Partridge took four for 108 and Peter Pollock three for 98, as Australia led by 173. Despite a third wicket stand of 128 between Tony Pithey (76 scored in 249 minutes) and Waite (77), the South African batsmen didn't quite manage to fashion the one big innings needed to rescue the Test. Their 306, scored at three an over, meant Australia needed 136 to win. This proved to be reasonably straightforward for the home team. They won at a canter before close on the fourth day. The South Africans could logically point to the loss of the toss as a determining factor in their defeat. Then again, perhaps they should have been bolder at the 'Gabba?

Self-belief

Minutes before the start of the third Test at Sydney, Denis Lindsay was told that the selectors had changed their mind. Lindsay had debuted at Brisbane in the first Test and was expecting to play, but at the last minute the powers that be opted for Halse, a fast-bowler. The reserve wicketkeeper was left to skulk to the hill. He spent most of the day boiling. 'I was pissed off, totally pissed off,' says Lindsay. 'I went over to the Sydney Hill and sat with the mob over there. You realise that you've been picked and geared yourself, but in hindsight, it was exactly what was required because we started to play with four seamers and that's how South Africa have played their best cricket – forever. There was a little bit of doubt about Peter's hamstring and Clive [Halse] played and it was perfect because you had Peter [Pollock], Joe [Partridge], Clive and Trevor [Goddard] as well as Eddie [Barlow]. Five. Eddie wasn't a great bowler in those days. He was a bit of a mix 'n match bowler but you had four absolutely first-class seamers.'

Peter, Clive and Joe bowled magnificently in the Australian first-innings at Sydney, this despite a challenging 100-run partnership for the sixth wicket between Brian Booth (75) and Benaud (43). The Australians were back in the hut for a mediocre 260 – Peter Pollock five for 83, Partridge four for 88 – but had managed to snare the important wicket of Barlow (six) before close. With South Africa balancing on a knife-edge at 11 for one, the start of day two loomed with special significance for the visitors. Despite young Graeme Pollock's debut Test century and a fighting 80 from their captain, the visitors just couldn't establish any kind of headway against a dogged home attack. Thanks to Bland's 51 down the order, they fought for a slight lead, but it was too small to prove significant.

With 88 from O'Neill, 89 from Lawry and 90 from Benaud, the Australians climbed to 450 all out in their second innings – a 408-run lead. Worryingly for Goddard and Viljoen, the Australians' runs flowed quickly. Peter Pollock took four wickets, but his 24 overs cost him 129 runs. Similarly, although he took five wickets, Partridge conceded 123 runs in his 32.5 overs. All in all the Australians batted for 100 overs and five balls, speeding to their impressive total through the third afternoon and well into the fourth day.

With the wicket taking turn, Benaud and Simpson were poised to come into their own on the final morning. Not only was the wicket taking spin, but Keith Miller doubted that the South Africans had either the will or the resources to mount a challenge. 'South Africa haven't the players to win Test matches against Australia – even this Australia. But she could go far nearer to winning a Test or two if she would first marshal her resources and play with a plan instead of dithering between the positive and the negative approach.'

Resuming on 61 for one, the Aussies were given a sniff when David Pithey was bowled by McKenzie for seven with the total on 67. But it was a false dawn. Goddard, playing masterfully, slowly shut them out. Lunch was taken with the addition of 80 runs in the session for the loss of Graeme Pollock, slashing at a wide one from Neil Hawke. At lunch it appeared to have been decided: despite having seven wickets in hand, South Africa wouldn't dash for victory. They finished the day on 326 for five (Goddard 84, scored in 265 minutes, Bland 85, Tony Pithey 53 not out), 83 runs short of squaring the series. In mounting desperation, the Australians tried eight bowlers, even Booth and Shepherd having a go. But it wasn't to be: the South Africans wouldn't budge.

Whether or not Goddard's team should have struck out boldly for victory at Sydney is a moot point. In retrospect, Tony Pithey has said that he was well satisfied with batting out more than a day on a turner. Naturally, Whitington was less easy to please. His *Rand Daily Mail* article after the Test contained the sentence 'They Played It Safe,' as a headline and the accusation 'Goddard lacked faith in his middle batsmen' as a sub-heading. Having established his credentials as the journalistic equivalent of the sniping back-bencher, Whitington was no doubt loath to change his tune. All in all, though, South Africa hadn't done badly, although decisive they were not.

Between the middle of January (when the third Test came to an end) and the 24th of January, when the fourth Test began, something important changed in the heart of the team. Whatever it was, it wasn't provided by Goddard or Viljoen. More likely, it was the dawning realisation, provided in part by Barlow but recognised intuitively by the Pollock brothers and Lindsay, that there was nothing to hold the tyros back. Paradoxically, the South Africans might have learned from their opponents. Batting first in the fourth Test at the Adelaide Oval, the Australians mustered 345. Four fifties were scored – two of them big ones, from Simpson, captain since the second Test, and Burge – but otherwise the home team were ensnared by Goddard. Back to his bowling best, the captain was the only South African bowler who was treated with respect. He took five for 60. Everyone else was dismissed, the 345 taking 93.6 overs.

The South Africans had at times batted adventurously in Australia but on day two of the fourth Test Barlow and Graeme Pollock exploded. Both Goddard (34) and Tony Pithey (nought) fell just after lunch on the second day with the total on 70. Pithey's dismissal brought Pollock to the wicket and he and Barlow were still there at the close – 225 runs later – with Barlow on 125, Pollock on 120. Graeme and Peter's dad, AM 'Mac' Pollock, was holidaying in Cape Town at the time. Unable to pick up anything on the radio, he had to phone the *Cape Times*' AC Parker to find out the news. 'Just before close of play, Mr Pollock phoned to find out how his son had fared,' writes Staff Reporter. 'The call was transferred to AC Parker of the sports department who told him the great news. With unconcealed pleasure Mr Pollock heard of how Graeme had hit 4,4,6,6 off successive balls from Simpson – described by Louis Duffus as "some of the severest punishment suffered by an Australian bowler." Mr Pollock was also told of Jack Fingleton's comment – "[that] 22 000 people were sent into rhapsodies of joy".'

On the third morning, the match situation posed an awkward problem for Simpson. According to Lindsay, the second new ball was due and Simpson misjudged things horribly. 'He had bowled his quicks to a stage where he thought he had about ten overs to go before the new nut was taken,' he says. 'At that stage he brought himself on to bowl and, in one over, two overs, maybe, he was just slaughtered by Graeme. Simpson bowled from the scoreboard end and Graeme popped him there and cover-drove him there. And then he didn't know at that stage whether to take it or not. His fast-bowlers were knackered, they'd bowled the opening spell in the morning, and he couldn't toss the new ball to them because it would have been no good. In any event he had to turn to the quicks because he couldn't keep on bowling himself and Benaud because they were getting slaughtered. Anyway, he brought the quickies back, and I think Hawkie took the new nut instead of [Ron] Gaunt. He also got thumped. That's where that super partnership came in, where it really took off.'

South Africa rocketed to 595, Barlow scoring 201 of them and Pollock 175. The runs were scored so quickly that the bowling figures are liable to vanish off the page in shame. Simpson's 10 overs cost him 59; Benaud's 20 overs cost him 101; Gaunt's 24 overs cost him 115. McKenzie's make the most miserable reading of all: his 30.1 overs cost him a whopping 156 runs. And, until he picked up Partridge, batting at 10, he was wicketless.

The South Africans' assault didn't force the Australians to creep from the Test in embarrassment. With savage application, they ground their way to 300 for four on the fourth day before Goddard could take Barlow's pestering no longer. Late in the day, he tossed the ball to the nominal allrounder, no doubt expecting the worst. In Barlow's first over, Shepherd mistimed a pull off a long-hop and Lindsay took a splendid running catch in the deep. Shortly afterwards, Benaud dragged on and then McKenzie provided Barlow with a return catch after Barlow gifted him a full toss. Barlow's five overs had cost him six runs and he had taken three wickets. The Test had tilted definitively South Africa's way.

Wally Grout, the final Australian second innings wicket, fell early on the fifth morning, leaving South Africa needing 82 runs to win. They accomplished the task quite easily, with Barlow not out on 47 and Goddard not out on 34. 'It was the first time we realised that it was the way to play cricket,' says Lindsay.

The ten-wicket win at Adelaide was not only a triumph for South African cricket, it was a triumph for the players. They wrested control away from Viljoen and had taken the Australians on at their own game. The prime suspect in all of this was Barlow. 'They just couldn't handle him [Barlow],' says Lindsay. 'It was a case of, at times, they could see that there was something different happening. There was something totally different that was on the pace and I think you could see it. You didn't have to be a whiz-kid to know that a trend was changing. You know, in the sixties it was all flower power, wasn't it? The young guys in the side were part of that era – the flower children. It was the Elvis Presley situation.'

Duffus put it slightly differently. 'I am inclined to contend that he had more influence over South African cricket than any single other player I know. Perhaps it would be more accurate to say that he had more influence on the country's spirit, tempo of batting and approach to the game. He did more than anyone else to break down the timid, defensive tactics which for so many years kept South Africa a second-rate cricket country – and that, for me, is a tremendous achievement.'

'Where have you been... Joe Partridge?'

Before the fifth Test, Sir Robert Menzies, the Australian prime minister, told Goddard that there were limits to even his patriotism. 'Victory for you Springboks might clear away all this nonsense about your Test matches being regarded as unofficial,' he says.

In the event, the match spluttered to an unsatisfactory draw. Menzies' hope went unfulfilled and the respective teams were left to rue chances not taken – what if Goddard had made a mad dash for it at Brisbane? What if Benaud and Simpson had made more of the Sydney track in the third Test?

As it was, the final Test of the series was to turn out to be Partridge's final bow in Australia. The Rhodesian seamer took seven for 91 in helping to bowl Australia out for 311 batting first. He followed it up with two for 85 in the Australian second innings – a wonderful analysis without being quite good enough to steer the Test in South Africa's favour.

Partridge enjoyed bowling at Sydney, having taken nine wickets against NSW and nine wickets in the third Test. 'Until Joe cast his net at the Sydney Cricket Ground in that game against NSW,' writes Whitington, 'few people in Australia – officials, players, press or public – treated the Springbok threat at all seriously. This 1963/4 series was regarded as good match practice for England in 1964.' By the time Partridge got to the SCG for a third time he was an established favourite. 'In his spectacles, Partridge looked the bank officer he was and the Sydney spectators took to him,' writes the cricket historian, David Frith. 'He seemed inoffensive enough alongside the snorting Pollock and there was an absence of ostentation about him which added greatly to his appeal. Round after round of applause greeted him as he returned to his position on the boundary after each probing over. The third-man territory became known as "Joe's Corner." In two Tests and a State match at Sydney, Joseph Titus Partridge took 27 wickets (18.67) off 148.1 enthusiastic, accurate overs. He became one of the Hill's own.'

After the fifth Test, Partridge played six more, three against New Zealand in New Zealand and three against England in 1964/5. He retired from first-class cricket at the end of the 1966/7 season, aged 34. A subsequent job for Rhodesian Breweries was to prove both a saviour and his undoing – Partridge developed a drinking problem. He separated from his wife and committed suicide after failing to settle a hotel account in Harare in June 1988. Partridge killed himself by grabbing a police officer's revolver and shooting himself in the head.

Tony Pithey, the best man at Partridge's wedding, remembers happier times – in particular, the way in which Lawry was forced to revise his initial impression of Partridge in 1963/4. 'Joe was a very unusual bowler,' says Pithey. 'He had an economical, almost lazy, action but swung the ball in very late. He also had a leg-cutter. Lawry had great difficulty in reading his leg-cutter and I have vivid recollections of Bill being bowled having left the ball thinking it was swinging away. After the tour Bill admitted that Joe was just an ordinary seam bowler but had to drastically revise his opinion. Had Joe come from one of the major South African provinces he undoubtedly would have played far more cricket for South Africa.'

Two very different stories...

Two very different stories jostled for attention on the *Rand Daily Mail*'s front page on September 18, 1963, not a month before Goddard's team left for Australia. The one story represented the South Africa that had fought in the war, a South Africa of imperial certainties. It was a story about the death of 'Sailor' Malan, the World

War Two fighter ace. 'Group captain AG "Sailor" Malan, the South African air ace who shot down 35 German aircraft during the Battle of Britain, died in the Kimberley hospital yesterday, after being taken there earlier with pneumonia. Sailor Malan, who had been suffering from Parkinson's disease since 1959, was 52. He was taken to hospital yesterday morning after developing "virulent pneumonia" which his weakened system could not resist.'

The second story concerned anti-apartheid activist and poet, Dennis Brutus. Brutus had been shot the previous day while attempting to escape from police custody. 'Dennis Brutus, the banned 38 year-old Coloured teacher who fled to Swaziland five weeks ago, was last night shot in the stomach in Main street Johannesburg, two blocks away from Marshall Square police station. It was understood that he was shot by a policeman. He had been arrested in Lourenco Marques and was handed over to the South African authorities at the border on Monday. He was taken to Coronation hospital, where he had an emergency operation. Two policemen in surgical masks stood guard in the operating theatre. Late last night his condition was said to be serious and he was being given blood transfusions.'

Brutus survived the ordeal and fled to Canada where he became a leading administrator in the South African Non-Racial Olympic Committee (SANROC), an organisation formed with the express purpose of campaigning against white South African sport. As such, he contributed directly to the slow alienation of South Africa's sportsmen and sportswomen from the rest of the world as the decade continued. His and SANROC's initiatives were part of a coalition of forces which, combined with government recalcitrance within South Africa itself, led to the amputation of South African sporting ties at the end of the decade.

In a narrower sense, the sixties witnessed the slow alienation of the South African players from the South African Cricket Association. South African cricket was not part of the Imperial Cricket Conference but at times it seemed that their players were hardly part of the association itself. 'In 1966 and '67 we felt that we weren't village idiots anymore,' says Lance. 'We were members of King Arthur's round table. We knew that without us, the knights, King Arthur could do nothing. The band stood together. It wasn't one guy doing something because he was going to get more out of it than the other guy. The trust between us was there. The administrators could look us all in the eye and we could look back at them and tell them that we knew why they were eating crayfish and drinking fancy whisky up in the Long Room. It was because of us. We were still getting the polony, stale rolls and bowl of potato salad that had been made from the Test before. But we really began to appreciate our power.'

The problem with player power, such as it was, was that it was operating in an international context in which South Africa became increasingly shunned and therefore powerless. South African cricket, the ugly imperial duckling, couldn't rely indefinitely upon the support of her traditional allies – England, Australia and New Zealand.

The age represented by fighter ace Sailor Malan was at an end; the age represented by Dennis Brutus and his politics was only just beginning.

INDEX

Reid, John, 105, 158, 161-162, 164-165

Rhodes, Harold "Dusty", 148

Richardson, Peter, 48, 125, 127, 130

Richardson, Vic, 48

Ritchie, Gerald, 52, 125-126

Rorke, Gordon, 151

Rowan, Athol, 13, 14, 18, 24, 27, 32, 51, 53, 58, 65, 67-68

Rowan, Eric, 43, 45, 48, 55, 58-59, 61, 63, 67-71, 73-75, 100

Rowan, Peter, 14, 45

Rushmere, Colin, 159

Sabba Row, Raman, 150

Saggers, Ron, 57

Seymour, Kelly, 169-170

Shafto, Mike, 97, 100

Sharpeville, 147

Shepherd, Barry, 174

Simpson, Bobby, 142, 144

Simpson, Reg, 67

Singh, Swaranjit, 123

Smith, Ian, 27, 111, 141

Smith, Mike, 150

Smuts, Field-Marshall Jan, 11, 33, 37, 125

Sobers, Garry, 170

Stanyforth, Ronnie, 20

Statham, Brian, 73, 113, 129

Sutcliffe, Bert, 103, 105

Swanton, EW, 44, 117

Tallon, Don, 86

Tayfield, Arthur, 126, 136

Tayfield, Hugh, 60, 84-85, 88, 91, 95, 103-105, 110, 116-118, 127, 129-130, 132, 134-138, 141, 143-144, 155-157

Taylor, "Scotch", 127

Taylor, Herby, 18

Titmus, Fred, 111

Trueman, Freddie, 65

Tuckett, Len, 25

Tuckett, Lindsay, 25, 27, 30-31, 33

Valentine, Alf, 17

Van der Bijl, Peter, 43

Van der Merwe, Peter, 155, 169, 173

Van Ryneveld, Clive, 63, 67, 102, 130-131, 134, 136, 139, 142, 144-145

Veivers, Tom, 172

Verwoerd, Prime Minister Hendrik, 168

Viljoen, Carol, 168

Viljoen, Ken, 18, 25-26, 34, 53, 81, 92, 97, 110, 120, 168-169, 174

Voce, Bill, 20

Voortrekker Monument, 56

Wade, Billy, 40, 43, 53

Wade, Herby, 31

Waite, Johnny, 55-56, 66, 81, 84, 87, 89, 100, 111, 118, 130, 133, 141-144, 154-155, 162, 173

Wallace, Boon, 167

Walsh, Jack, 118

Walter, Ken, 161

Wardle, Johnny, 67, 112, 130

Washbrook, Cyril, 27, 41, 53

Watkins, John, 39, 60, 85, 96, 109, 128-129

Watson, Willie, 67, 117

Wesley, Colin, 147-148, 151

Westcott, Dick, 105, 141

White, "Butch", 148

Whitington, Dick, 57, 84, 97, 164, 168

Winch, Jonty, 58, 103

Winslow, Paul, 109, 111-112, 114-115, 119-120, 123

Woodley, Ray, 103

Wright, Ron, 87

Wynne, Owen, 12, 40, 41, 52, 56, 59-60

Yardley, Norman, 27, 29